Charcoalblue

Char

Hugh Pearman
with a Foreword by David Lan

LUND HUMPHRIES

coalblue

Designing for Performance

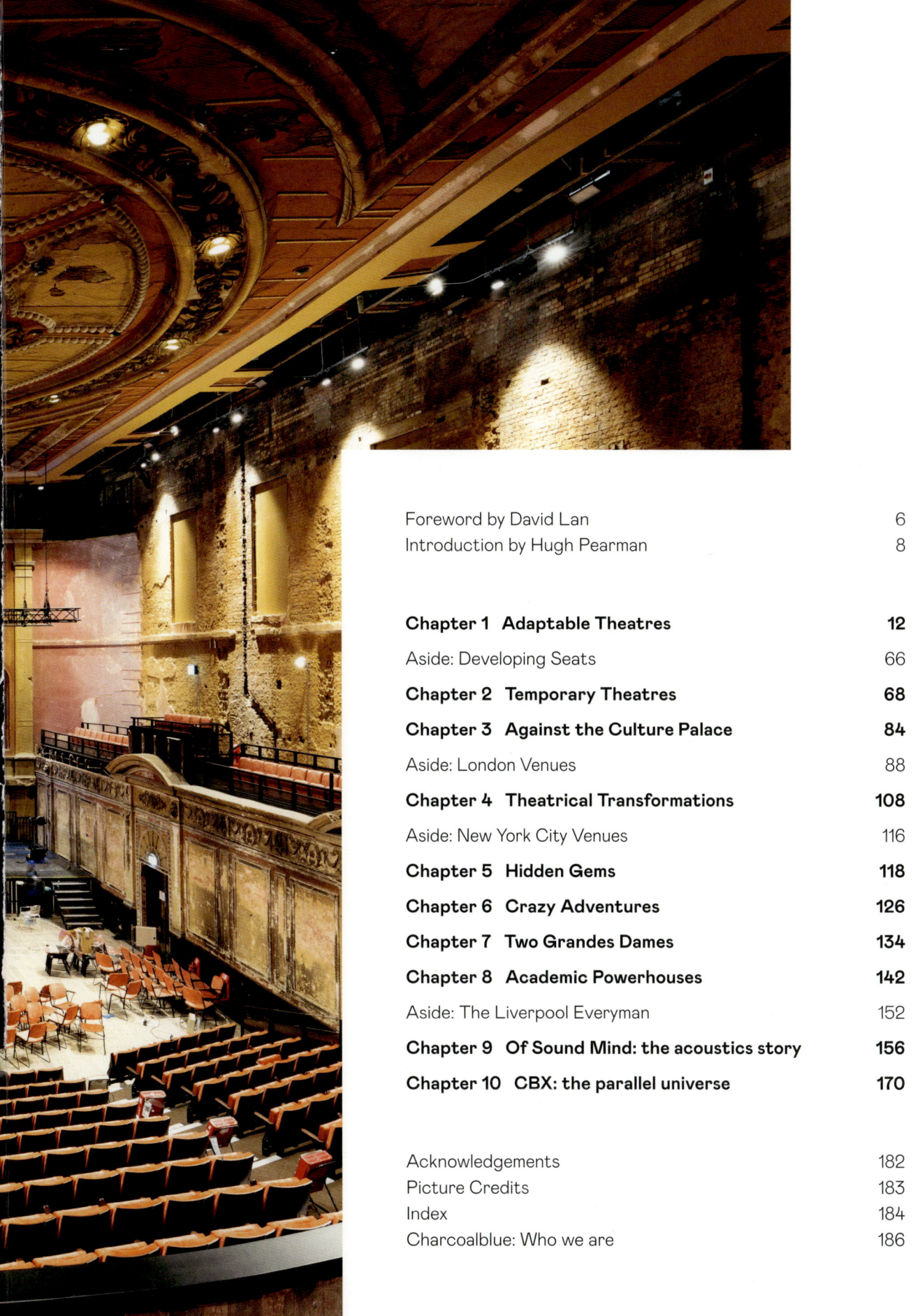

Foreword by David Lan	6
Introduction by Hugh Pearman	8
Chapter 1 Adaptable Theatres	**12**
Aside: Developing Seats	66
Chapter 2 Temporary Theatres	**68**
Chapter 3 Against the Culture Palace	**84**
Aside: London Venues	88
Chapter 4 Theatrical Transformations	**108**
Aside: New York City Venues	116
Chapter 5 Hidden Gems	**118**
Chapter 6 Crazy Adventures	**126**
Chapter 7 Two Grandes Dames	**134**
Chapter 8 Academic Powerhouses	**142**
Aside: The Liverpool Everyman	152
Chapter 9 Of Sound Mind: the acoustics story	**156**
Chapter 10 CBX: the parallel universe	**170**
Acknowledgements	182
Picture Credits	183
Index	184
Charcoalblue: Who we are	186

Foreword

David Lan

I first became aware of Andy Hayles as a presence that, day after day, turned up in the viewfinder of my camera while I filmed the reimagining and redesigning of the Royal Court Theatre. From 1995 to 1997 I was playwright-in-residence, but, rather than write a play, I made a fly-on-the-wall documentary for the BBC following Artistic Director Stephen Daldry and architect Steve Tompkins and their teams — and also this other guy — on design meetings, on research trips abroad and deep into the dark, dusty bowels of the building.

As we edited some 70 hours of footage, a key question was who would emerge as the leading characters. Would Andy? Indeed he did — and, in retrospect, how could he not have featured strongly in that story, as he has in the stories of so many new and reconceived theatres over the last two decades.

The rapport he struck up with Steve as well as with Roger Watts and Eric Lawrence of Haworth Tompkins, for whom the Royal Court was a breakout building, formed the basis of an enduring, and now globally celebrated, design double act.

By 2000 I was Artistic Director of the Young Vic. In tune with the 'let's-do-the-show-right-here' spirit of the late 1960s, it had been built on a bomb site/parking lot in London's Waterloo to a spec that anticipated a five-year life span. By the time I got the job of running it 30 years later, the local council was demanding that the disintegrating structure be shut down. Most of it was not worth saving, but, as with the Court's 'Italian' proscenium auditorium, though in a radically contrasting style, the Young Vic thrust-stage auditorium was a classic.

The Tompkins/Hayles duo won the design competition. Together with my team, working with a rigorous, highly collaborative and, in fact, revelatory intimacy, they came up with the idea of generating a new shell around the auditorium. By adding two new studio spaces, they created a three-auditoria complex, an invitation to the finest theatre artists of the country, of the world and, at the same time, of the neighbourhood to create the shows they couldn't make, and perhaps wouldn't even think of making, anywhere else.

Just as construction was getting going, Charcoalblue was founded by Andy alongside Gavin Green, Jon Stevens and Jack Tilbury with their first employee, Katy Winter, who later took over from Tilbury as a senior partner. Thus I became one of the first clients of the new outfit, alongside the Roundhouse in Camden and Siobhan Davies Studios in Southwark. The finished theatre was named RIBA London Building of the Year.

In 2013 I was hired to write the artistic and architectural brief for a proposed new performance art complex at Manhattan's World Trade Center and to help select the architect. The project leaders' preference was to work with a New York architectural practice. By now Charcoalblue had opened an NYC outpost, and one of my first interventions was to suggest that they join the team.

David Lan at the Young Vic and the theatre itself on The Cut, London, just around the corner from the Charcoalblue studio.

After a year and a half of a-week-a-month research trips among NY theatre, dance and opera artists, much of the discussion about how to transform all those dreams and aspirations into a producing house of maximum utility and benefit to the city took place in the cafe-foyer of the Young Vic. (Perhaps it's no coincidence that the soon-to-open Perelman Performing Arts Center designed by REX Architects is another three-auditoria complex.)

Charcoalblue do what they do so imaginatively, so effectively and with such confident and deep engagement and care that the name has become virtually a synonym for world-beating theatre design. If it's not yet a verb, it no doubt soon will be.

Foreword

Introduction
Hugh Pearman

It was an eye-opening business, visiting the construction site of the enormous performance-space complex in Manchester known as Factory International, down by the River Irwell. It was the beginning of May 2023, and 400 workers were swarming over the site, their task being to get the building to a point where it could open for that summer's Manchester International Festival.

This is always the point in a building project when – with last-minute changes going on – everyone has to keep their nerve. What struck me was that, amid what looked, as usual, like controlled chaos, Charcoalblue's responsible director, Jenni Harris, was calmness personified. No doubt her experience of working in theatres and touring companies before joining Charcoalblue had accustomed her to the last-minute whirl of productions. We were in one sense in the middle of a battle scene, the important difference being that everyone was on the same side, but from different battalions. We went up beyond the 'gods' to walk on the technical grid and check that the various pieces of flying equipment, capable of handling great weights, were installed and operating smoothly: they were. It was just one aspect of a wide-ranging consultancy role.

Another metaphor comes from the name. Factory International, designed by Rotterdam-based architects OMA, is a brand-new industrial-scale building, and its form and intent is inspired by the cultural events that the city's inhabitants used to stage in otherwise abandoned factory and warehouse buildings. The whirl of activity and the noise it generated was indeed industrial. A very large thing was

OPPOSITE Aviva Studios, Manchester. A bold new creative venue surrounded by an industrial heritage.
ABOVE Aviva Studios, Manchester, foyer and new event space, with its own DJ booth.
FOLLOWING PAGES Perelman Performing Arts Center, New York. Inside at 'play' level, looking towards the translucent glass and marble cladding.

being manufactured, with such innovations as full-height retractable walls to allow it to be used as two or three performance spaces, or one vast interconnected one. This displays a level of operational flexibility also apparent in a much smaller but very prominent new theatre complex across the Atlantic that was coming to completion at the same time: the glowing cube of the Perelman Performing Arts Center in Manhattan (REX Architects), part of the World Trade Center redevelopment. Both theatres are equally devoted to the creation and staging of new kinds of performance.

Although a significant aspect of Charcoalblue's work today is in the digital realm, with the electronic systems that such places need to operate smoothly, it is good to acknowledge the industrial, physical, people-heavy side of the theatre world, because Charcoalblue emerged as a consultancy from just such a hands-on milieu. Its way of operating is inclusive of everyone in the business, from actors and musicians, producers and directors, to engineers and architects. While the team now also works across the corporate and educational worlds, it is that theatrical show-must-go-on bloodline that runs through what they do.

Introduction

As David Lan touches on in his Foreword, the origin story of Charcoalblue goes back to a key UK cultural project of the late 1990s lottery-funded boom, the remaking of London's Royal Court Theatre, when its founders were working for the long-established consultancy Theatre Projects. By the turn of the new millennium, while working on Lan's equally radical-fringe Young Vic, they were ready to strike out on their own. The four who took this step in 2004 were Andy Hayles (chief electrician), Jon Stevens (lighting and sound engineer), Gavin Green (architectural design) and Jack Tilbury (production manager). Katy Winter, who started as the first ever Charcoalblue employee in 2004, was also crucial in the founding of the firm, later replacing Tilbury as a senior partner.

As for the name, that was inspired by jazz saxophonist Wayne Shorter's 1964 Blue Note recording 'Charcoal Blues', which jazz aficionado Hayles had playing while planning out the first job for the new consultancy, Siobhan Davies Studios by architect Sarah Wigglesworth. According to Hayles, the name encompasses the move from initial concept – a charcoal sketch – to the technical authority of a blueprint or working drawing. But it's jazz-inflected because collaborative improvisation in creative endeavour is crucial.

Looking back now on their subsequently rapid rise to prominence, what came next was a highly significant leap in scale: the Royal Shakespeare Company in Stratford-upon-Avon. For a fledgling consultancy to take on two 1,000-seat theatres in rapid succession for such an august company – first the temporary Courtyard Theatre with architect Ian Ritchie, then the rebuilt permanent main house with Bennetts Associates – was remarkable. Change was in the air: theatrical institutions were reinventing themselves for the 21st century and wanted their buildings to embody the same spirit. The founding five had picked just the right moment.

Word got around: American and Pacific-region venues came calling and Charcoalblue scaled up, taking on new specialisms – acoustics, led by Byron Harrison, being a case in point. Scaling up meant delegating responsibility, and so each of Charcoalblue's venue design offerings now had its own founder and leader: the US founded by John Owens and now led by Kate Nolan, Australasia by Eric Lawrence and the UK and EMEA by Gary Sparkes.

So, some 20 years later, the one-time start-up is an international business employing hundreds of people involved in every aspect of what may broadly be described as performance, whether the location is a theatre, concert hall, event space, sporting venue, corporate HQ or community centre.

Not everything makes it to the construction stage by any means. A case in point would be London's Centre for Music, a multi-level affair proposed near the Barbican on the vacated home of the Museum of London, but never built. This would essentially have been the first-rate orchestral concert venue and performing arts school, championed at the time by conductor Sir Simon Rattle, that the capital still inexplicably lacks, despite improvements made over the years

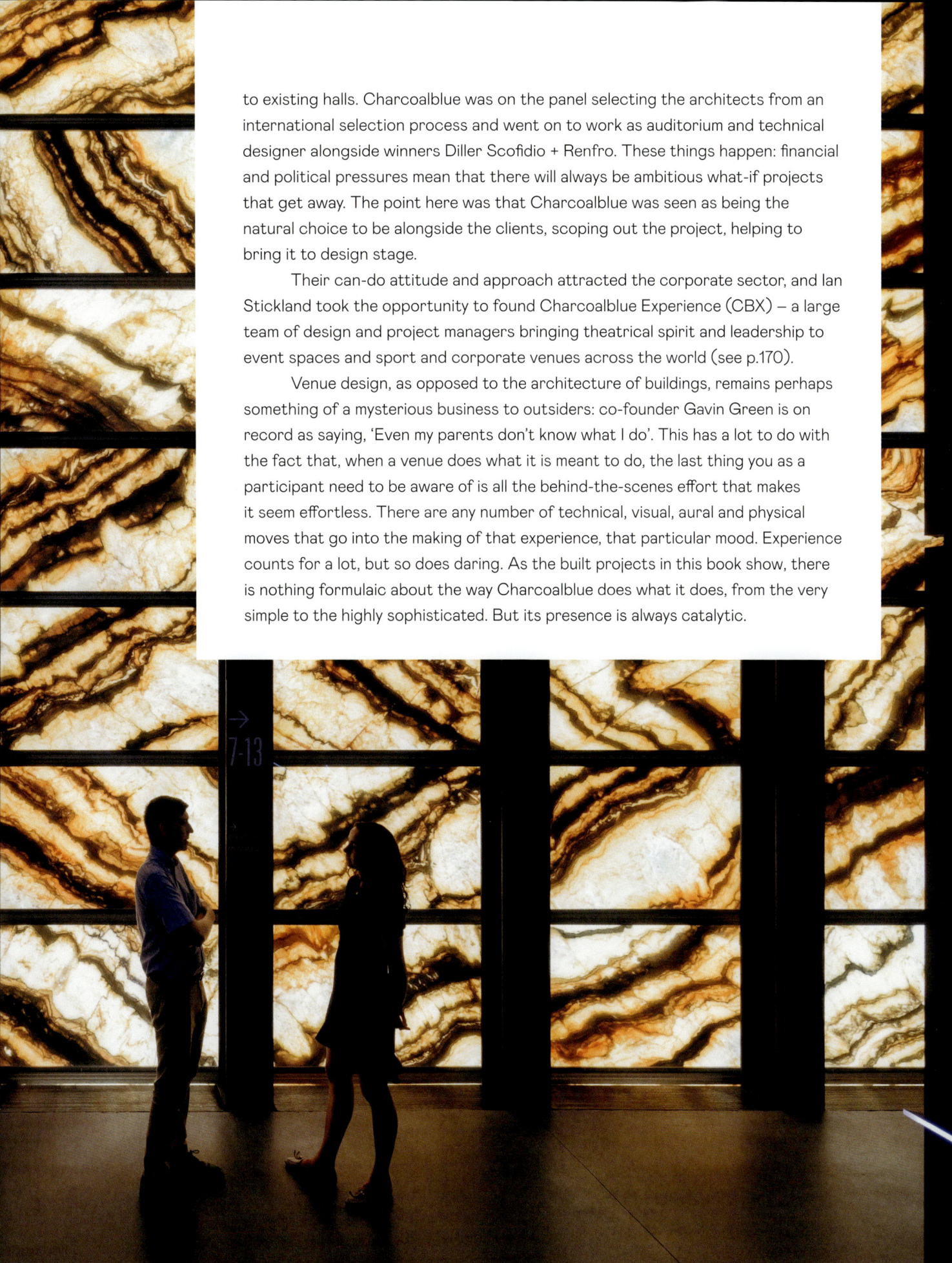

to existing halls. Charcoalblue was on the panel selecting the architects from an international selection process and went on to work as auditorium and technical designer alongside winners Diller Scofidio + Renfro. These things happen: financial and political pressures mean that there will always be ambitious what-if projects that get away. The point here was that Charcoalblue was seen as being the natural choice to be alongside the clients, scoping out the project, helping to bring it to design stage.

Their can-do attitude and approach attracted the corporate sector, and Ian Stickland took the opportunity to found Charcoalblue Experience (CBX) – a large team of design and project managers bringing theatrical spirit and leadership to event spaces and sport and corporate venues across the world (see p.170).

Venue design, as opposed to the architecture of buildings, remains perhaps something of a mysterious business to outsiders: co-founder Gavin Green is on record as saying, 'Even my parents don't know what I do'. This has a lot to do with the fact that, when a venue does what it is meant to do, the last thing you as a participant need to be aware of is all the behind-the-scenes effort that makes it seem effortless. There are any number of technical, visual, aural and physical moves that go into the making of that experience, that particular mood. Experience counts for a lot, but so does daring. As the built projects in this book show, there is nothing formulaic about the way Charcoalblue does what it does, from the very simple to the highly sophisticated. But its presence is always catalytic.

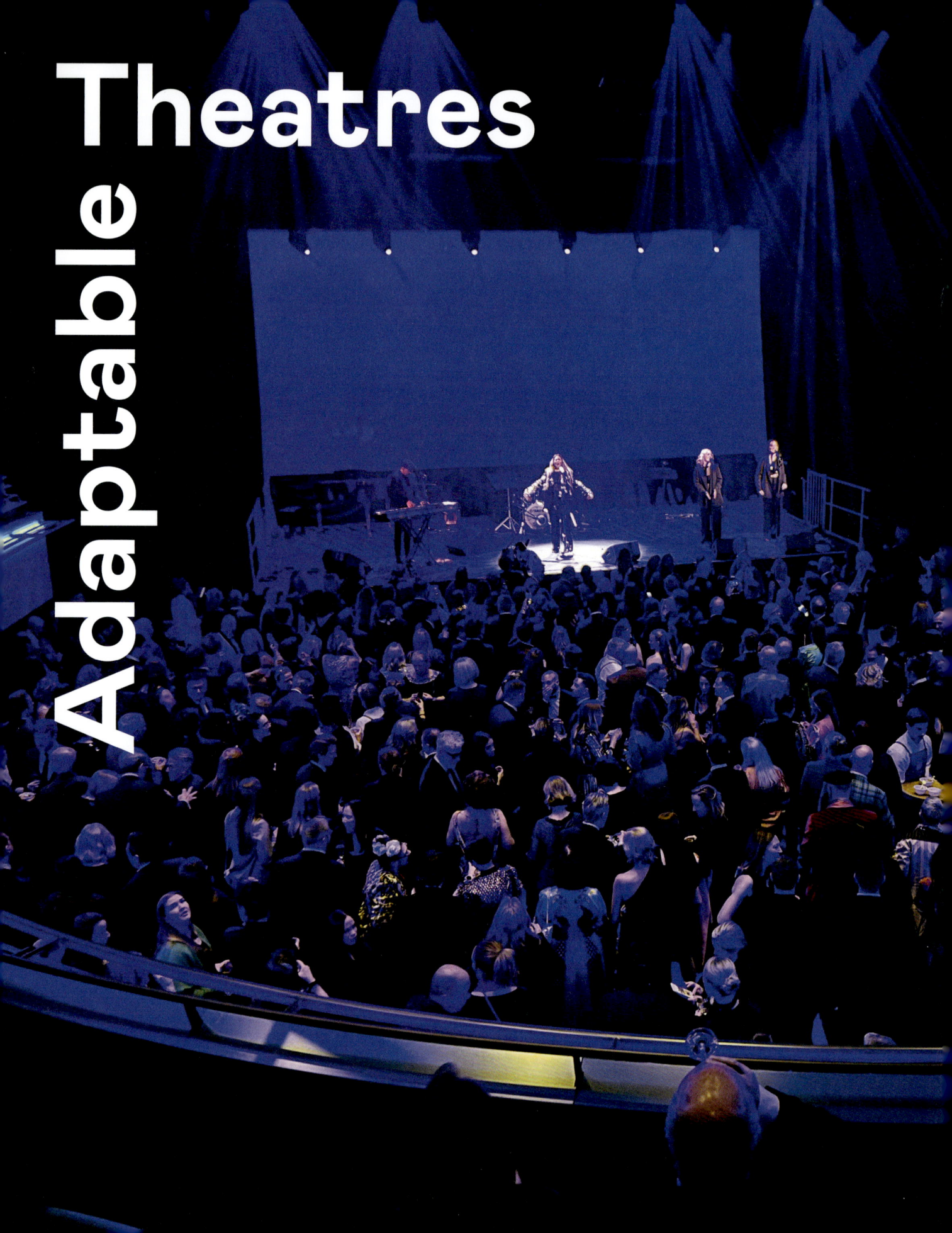

Adaptable Theatres

In the 21st century, Charcoalblue has more than led the way in creating a variety of highly adaptable theatre spaces in which there are movable elements of one kind or another. Both working solo and with a number of theatre architects, they have essentially defined the sector and enabled considerable innovation in the kinds of shows staged. Some long-term collaborative relationships and friendships have developed along the way.

Earlier generations of 'flexible' theatres could suffer from compromise, rather like sofa beds: too often not very satisfactory as either sofa or bed. But although larger budgets can buy more clever technology, the answer at all budget levels is always found in the basic design. Whatever configuration the theatre morphs into, that must always feel inevitable, the way it was meant to be.

There has long been a growing desire for change, for flexibility, even as the conventional fixed proscenium/orchestra pit format of typical Victorian-era theatres continued. Consider the 'Total Theatre' envisaged by architect and Bauhaus director Walter Gropius in 1926 for the Berlin Communist theatre director and producer Erwin Piscator, a leading proponent of epic-scale political drama.

Whatever configuration the theatre morphs into, that must always feel inevitable, the way it was meant to be.

Gropius designed the theatre with a large circular section of stage and auditorium that revolved. Considerably more sophisticated than mere revolving sections of stage, which had long existed, this would allow multiple configurations, from proscenium to in-the-round. Such a theatre was never built in his lifetime and came to be seen as 'endlessly influential and eminently unworkable'. But some theatres began to have a go at the Gropius concept, not least the 1973 New London Theatre in Drury Lane by Croatian architect Paul Tvrtković and scenic designer Sean Kenny. Its analogue mechanical contrivances (always a staple of stagecraft) suited the theatre of spectacle, especially fast-moving musicals. There wasn't to be another all-new West End theatre for 50 years – I'll come to that.

But before that delayed innovation had come the postwar rediscovery of the Shakespearean thrust stage, in-the-round formats and the arrival of supposedly ultra-flexible 'black box' theatres. Shortly afterwards, the 'courtyard theatre', a usually rectangular enclosed space lined with galleries, made a comeback. Add to this assortment 'found space', the always-seductive idea of co-opting a building originally designed for another purpose. All of these approaches have their various merits and demerits depending on what you want to stage, but what theatre

Adaptable Theatres

directors increasingly want is a space that can shape-shift so as to be able to handle anything — or as much as possible, anyway; a multiplicity of auditorium configurations and production types, within the one building.

An exemplar of this approach is Susan Feldman's St. Ann's Warehouse performing arts centre in the rapidly reviving DUMBO historical north-western waterside district of Brooklyn, across the East River from Manhattan. Founded in 1980 in a church that gave it its name, the company later moved to a former spice-milling factory on Water Street. That was very close to a potential larger space in a fire-gutted former tobacco warehouse virtually beneath the Brooklyn Bridge. St. Ann's acquired it. Feldman had a list of new theatres elsewhere that she admired. These included an English pair from 2006, both early Charcoalblue projects: the reconfigured Young Vic in London's Waterloo with Haworth Tompkins, and the temporary Courtyard Theatre for the Royal Shakespeare Company (RSC) in Stratford-upon-Avon, architect Ian Ritchie. The latter was a full-scale test-bed theatre designed in six months and built in 11.

PAGE 12 Storyhouse Theatre at the Geelong Arts Centre, Australia.
RIGHT Former St. Ann's Warehouse technical director Owen Hughes, now with Charcoalblue.
BELOW Concept sketch by Andy Hayles, Charcoalblue: technical level across the warehouse.
LEFT Site in construction: studio and administration steelwork taking shape.

The Young Vic had itself originally been viewed as temporary when established in 1970, but its low-budget design by architect Bill Howell worked so well that it became permanent and lasted 30 years before its rebuild. Something similar, but faster, happened to the much newer oxidised-steel box of the RSC Courtyard, a 1,000-seat galleried thrust-stage affair built to house the Royal Shakespeare Company (RSC) and test new designs for its main house, which was about to enter redevelopment (see p.86). Once that was done, the Courtyard was reconfigured as a permanent expansion of the RSC's experimental small third auditorium, The Other Place, again with Ritchie.

What interested Feldman and her GM Erik Wallin, however, was not how long these theatres would last, but how adaptable they were. In a way, it amounts to the same thing. She invited Charcoalblue to work with a series of architects on the St. Ann's Warehouse project from 2010 onwards, and this proved to be a breakout commission for the growing practice internationally. When the 'new' St. Ann's Warehouse opened in 2015 with all the back-office as well as performance space and a garden included, the intended design lifetime was 50 years. Having

Adaptable Theatres

OPPOSITE Hurricane Sandy flooding tideline.
ABOVE Charcaolblue's acoustic challenges in a built-up neighbourhood.
RIGHT St. Ann's Warehouse Artistic Director Susan Feldman and Charcoalblue's Gavin Green walking the site.

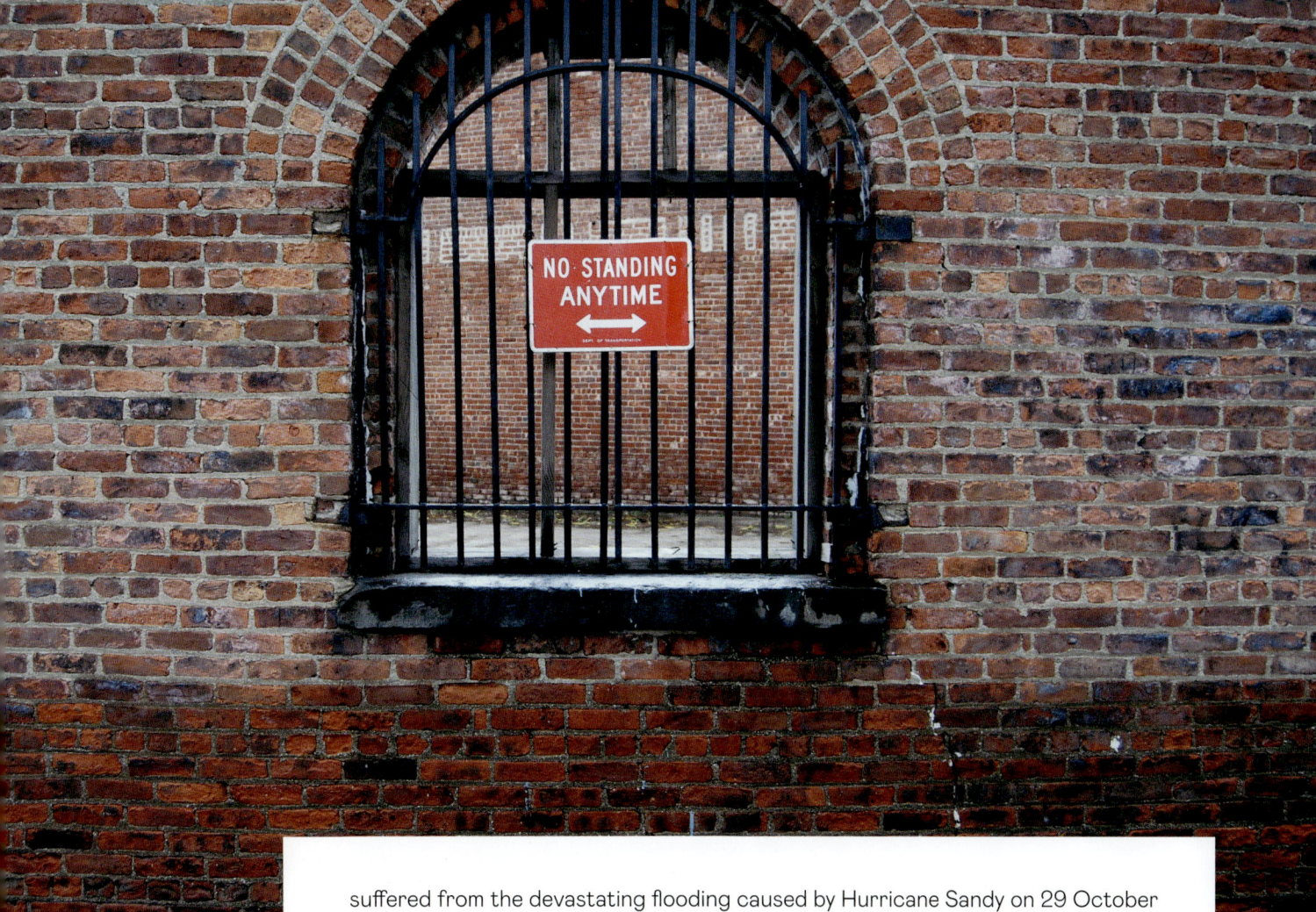

suffered from the devastating flooding caused by Hurricane Sandy on 29 October 2012, the design of the site was developed to bring power and other services down from above, thereby keeping them dry should such an event recur.

It was built with Marvel Architects within the consolidated walls of the pre-Civil War warehouse. The previously reduced-height walls were raised by a storey with a glass-block lantern extension to bring in daylight (exceptionally rare in theatres, and capable of rapid blackout when required) and provide height for the lighting rigs, air handling and their associated catwalks. The theatre has a highly adaptable 10,000 square foot main auditorium for 300 to 800 people depending on configuration and a 1,000 square foot studio space. However, it does not confine itself to these two auditoria. With a history of using 'found space' in other buildings, Feldman and her team had a desire to keep that openness when building afresh. There are few dividing walls and no doors. The catwalks and rigging mounts extend right through the building, including the foyer. Performances (St. Ann's is known equally for music, theatre and all combinations thereof) can take place anywhere at all in the building.

So, while the spaces you inhabit within the old walls might seem very simple — flat-floor, mostly blank walls, seating raking any way you want, bringing out the character and texture of the place — all the desired flexibility is provided by the very hard-working top layer signalled by those glass blocks. With no

ABOVE End-on seating arrangement and flexible catwalk ceiling spanning the entire warehouse.
OPPOSITE TOP St. Ann's Warehouse, early concept sketch, Gavin Green, Charcoalblue.
OPPOSITE *Oklahoma* production, staged in traverse, 2018.

Charcoalblue

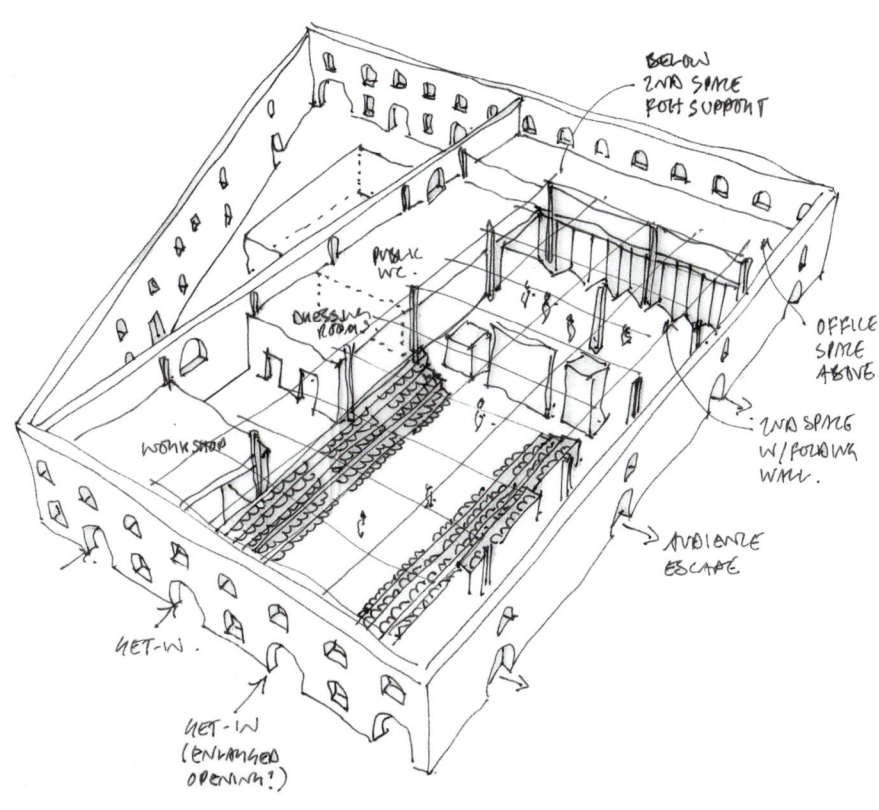

Adaptable Theatres

St Ann's Warehouse, DUMBO, New York. A beautiful pre-Civil War structure overlooking Manhattan Island. The building, designed alongside Marvel Architects, includes a large flexible performance space; seating 300 to 700 for theatre, music and large-scale festivals; a multi-purpose studio for local artists and community groups and the Max Family Garden; and an open-air triangular garden designed by Brooklyn Bridge Park landscape architects Michael Van Valkenburgh Associates.

flytower, this layer contains all the technical guts of the theatre, controlling light, acoustics, ventilation and access for the technicians. And every part of the space is designed to allow the unamplified human voice to be heard clearly, without distraction, from anywhere in the building.

Meanwhile, the garden created in a large existing triangular subdivision of the warehouse by landscape architects Michael Van Valkenburgh Associates has an urban-salvage feel in keeping with the public realm of this unique post-industrial district with its necklace of former wharfside parklets. It is the point where that realm intersects with the world of theatre.

The success of St. Ann's led to an expanding portfolio of other North American projects. Two big-name Chicago venues followed: the celebrated Steppenwolf Theatre and the Chicago Shakespeare Theater (CST). Steppenwolf is historically akin to London's Young Vic in some ways – also founded in the early 1970s, also originally in adapted found space, also birthing productions that subsequently achieved mainstream success, also needing to expand – but beyond that the model is different. Steppenwolf is a company as much as a building, famously including John Malkovich among its founding members, and already had a significant rebuild in 1991. It remains true to its brand of 'natural theatre', inviting intimacy with the audience.

ABOVE LEFT Steppenwolf's Liz and Eric Lefkofsky Arts and Education Center, N Halsted Street, Chicago.
OPPOSITE Inside Steppenwolf's purpose-built and flexible in-the-round theatre.

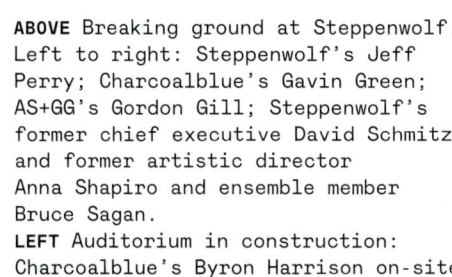

ABOVE Breaking ground at Steppenwolf. Left to right: Steppenwolf's Jeff Perry; Charcoalblue's Gavin Green; AS+GG's Gordon Gill; Steppenwolf's former chief executive David Schmitz and former artistic director Anna Shapiro and ensemble member Bruce Sagan.
LEFT Auditorium in construction: Charcoalblue's Byron Harrison on-site.
BELOW Auditorium one-to-one mock-up and exploring the room using virtual reality.

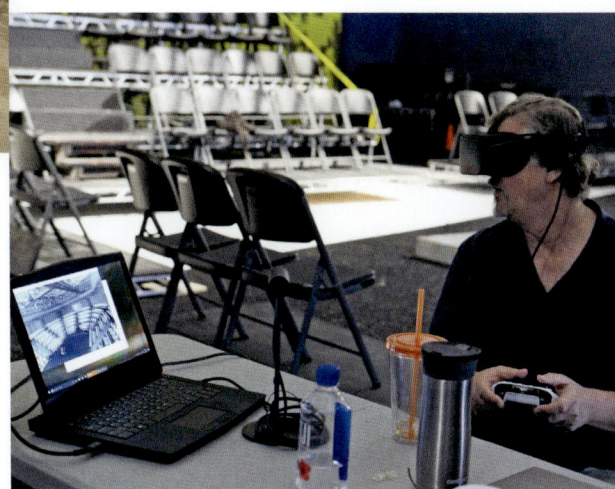

Adaptable Theatres

Here an ambitious three-phase project started which added new theatres and facilities at both the north and south ends of the 1991 block on North Halsted Street at the point where the northern suburbs give way to industry. It then concluded by adapting and upgrading that building too.

First was a new 88-seat cabaret theatre, experimental studio space, bar and cafe at the north end, previously occupied by a furniture store. Next came the building of the Liz and Eric Lefkofsky Arts and Education Center at the south end on what had been an open parking lot. It includes the very intimate in-the-round Ensemble Theater with (depending on configuration) a maximum of 400 seats arranged across only six rows all round. There the architect was Gordon Gill of AS+GG, whose local theatre this is.

Both of these moves served to bookend and visually open up what had previously been a somewhat forbidding-looking building. Finally, Charcoalblue returned to the 1991 building, working with John Morris Architects to improve the existing Downstairs Theater – especially technical equipment and front of house – and to convert the previous Upstairs Theater and dressing rooms into two rehearsal halls for the whole expanded complex. All in all, this was a 12-year programme that saw collaboration with three separate artistic directorships, Martha Lavey and Anna Shapiro having particular influence and impact. The result of all this is that Steppenwolf now has a multiple-configuration urban theatre campus with a much greater public presence and enhanced facilities, occupying about half of its city block.

Three and a half miles south-west of Steppenwolf is a very different proposition. Chicago Shakespeare's Yard Theater is inside the Skyline stage, a large rigid canopy on the Navy Pier, projecting out into the harbour in Lake Michigan. Revived as a public promenade and visitor attraction in the early 21st century, the pier has many attractions, from a children's museum to funfair rides. But also Shakespeare.

This is a relatively new institution in world terms. CST, then called the Chicago Shakespeare Workshop, put on its first performance of *Henry V* on a pub rooftop in 1986. Its rapid success and growth led it to establish a three-stage campus on the Navy Pier by 1999. This consisted of a 500-seat Shakespearean-format galleried auditorium with thrust stage, a 200-capacity experimental 'black box' auditorium upstairs, and the outside Skyline Stage, beneath a domed glass-fibre fabric roof. By that time, the company was also staging new plays and welcoming other theatre companies from around the world.

The time came when the always-ambitious CST, driven by its founder-directors Barbara Gaines and Criss Henderson, decided to build a new year-round venue on the site of Skyline Stage. Looking for a relatively inexpensive but also highly adaptable auditorium, they had seen the success of the temporary Courtyard in Stratford-upon-Avon, and wanted something akin to that. Henderson met up with Andy Hayles over tacos at a Dallas theatre conference and, with a napkin sketch, the project was born.

24 Charcoalblue

ABOVE Concept sketch by Gavin Green, Charcoalblue: section through Skyline Stage and new Yard Theater.
BELOW The Yard Theater in construction: movable towers linked together.

ABOVE Yard Theater auditorium in horseshoe format from stage.

Adaptable Theatres

28   Charcoalblue

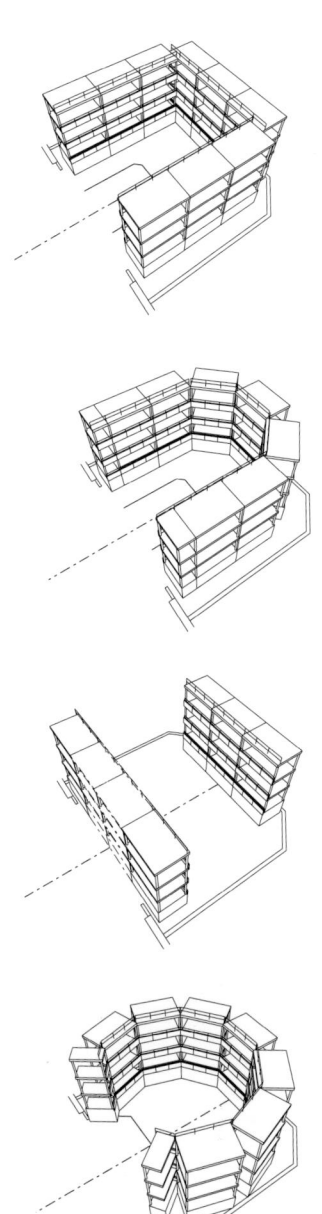

The project had the advantage of being able to reuse some elements of the Skyline Stage, most notably its backstage areas – rather as the Courtyard had been able to use parts of the pre-existing Other Place in Stratford-upon-Avon. As built, in one configuration it looks similar, with its tiers of galleries curving round the back of the auditorium, and there's even an echo of the Stratford auditorium in its name – The Yard. But this place can be almost any other kind of theatre layout: proscenium house, thrust or traverse stages or in-the-round. You'd have to be a very loyal patron to see The Yard in all its permutations. The Charcoalblue slogan for this was: 'It's not just what's ON the stage, it's where IS the stage?'

This flexibility is achieved by moving big stuff around. Nine four-storey, movable seating towers, each the size and weight of a double-decker London bus, are the building blocks. Depending on how you arrange them, you can make any of 12 different stage formats, seating between 150 and 850. So it can be the smallest or largest house in the CST campus, or anything in between.

Charcoalblue were the lead consultants, working again with Steppenwolf colleagues AS+GG for the design of the building's shell and foyer, which includes a photochromic south-facing glass facade that darkens like sunglasses in bright light. Meanwhile, Charcoalblue took sole charge of all aspects of the auditorium, which is a marvel of ingenious design. Each of the movable towers carries all the services a theatre needs: stage and house lighting, audiovisual systems, mechanical and electrical systems and fire sprinklers. Remarkably, each tower needs only three technicians to decouple it and slide it around on an air cushion system like a hovercraft.

Despite all this, the auditorium has its own character. Nobody going to the theatre wants to feel they are sitting in a machine. So whatever configuration is adopted, that – while you are there – is the fixed theatre, playing its part in bringing actors and audience together, feeling as if it was always that way. And for the next production, it may be utterly different, but still have that air of rightness about it.

OPPOSITE ABOVE Curtain call of Chicago Shakespeare Theater's North American premiere of *SIX*, directed by Lucy Moss and Jamie Armitage, in The Yard at Chicago Shakespeare, 2019.
OPPOSITE BELOW Concept sketch by Gavin Green, Charcoalblue: the Yard's in-the-round stage.
LEFT Concept model illustrating movable towers and stage formats.

Adaptable Theatres

By no means everything in the world of adaptable theatres needs to be on that level of ingenuity, however. An early project, which started as a feasibility study in 2007 and was finally completed in 2011 with architects Miller Bourne, is the **Ebert Room** at Glyndebourne, first and best of the country-house opera festivals. This was a 1959 scenic-rehearsal room, and the question was – what more could it be? Today it is an accessible multi-use space for up to 130 people on a fixed balcony and powered bleacher seating which can stage complete small operas, with all the necessary technical equipment for that, including air handling and heating/cooling. Or it can be used for educational and special events, pre-performance talks and rehearsals of all kinds, including a seated 60-strong chorus.

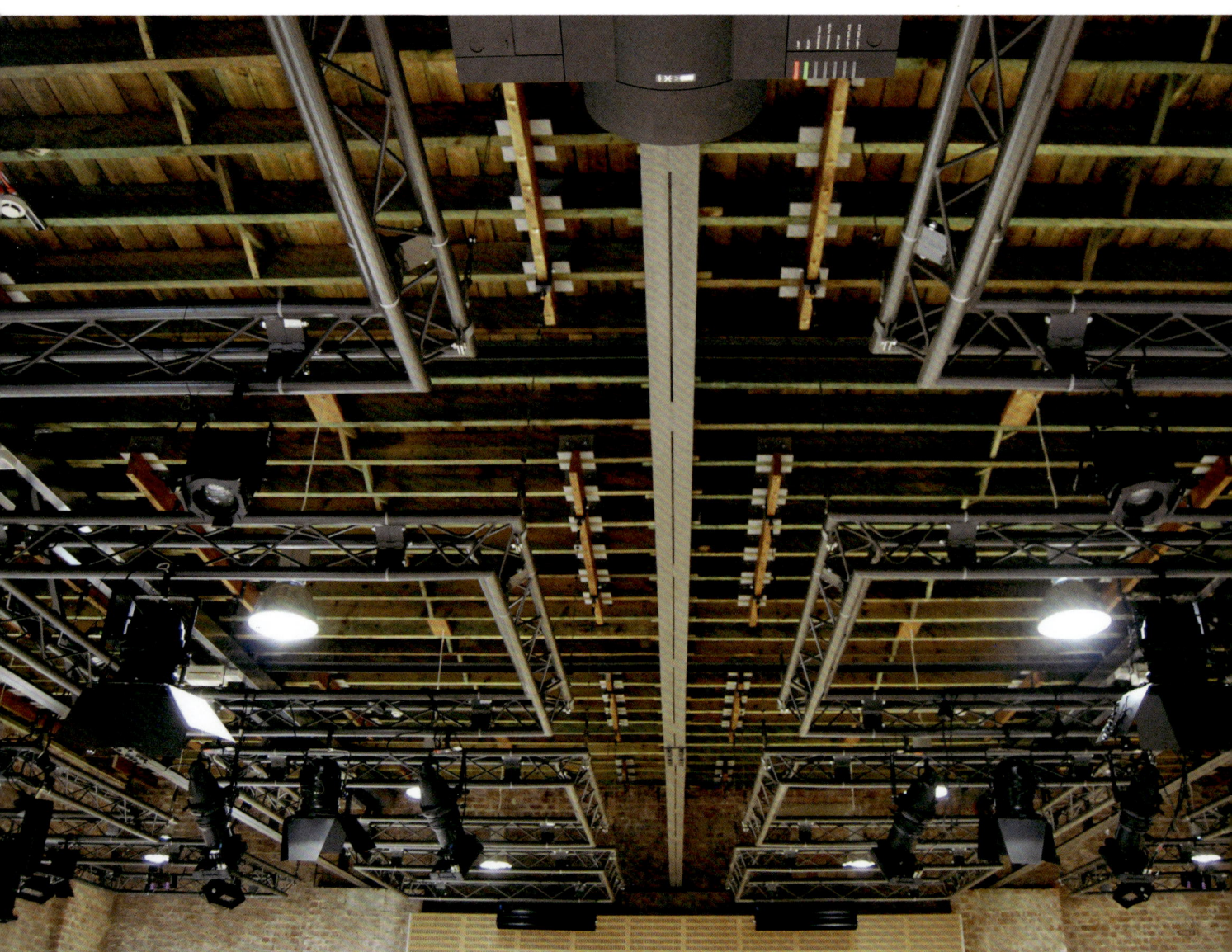

OPPOSITE Motorised truss grid units – Simple and easy to operate.
ABOVE Glyndebourne's Ebert Room seating extended for choir in rehearsal.
RIGHT Ebert Room concept sketch by Gavin Green, Charcoalblue.
BELOW Design development computer model.

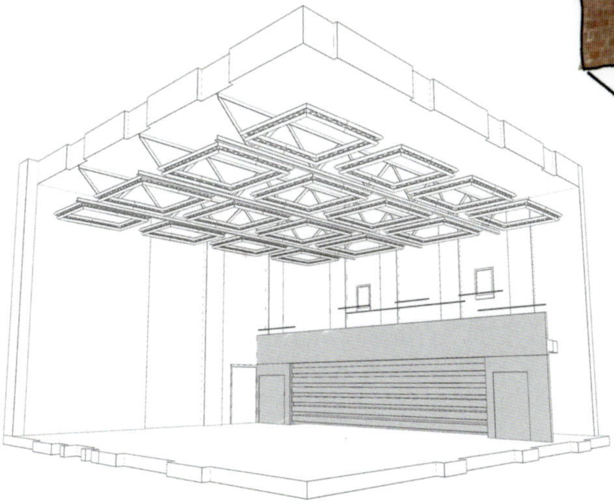

Adaptable Theatres

A further brace of British theatres took this much further: Storyhouse in Chester, north-west England, and the Kiln Theatre in Kilburn, North London. The former is an all-new theatre springing from an existing building, while the latter is a thorough reworking of a much-loved existing theatre, previously the Tricycle, which started life in 1980 as a highly successful attempt to build an ultra-cheap, intimate theatre of Georgian proportions and layout within an existing hall.

Storyhouse was a further collaboration with architects Bennetts Associates following on from the RST in Stratford-upon-Avon (see p.86), together with Storyhouse CEO Andrew Bentley and its Artistic Director Alex Clifton. It's an unusual complex, an arts centre containing a multi-format theatre for everything from drama to literary discussions, but also a cinema, public library and restaurant. This mix of uses gravitated together over the years along with the growing sense that it was better to be in the city centre than on the outskirts, and that an existing Grade II listed 1930s Odeon cinema could be the key to it.

A very theatrical device lies at its heart. With the later partitioning removed, the shape and plasterwork of the original Odeon, with its enormous proscenium arch containing the screen, became apparent. Now, you step through this: it has become the portal through to the new theatre beyond, which is Charcoalblue's territory. Meanwhile a new smaller cinema is placed up at what would have once been balcony level, further back. A library and cafe occupy the rest of the old building.

The new theatre extends the footprint of the cinema westwards in sympathetic materials of textured brick and copper. With a 500-to-800-seat main auditorium and a 200-seat studio theatre above, it doubles as a thrust-stage festival theatre during the summer months and a more conventional proscenium theatre, complete with flytower, for receiving production over the winters. The multiple uses of the whole complex keep it busy throughout the day and year-round.

LEFT Storyhouse: remodelled from the old Odeon cinema.
BELOW Concept sketch of Storyhouse by Gavin Green, Charcoalblue.

Adaptable Theatres

34 Charcoalblue

OPPOSITE Computer concept models of Storyhouse by Charcoalblue's Ben Hanson, left in 'end-stage', right in 'thrust' format (and the auditorium volume compressed for a more intimate room).
ABOVE Storyhouse auditorium from stage in thrust format.

Adaptable Theatres

Down in North London, the Kiln was to an extent sacred ground, a noted success as a space originally co-designed as the Tricycle Theatre by Tim Foster and Iain Mackintosh, for whose company Charcoalblue's founders had previously worked. A high-street theatre, it is flanked by shops, but a narrow arcade leads you into a large hall at the rear, which shares its foyer with the late 1990s Kiln Cinema, set to one side. The proportions of the Georgian theatre in Richmond, Yorkshire, on which the original Tricycle Theatre was modelled, seemed to have great geometric significance. Rebuilt more or less the same in 1989 after a fire, it was by now showing its age and its limitations. However, its particularly intimate character as a semi-courtyard theatre, stimulating some trail-blazing performances down the years and making it a favourite for both actors and producers, had to be kept.

Working with inspirational Artistic Director Indhu Rubasingham and Chapman Architects, Charcoalblue introduced some modest but effective measures, expanding the theatre's footprint up to the existing Foresters' Hall side walls to increase the capacity from 235 to 294. The rear and side galleries were reinstated, as was the sunken stalls level – made fully accessible along with the rest of the building.

LEFT Entrance to Kiln Theatre from Kilburn High Road.
ABOVE Concept sketch by Ben Hanson, Charcoalblue – view from stage.

The key change beyond that, other than necessary technical upgrades for both stage and auditorium and new seating, was in flexibility. Previously it was a fixed end-on theatre. That remains its default setting because it is a proven success, but now it can also adopt different settings: in-the-round, long and short traverse, and wholly or partly flat-floor. It made a very convincing London pub for Zadie Smith's acclaimed first play, *The Wife of Willesden*, a platform for telling her bawdy tale in Chaucerian fashion.

These format changes are not done by pushing buttons, but by the old method of pushing things around. The front half of the stage breaks down into 72 component parts that can be rearranged like building blocks. The stalls seating stows away by clipping onto the below-floor structure of these 'rostra'. In its way, it's the grandchild of the original 1980s Tricycle, which was built with a proprietary scaffolding system. There's a lot to be said for a well-designed kit of parts.

Adaptable Theatres

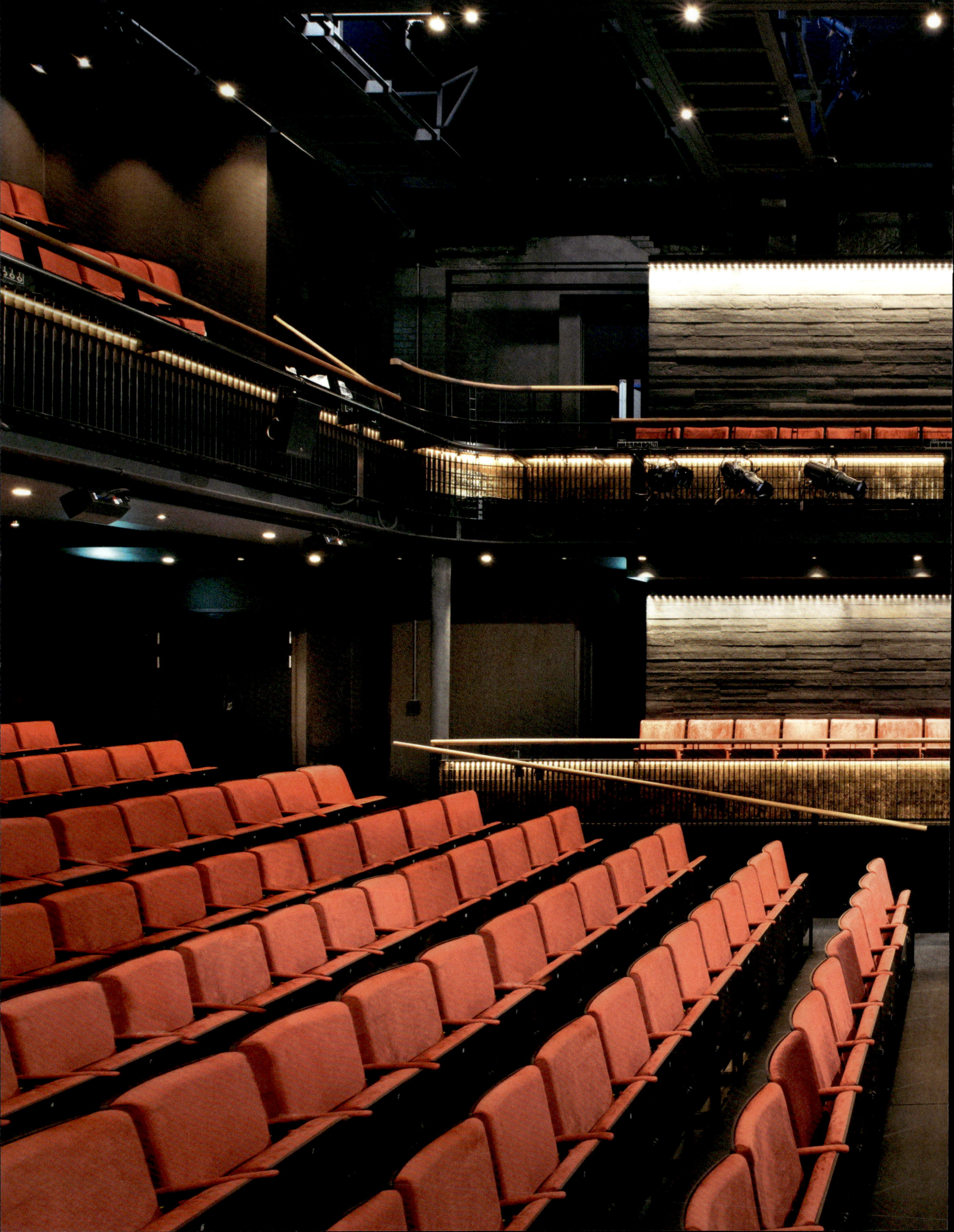

LEFT Kiln auditorium from side slips with historic chapel behind the new side balcony.
ABOVE Kiln balcony front and lighting bar mock-up.

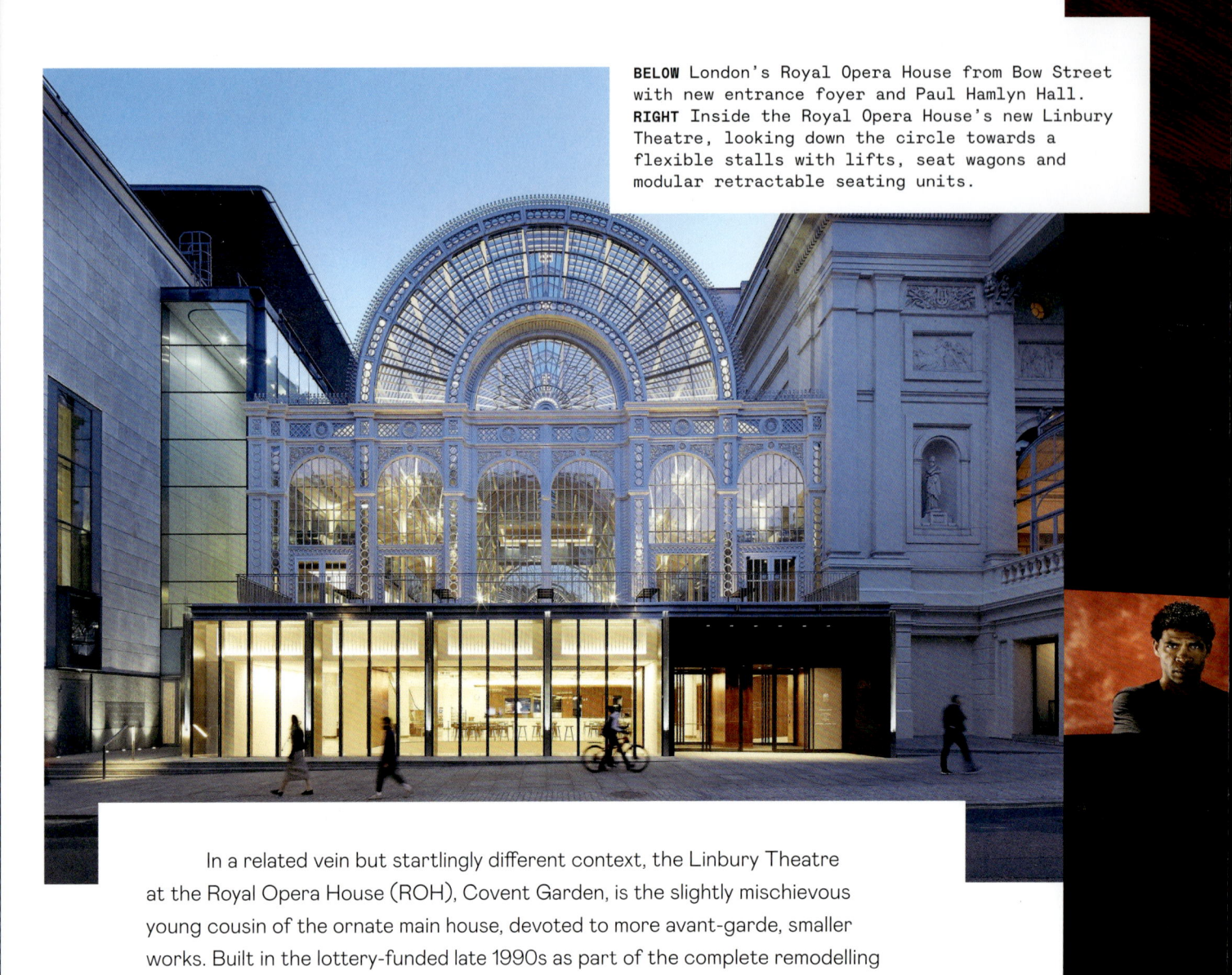

BELOW London's Royal Opera House from Bow Street with new entrance foyer and Paul Hamlyn Hall.
RIGHT Inside the Royal Opera House's new Linbury Theatre, looking down the circle towards a flexible stalls with lifts, seat wagons and modular retractable seating units.

In a related vein but startlingly different context, the Linbury Theatre at the Royal Opera House (ROH), Covent Garden, is the slightly mischievous young cousin of the ornate main house, devoted to more avant-garde, smaller works. Built in the lottery-funded late 1990s as part of the complete remodelling and extension of the entire complex, it felt like something of an afterthought: an austere functionalist 'black box' 400-seat auditorium which was adequate but (unlike the old Tricycle) without much of an identity of its own, or sense of being a complementary part of a larger whole.

Fifteen years later, the ROH began another big overhaul, called 'Open Up', concentrating on expanding and improving public areas in the building – but also on promoting the Linbury as a nimble small auditorium of greater importance and wider appeal.

Charcoalblue found themselves on the roster of three of the five design teams competing for this project, but not, to begin with, on the team of the winners, architects Stanton Williams. However the ROH valued Charcoalblue's ideas, and brokered a marriage. Another collaborative partnership was born.

Although the shell of the below-ground Linbury remained the same, its interiors were completely remade and the approach to it was literally opened up

Adaptable Theatres

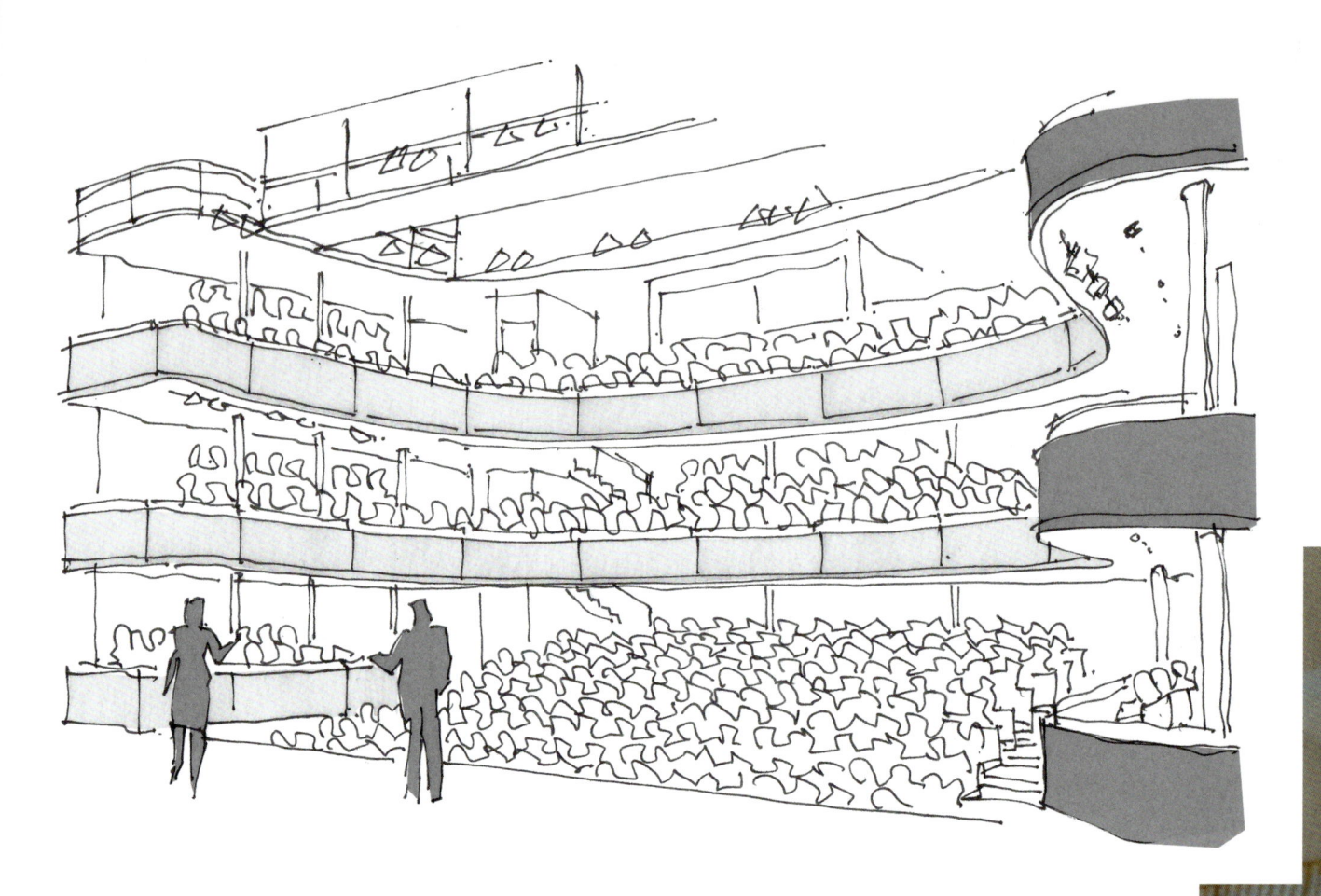

ABOVE Concept sketch of Linbury Theatre by Gavin Green, Charcoalblue.
BELOW Prototype tier front with lighting bar and rigging.
RIGHT Charcoalblue competition concept model.

Charcoalblue

— visually from Bow Street at the front by a glazed extended frontage, and from inside by cutting back the floor of the main concourse with a new marble staircase approach and a double-height foyer that doubles as an informal performance place, animating the public areas visibly and audibly.

In the auditorium, Charcoalblue got to work, keeping the same seating capacity but in a much more intimate horseshoe plan acknowledging the main house and many leading opera houses worldwide. Materials are richer. Much-improved seats and technical rigs play their part, the seating rake and size of orchestra pit can both be adjusted, an electro-acoustic system has been installed, but key to the whole thing is the theatre's new-found ability to work in any of the five main formats: thrust stage, end-on stage, traverse, in-the-round and flat-floor.

The Linbury has grown up, matured into a proper theatre much better suited to its context. It greatly extends the reach of the ROH in the variety of art forms and productions it can stage and the audiences it can attract.

ABOVE @sohoplace auditorium mock-up to test room proportions as well as stalls and balcony sightlines with Charcoalblue's Elena Giakoumak and Elina Pieridou on stage.
OPPOSITE Charcoalblue section through the @sohoplace auditorium.

@sohoplace Theatre

Theatres can insinuate themselves anywhere – what's wrong with a church hall or a room above a pub, anyway? The best of these will always graduate to steadily larger and more permanent premises. There's also a tradition of previously existing theatres being rebuilt inside commercial developments, sometimes including elements of the original building, but more often not. Too often in those cases the theatre was shoved into a basement or perched above other uses. But @sohoplace, the first all-new West End theatre for 50 years (since the aforementioned 1973 New London Theatre), takes pride of place right at street level, rises through five storeys and has an off-set block of offices separately accessed above that.

The precursor here was the Astoria, a shabby but beloved Soho music venue and nightclub originally built in the 1920s as a cinema. But that had to be demolished in 2009, along with a swathe of other buildings, to make way for the building of a key new Elizabeth Line station with all the engineering spaces that an underground railway needs, including a large vent shaft. Once all that was done, the owners

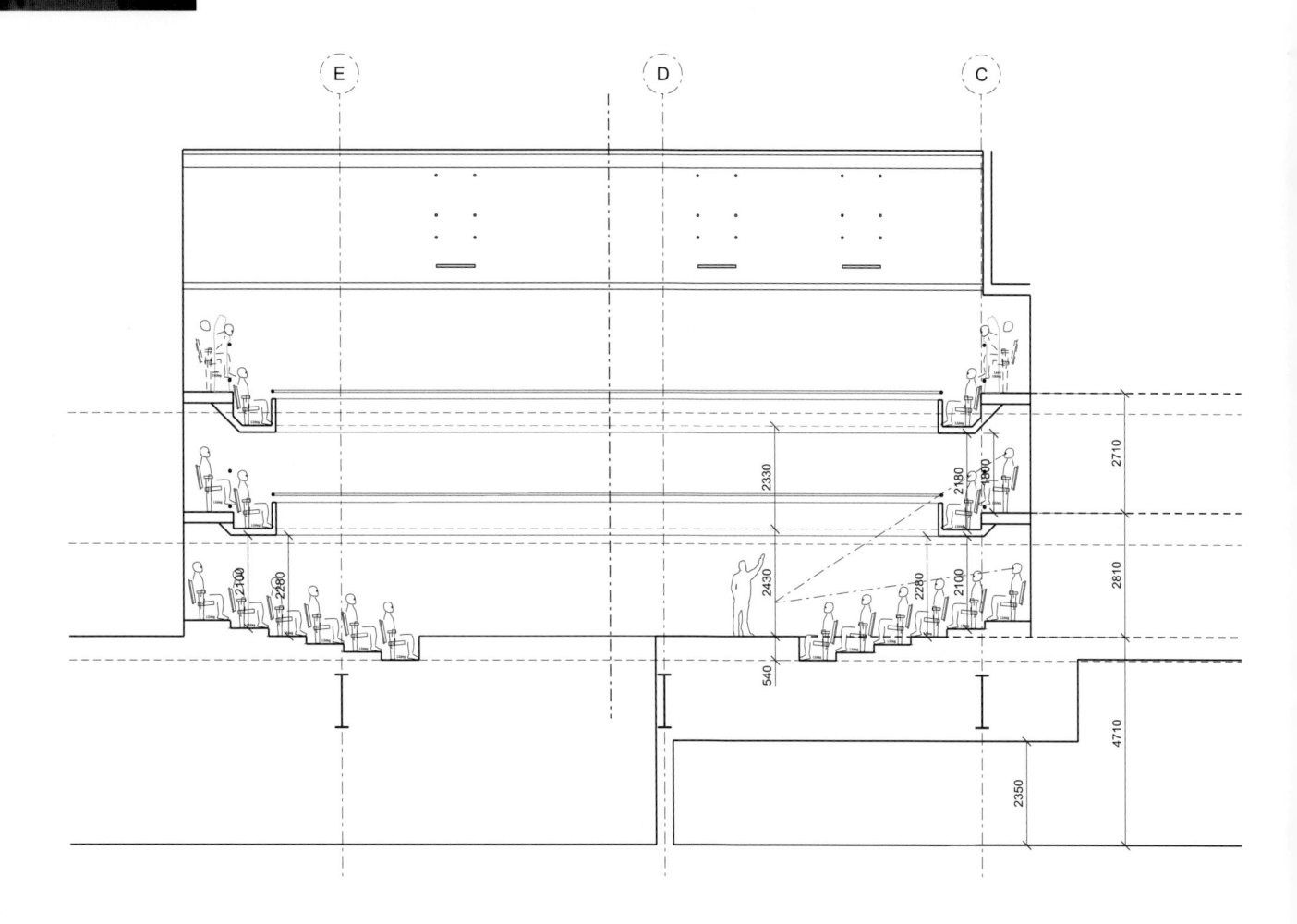

Adaptable Theatres

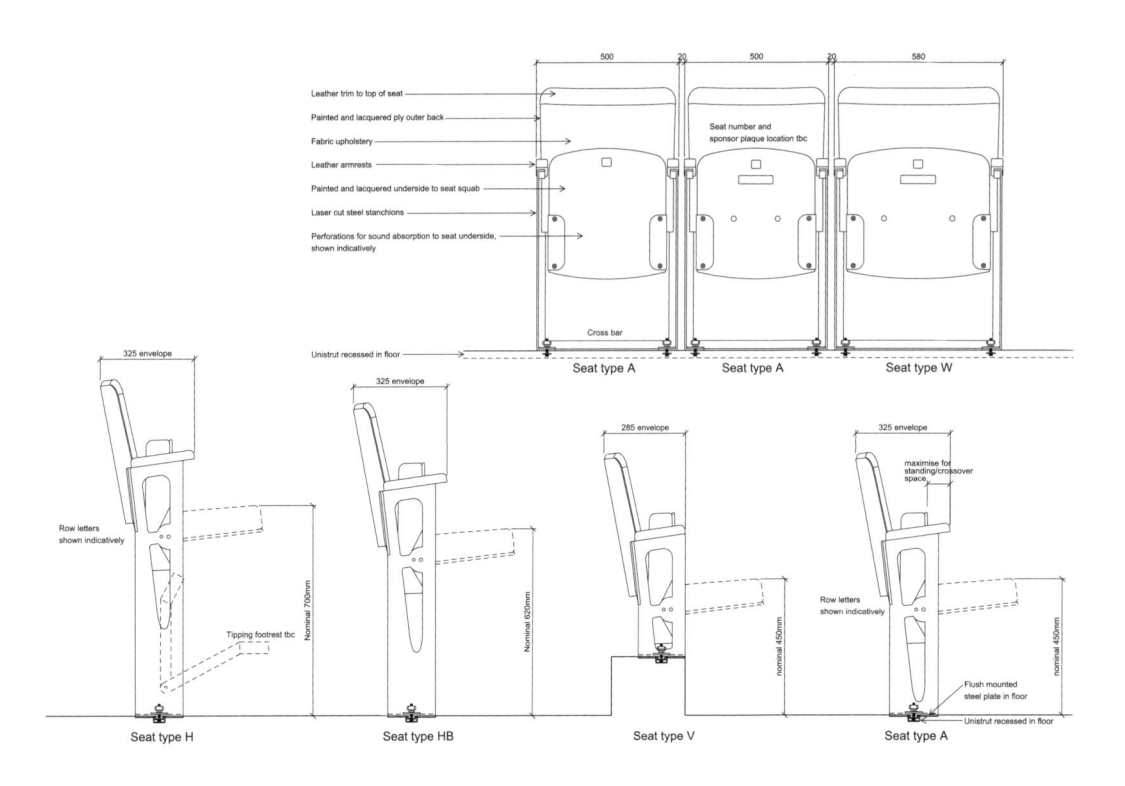

of the site, Derwent London, included a new 600-seat theatre in their 'oversite' redevelopment plan called Soho Place. So the @sohoplace theatre came to be.

Charcoalblue's frequent collaborators Haworth Tompkins worked with them on the design of the theatre auditorium within a building by architects AHMM. All were closely guided by the theatre's owner-to-be, founder-director-producer Nica Burns of Nimax Theatres (alongside Operations Director Geoff Summerton). She knew what she wanted, having consulted widely among the theatre community. 'They dreamt of a flexible auditorium, perfect acoustics and audience/stage intimacy. An ability to create on-site with the dream of a rehearsal room, a Green Room and a bar all in the same building. So that's what we built — with a few extras including an outside terrace,' she says.

Getting to that point on this site, given the proximity of noise-generating railways and their equipment, was not easy. So structural engineers Arup created an acoustically isolated 'box in box', and within that Nica's sumptuous room took shape. It's a broad rectangle in plan, ideal for in-the-round, but can also be changed to a thrust stage. Above the main seating area are two balcony levels. All of this is serviced from above: as in a factory, elements such as drop-in balcony cassettes can be swung out and placed by overhead gantries. Nica's dream of everything a proper theatre needs being together in one place has happened, with a full-size rehearsal room sitting above the theatre, a stage basement beneath and a restaurant at ground level. Invisibly and soundlessly beneath that is the subterranean domain of the Elizabeth Line.

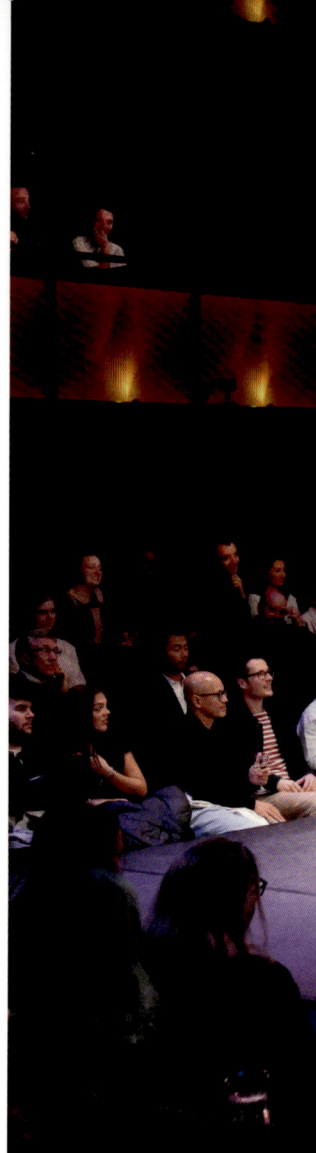

OPPOSITE Seating types: high seats, beam-mounted and standard, Charcoalblue.
ABOVE Test performance, @sohoplace auditorium in-the-round.
LEFT Balcony front and lighting bar mock-up @sohoplace, with Ian Albury, Steve Tompkins and Nica Burns.

Adaptable Theatres

Manhattan and Manchester

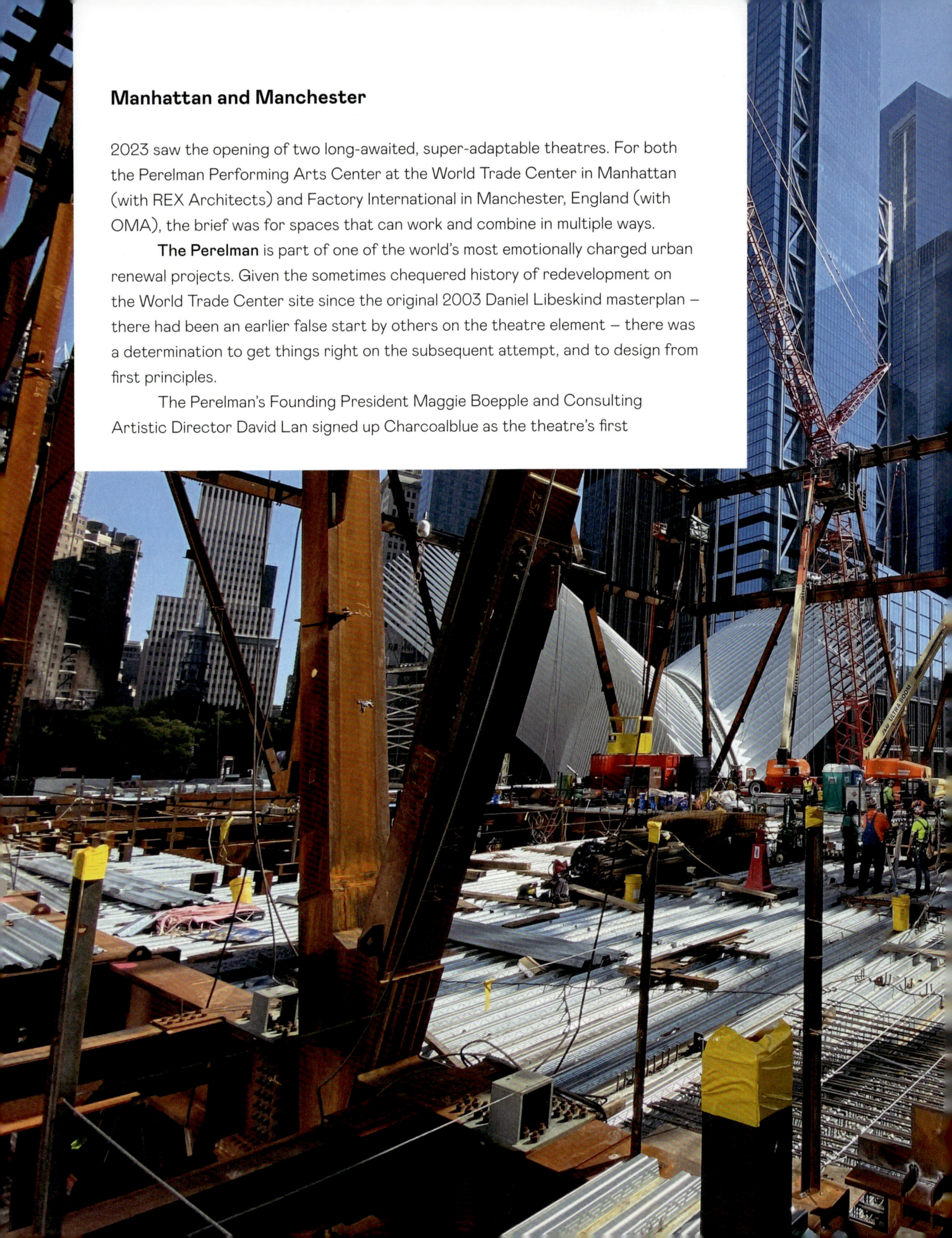

2023 saw the opening of two long-awaited, super-adaptable theatres. For both the Perelman Performing Arts Center at the World Trade Center in Manhattan (with REX Architects) and Factory International in Manchester, England (with OMA), the brief was for spaces that can work and combine in multiple ways.

The Perelman is part of one of the world's most emotionally charged urban renewal projects. Given the sometimes chequered history of redevelopment on the World Trade Center site since the original 2003 Daniel Libeskind masterplan – there had been an earlier false start by others on the theatre element – there was a determination to get things right on the subsequent attempt, and to design from first principles.

The Perelman's Founding President Maggie Boepple and Consulting Artistic Director David Lan signed up Charcoalblue as the theatre's first

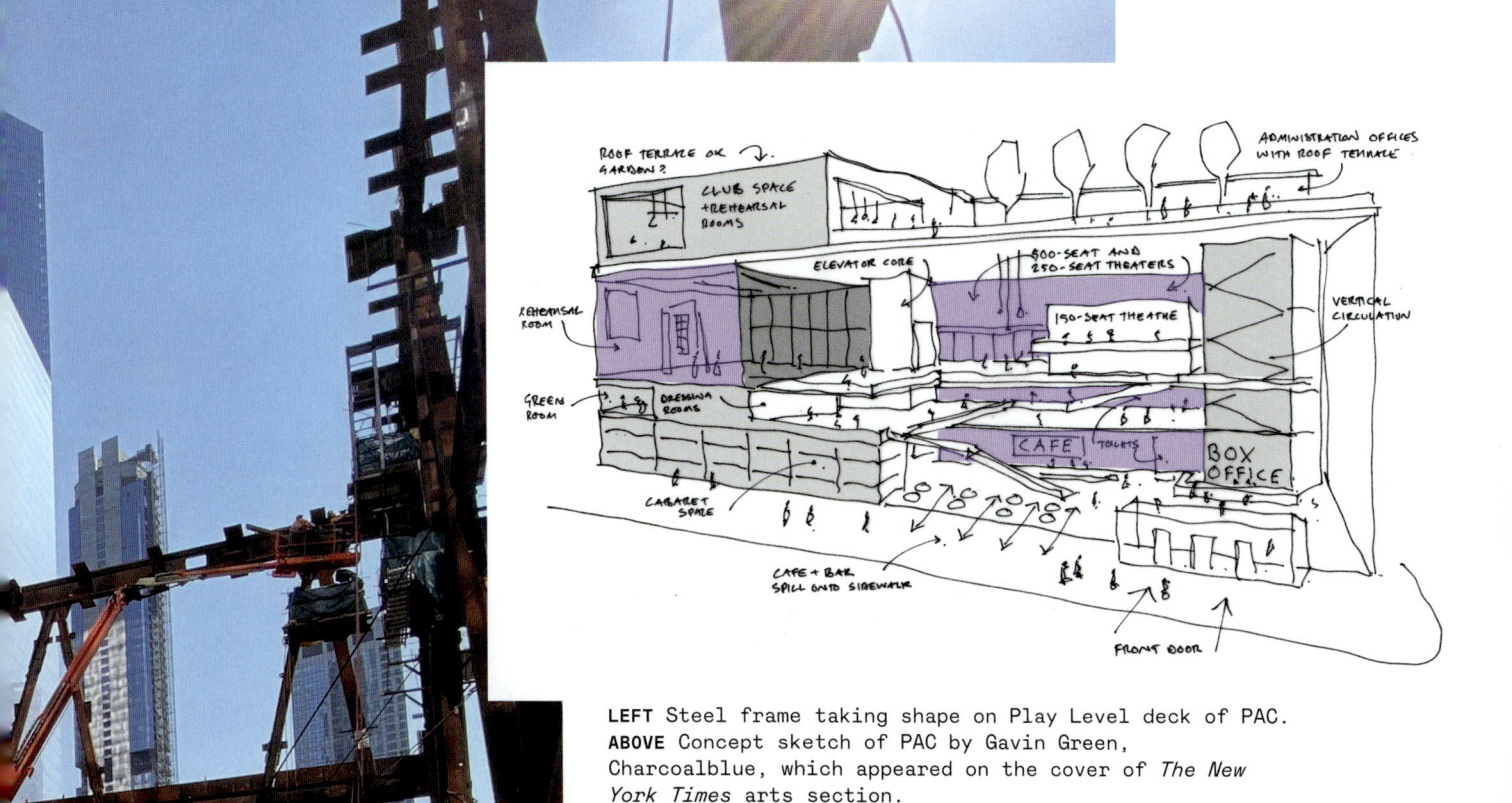

LEFT Steel frame taking shape on Play Level deck of PAC.
ABOVE Concept sketch of PAC by Gavin Green, Charcoalblue, which appeared on the cover of *The New York Times* arts section.

consultant in 2013, with a brief to come up with design concepts for the auditoria. What emerged from this was a three-auditorium theatre in which the performance spaces could be multiply configured, individually or collectively, merging when required to make a performance space – for a concert, say – of 1,200 seats. Otherwise, they range individually from 99 to 499 seats. Every performance art form in drama and music is catered for.

All this is placed in a glowing marble-clad building by REX Architects, described as 'a 129,000 square foot mystery box'. The mystery comes from the translucent Portuguese marble, sandwiched in insulated glass panels, which forms the building's cladding. Daylight filters through this by day, while at night it becomes a lantern. This pure geometric form rises to the occasion of its extraordinary and dignified site, with its memorial pools, museum and landmark transit station as key pieces in the masterplan.

The new artistic team, led by Artistic Director Bill Rauch and Executive Director Khady Kamara, announced their first season with the promise of 'genre-

Adaptable Theatres

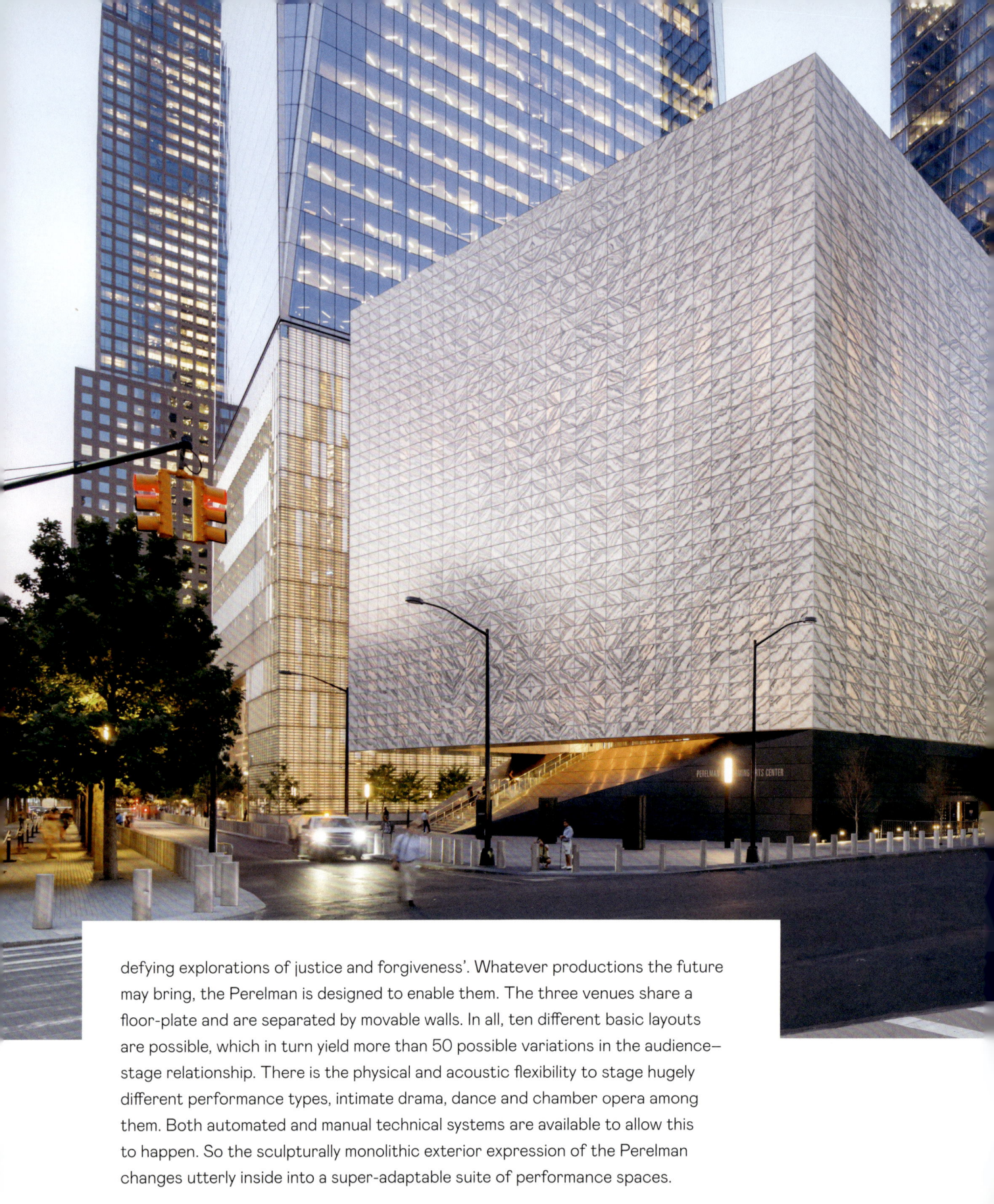

defying explorations of justice and forgiveness'. Whatever productions the future may bring, the Perelman is designed to enable them. The three venues share a floor-plate and are separated by movable walls. In all, ten different basic layouts are possible, which in turn yield more than 50 possible variations in the audience–stage relationship. There is the physical and acoustic flexibility to stage hugely different performance types, intimate drama, dance and chamber opera among them. Both automated and manual technical systems are available to allow this to happen. So the sculpturally monolithic exterior expression of the Perelman changes utterly inside into a super-adaptable suite of performance spaces.

LEFT The new marble facade and entry steps of PAC.
ABOVE Concept sketch by Elina Pieridou, Charcoalblue.
BELOW Charcoalblue's Jon Sivell's punch list.

Adaptable Theatres

Charcoalblue

OPPOSITE ABOVE Charcoalblue's Gavin Green presents the in-the-round format sketch model to clients Maggie Boepple and David Langford.
OPPOSITE BELOW Charcoalblue's Elina Pieridou setting out seats and testing sightlines at the PAC.
ABOVE Inside the John E. Zuccotti Theater, PAC, one of the three interconnected spaces.

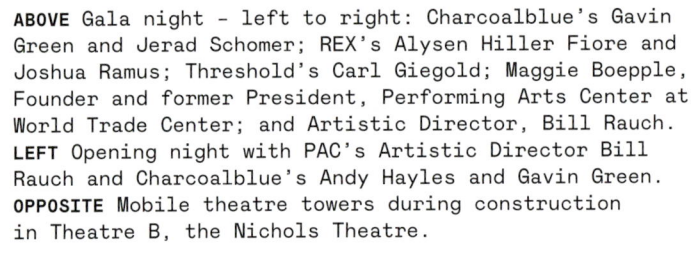

ABOVE Gala night – left to right: Charcoalblue's Gavin Green and Jerad Schomer; REX's Alysen Hiller Fiore and Joshua Ramus; Threshold's Carl Giegold; Maggie Boepple, Founder and former President, Performing Arts Center at World Trade Center; and Artistic Director, Bill Rauch. **LEFT** Opening night with PAC's Artistic Director Bill Rauch and Charcoalblue's Andy Hayles and Gavin Green. **OPPOSITE** Mobile theatre towers during construction in Theatre B, the Nichols Theatre.

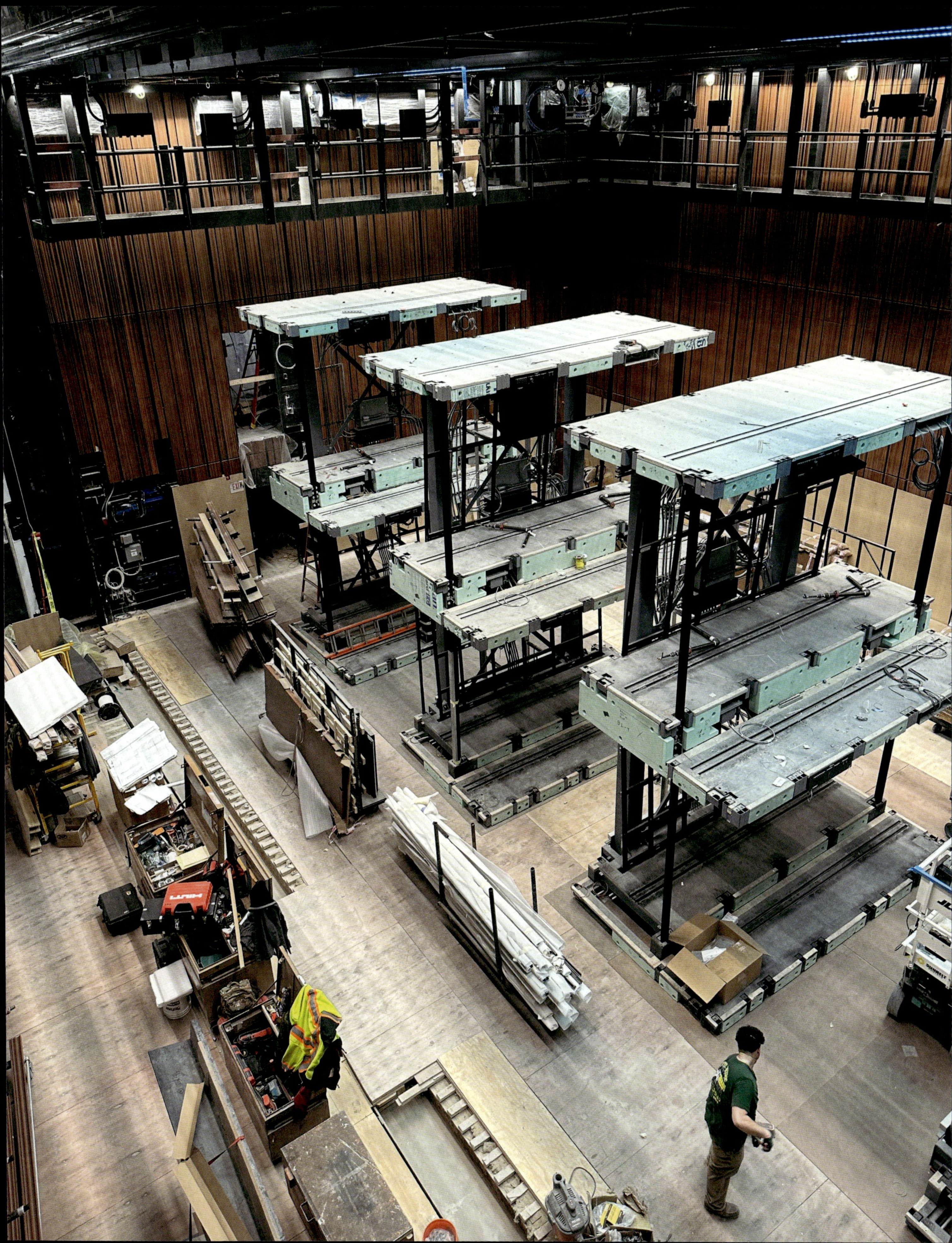

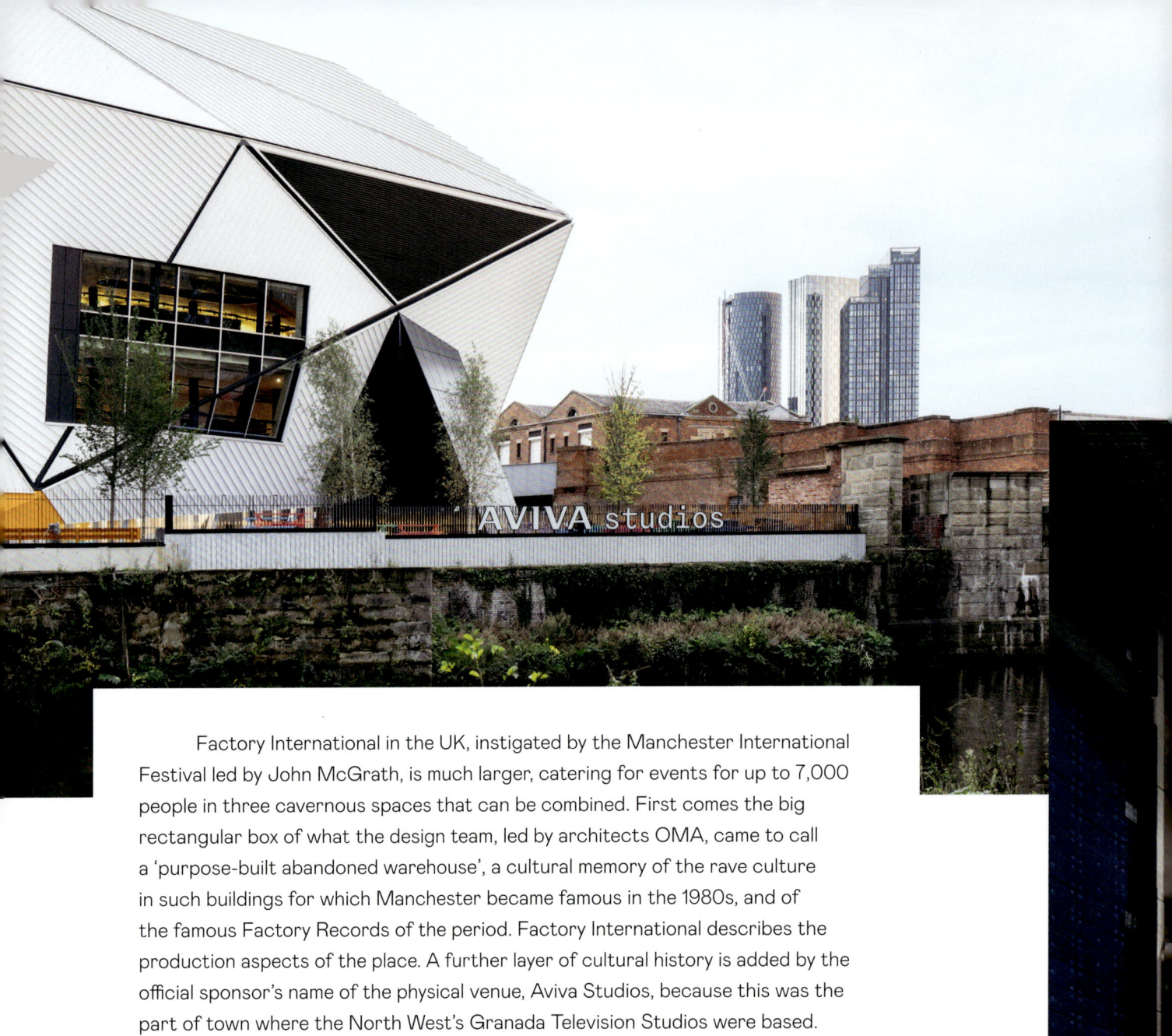

Factory International in the UK, instigated by the Manchester International Festival led by John McGrath, is much larger, catering for events for up to 7,000 people in three cavernous spaces that can be combined. First comes the big rectangular box of what the design team, led by architects OMA, came to call a 'purpose-built abandoned warehouse', a cultural memory of the rave culture in such buildings for which Manchester became famous in the 1980s, and of the famous Factory Records of the period. Factory International describes the production aspects of the place. A further layer of cultural history is added by the official sponsor's name of the physical venue, Aviva Studios, because this was the part of town where the North West's Granada Television Studios were based.

The main box can convert into two acoustically isolated hangar-like spaces. Attached to the box like an organic growth is a more conventionally recognisable raked 1,600-seat flexible theatre known as the 'hall'. This opens up into the box via a 20m-wide stage opening. The various performance spaces throughout the complex are defined and separated by enormous sliding acoustic doors.

This is where theatre design and the world of arenas come together. Large physical objects and equipment can be hung or lowered — 200 tonnes of them in the main warehouse space. Like the smaller Perelman, the auditoria can work independently or combine to make a larger entity. Both also have great digital capability through bespoke fibre-optic networks.

At this level of ambition — which plays into OMA founder Rem Koolhaas's theories on 'Bigness' — one of the prime determinants is exploiting the enormous scale. Here the world of performance becomes an industrial production too, complete with cranes in the roof to move items around the spaces. Moving within it, you cover considerable distances: a city within the city.

Built on a highly complex site incorporating an existing historical railway viaduct, this is a cultural centre of national importance, attracting the most public funding of any such project since the Tate Modern art gallery in London.

OPPOSITE OMA's external folding skin wrapping Aviva Studios new 'Hall' auditorium.
BELOW Inside Aviva Studio's vast new 'Warehouse' space.

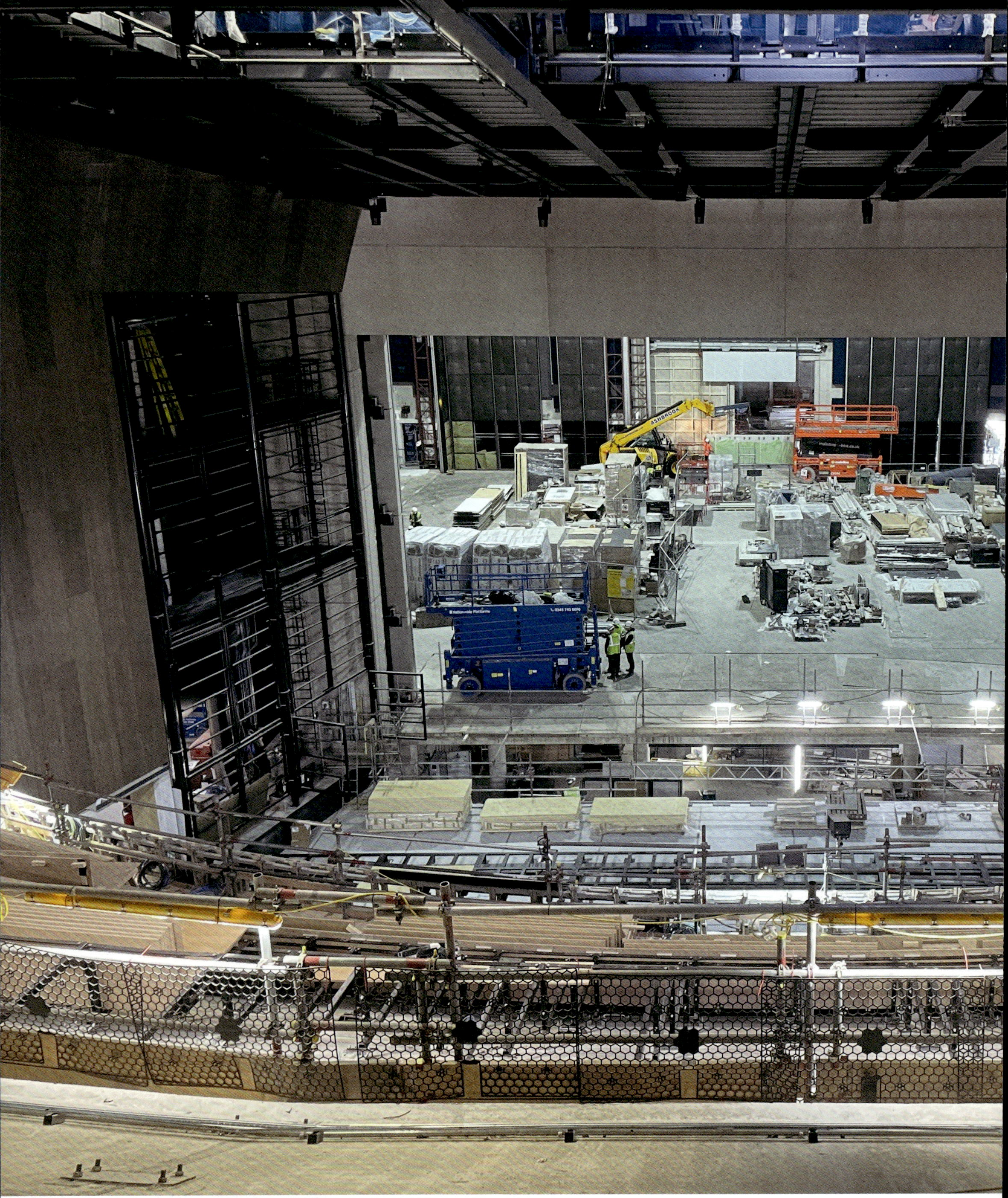

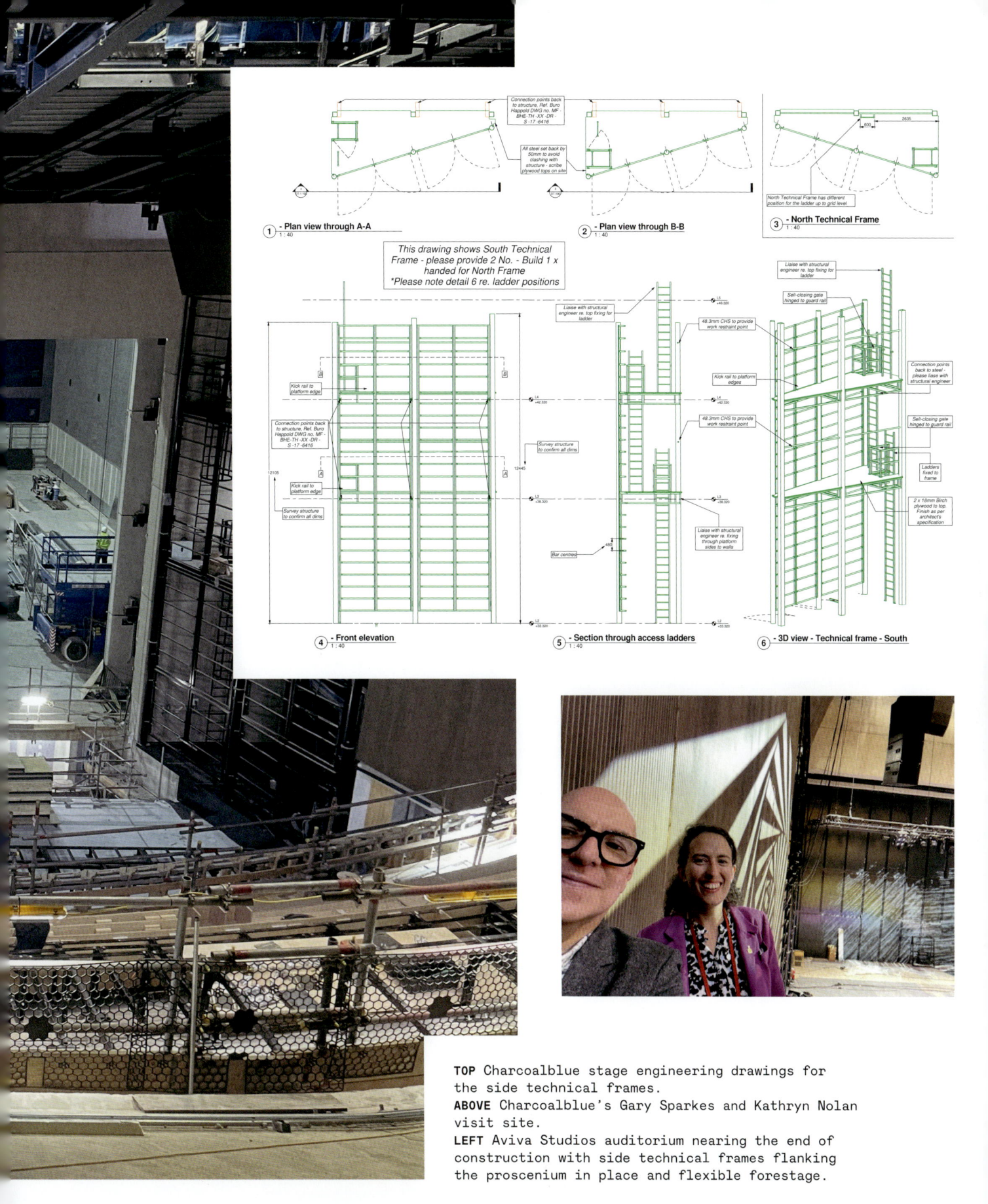

TOP Charcoalblue stage engineering drawings for the side technical frames.
ABOVE Charcoalblue's Gary Sparkes and Kathryn Nolan visit site.
LEFT Aviva Studios auditorium nearing the end of construction with side technical frames flanking the proscenium in place and flexible forestage.

Adaptable Theatres 59

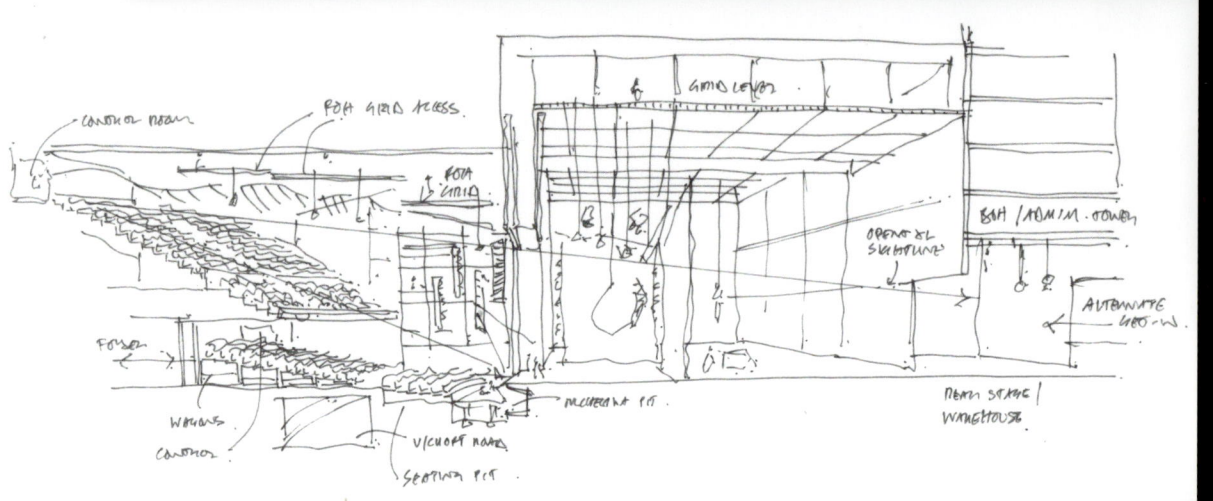

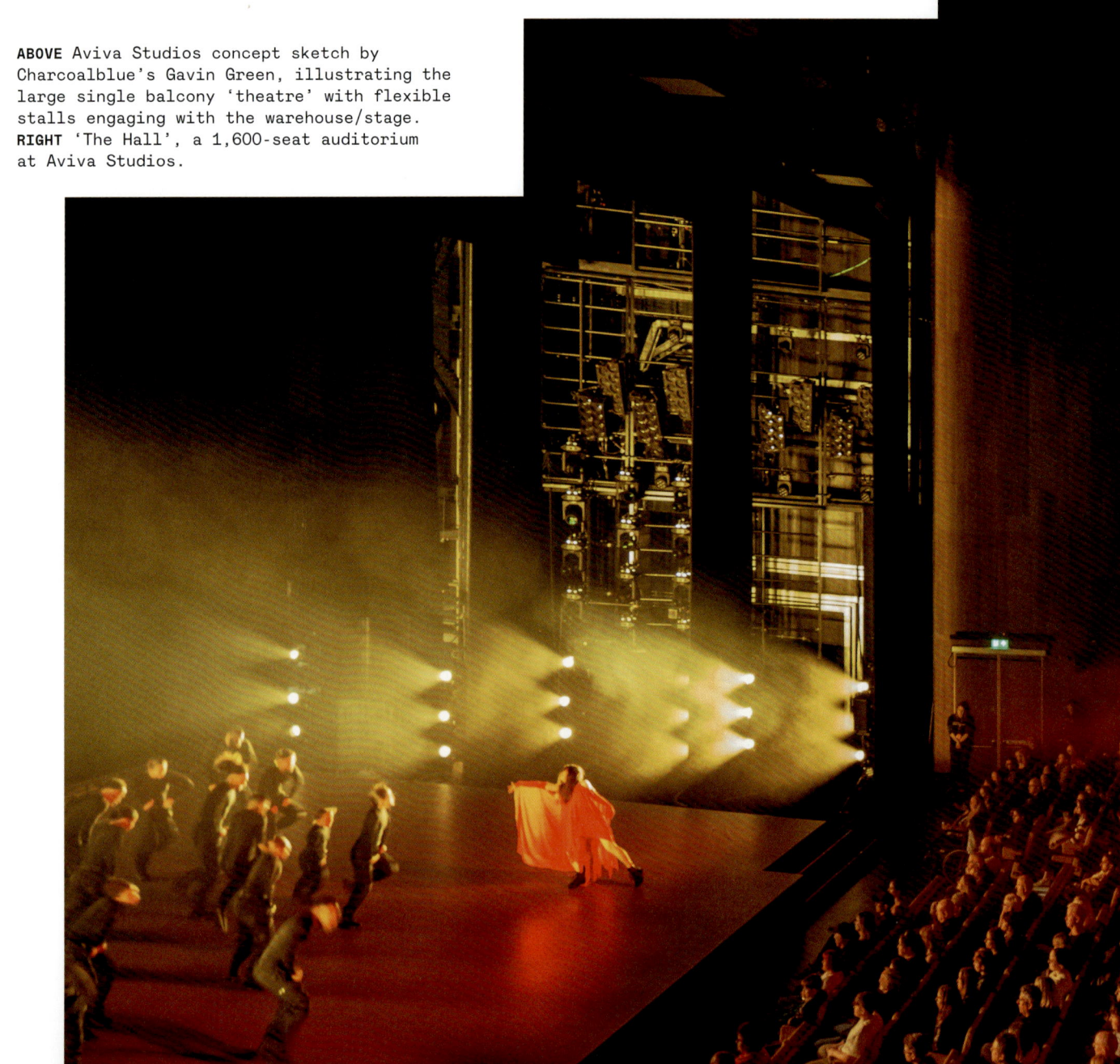

ABOVE Aviva Studios concept sketch by Charcoalblue's Gavin Green, illustrating the large single balcony 'theatre' with flexible stalls engaging with the warehouse/stage.
RIGHT 'The Hall', a 1,600-seat auditorium at Aviva Studios.

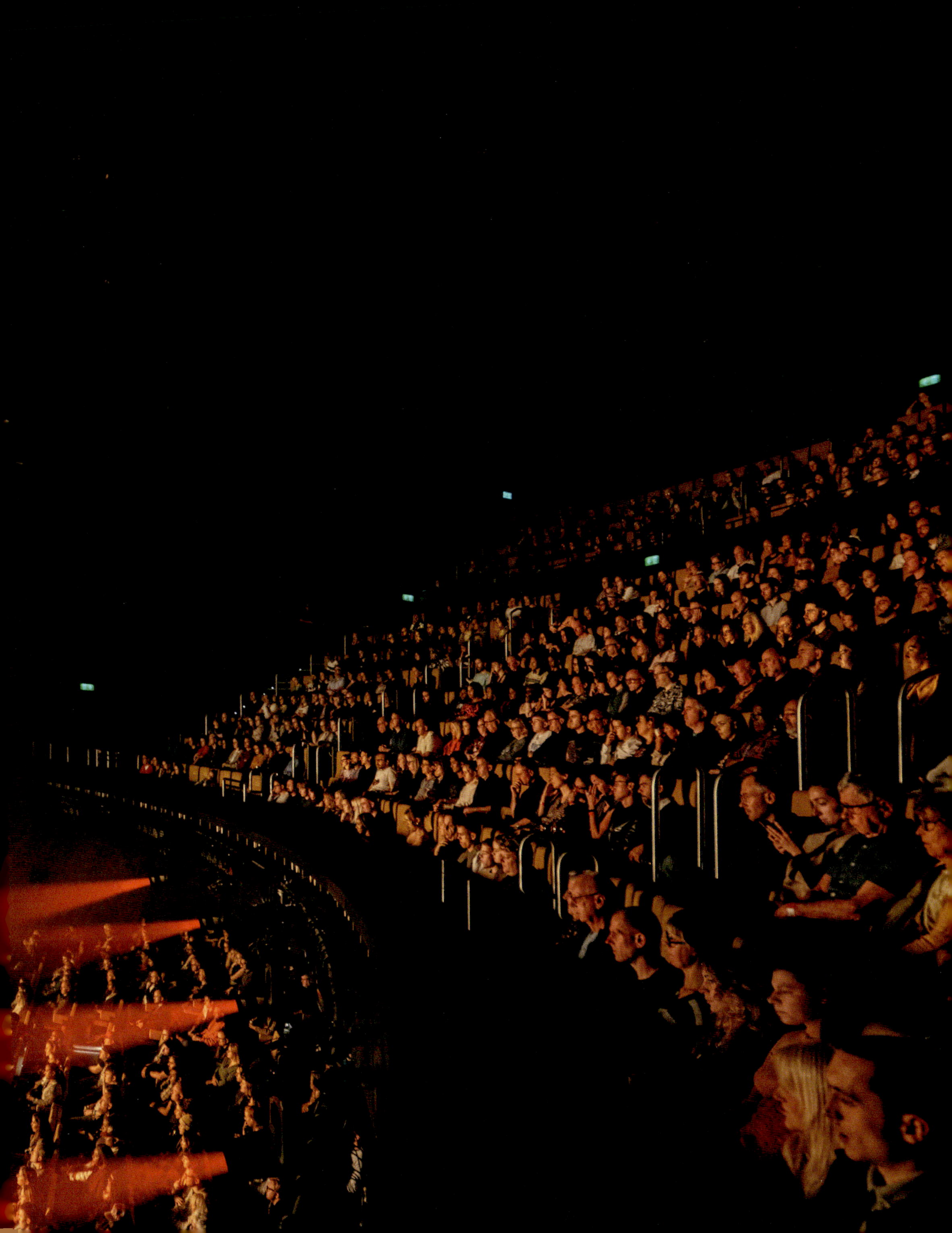

Geelong Arts Centre Phase 3, Australia

Geelong lies 75km south-west of Melbourne on Corio Bay, itself opening onto the large enclosed bay of Port Phillip. It is far enough away from the state capital to be a place with a strong identity of its own, a colonial town founded in 1838 on Wadawurrung lands which grew into a large grid-plan manufacturing city and transport centre in the 20th century. Today, alongside the area's shift towards service and creative industries, the Geelong Arts Centre, founded in 1981, has been growing to meet rising cultural demand. Extra stimulus was given by Geelong's designation as a UNESCO Creative City in 2017.

Phase 3 is a thoroughly individual building on Little Malop Street, designed by architects ARM for Artistic Director Joel McGuiness. Its narrative architecture sets out visually the history of performance in the area, including travelling circuses, with its four internal and external levels incorporating work by First Nations artists depicting their creation narratives. Within this are two

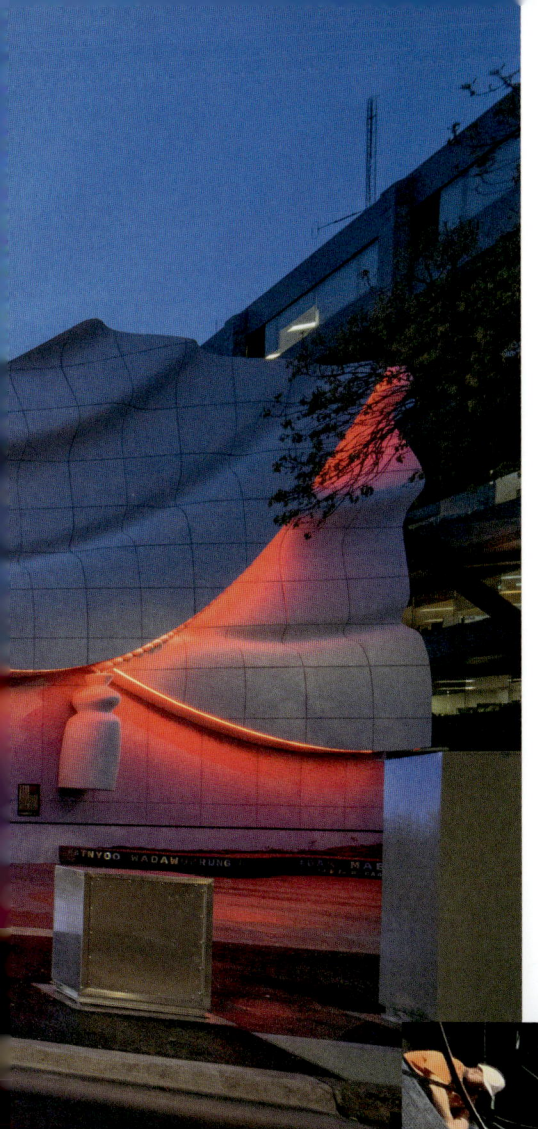

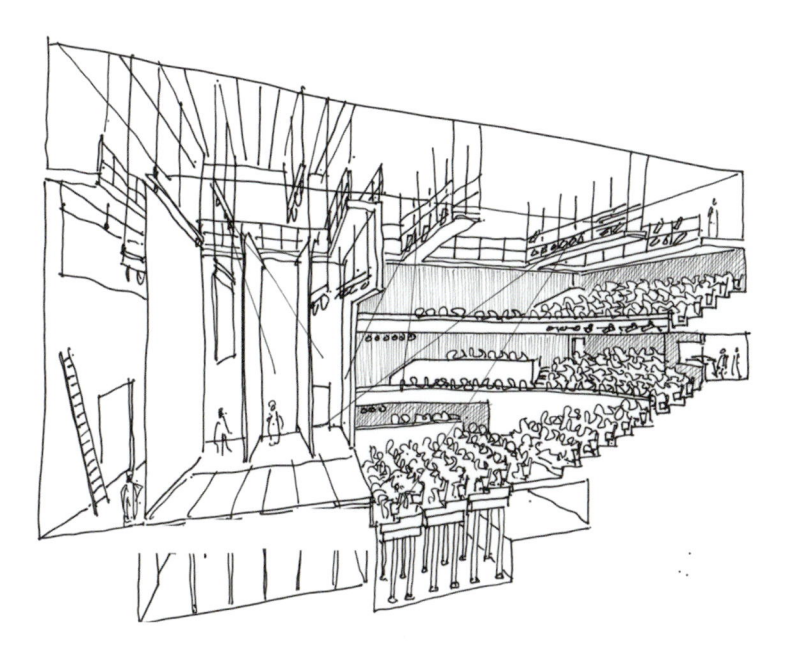

LEFT Geelong Arts Centre fronting Little Malop Street
ABOVE Concept sketch by Gavin Green and Ben Hanson for the principal theatre space.
BELOW Storyhouse Theatre in construction.

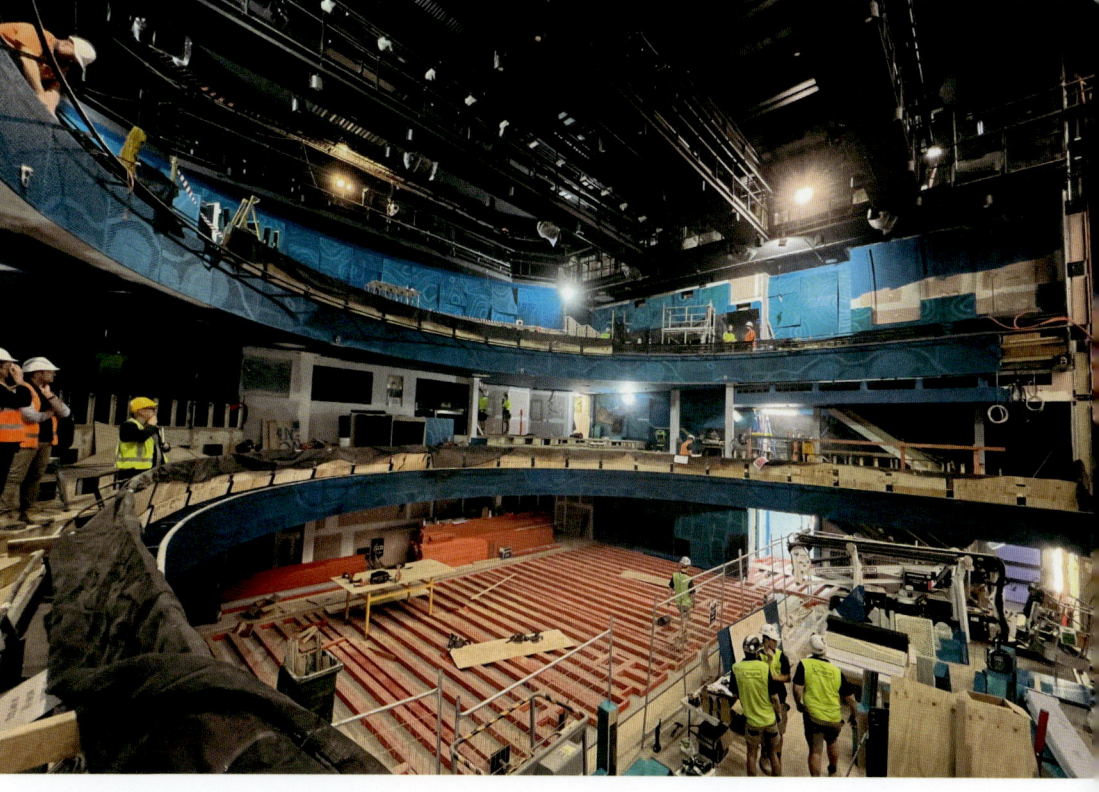

Adaptable Theatres

auditoria: a 550-seat flexible theatre for drama, dance, music and banquet/cabaret, and a 300-seat warehouse-format flexible space suitable for a variety of configurations and events. The latter has a large opening door to the street and a floor designed to take trucks, so that the place can be set up as a festival venue that works both with the very adaptable larger auditorium and its foyer and with the park opposite.

This is an urban-scale project, a state-funded facility and, at the time of writing, the largest scheme that Charcoalblue has undertaken in Australia. In addition to the new auditoria – which complement the pre-existing proscenium-format Playhouse Theatre at the centre of things – there are also links and public event spaces threaded across this arts campus connecting the public foyers. Charcoalblue's role was to provide theatre planning and auditorium design services alongside a full suite of technical design for all performance spaces, plus back-of-house and administration areas.

Adaptability is built into the brief: in contrast with the common scenario of upgrading long-established performance spaces, here the challenge was to help a relatively young arts institution progress its aims for inclusivity and growth.

OPPOSITE A flexible second space, the Open House, opens to the adjacent street. **ABOVE** The new Storyhouse Theatre in flat-floor configuration for a concert. **RIGHT** Charcoalblue's Erin Shepherd setting seats out.

Adaptable Theatres

Aside: Developing Seats

There is no 'do everything' standard formula for theatre seating. The seats are part of the character of the place as well as being essential for audience satisfaction, which is not necessarily the same thing as comfort: you need to stay alert and ergonomically supported, not fall asleep. The technical demands on seating, especially in the adaptable theatres that are Charcoalblue's forte, are high. They must be capable of rapid reconfiguration for different layouts; they must allow for proper accessibility; they are part of the overall acoustic set-up; they must allow clear sightlines; and sometimes they must do a disappearing trick.

At the Liverpool Everyman (see p.152), a cue was given by the previous theatre. Its somewhat ad-hoc audience arrangements had included repurposed rows of old cinema seats, those familiar tip-up plush chairs mounted on stout metal frames. Working with architects Haworth Tompkins and manufacturers Kirwin & Simpson, a design evolved that was inspired by these. Each can stand by itself or in combination with others in any of the possible auditorium configurations. For maximum accessibility, there are many 'specials', including some with a removable arm to go next to wheelchair spaces, and a 'high seat' variation for the rear two rows of the facing stalls so as to allow a clearer floor. All share the same design aesthetic. Variety still rules: in an auditorium of only 400 seats, there are now more than 27 different types.

For the Dorfman Theatre at the National (see p.98), also with Haworth Tompkins, the requirement was as different as could be. The need there was for the seats to fold away when required so as to create a wholly walkable floor, but at the same time they had to be proper theatre seats with no sense of compromise about them.

TOP Everyman Theatre seating manufacturer tender prototypes: Kirwin & Simpson and Race
ABOVE New Everyman Theatre seat concept model

Charcoalblue had prototyped early seats like this at the Royal Shakespeare Theatre in order to make easily arranged wheelchair spaces. Senior Partner Gavin Green describes this variety as folding down into concealed 'tea chests'. For the Dorfman, where the challenge was to make all 200 seats in the stalls disappear into the floor, he describes the hidden containers as 'suitcases'. It's quite a trick: the seats are pretty substantial — more generous in size and spacing than the previous set-up at what had been the Cottesloe — but they can do their magic disappearing act in pairs, two by two, with the adjustable floor set level with the stage.

The advantage of this is that the changeover time between auditorium configurations is dramatically speeded up. Nothing needs to be taken out or put into storage, nor is there a large retractable system to hide in the volume of the theatre when it is not in use. Made by Race Furniture, these are not the only example of seating innovation at the Dorfman, however. Here the Charcoalblue team also introduced 'dickey seats' or 'strapitains', common in France but previously unknown in the UK, which attach to the ends of rows and spring up out of the way when you stand up: handy when you have a capacity crowd, and contributing significantly to the atmosphere of a full house by seeming to fill the aisles (safely) with people.

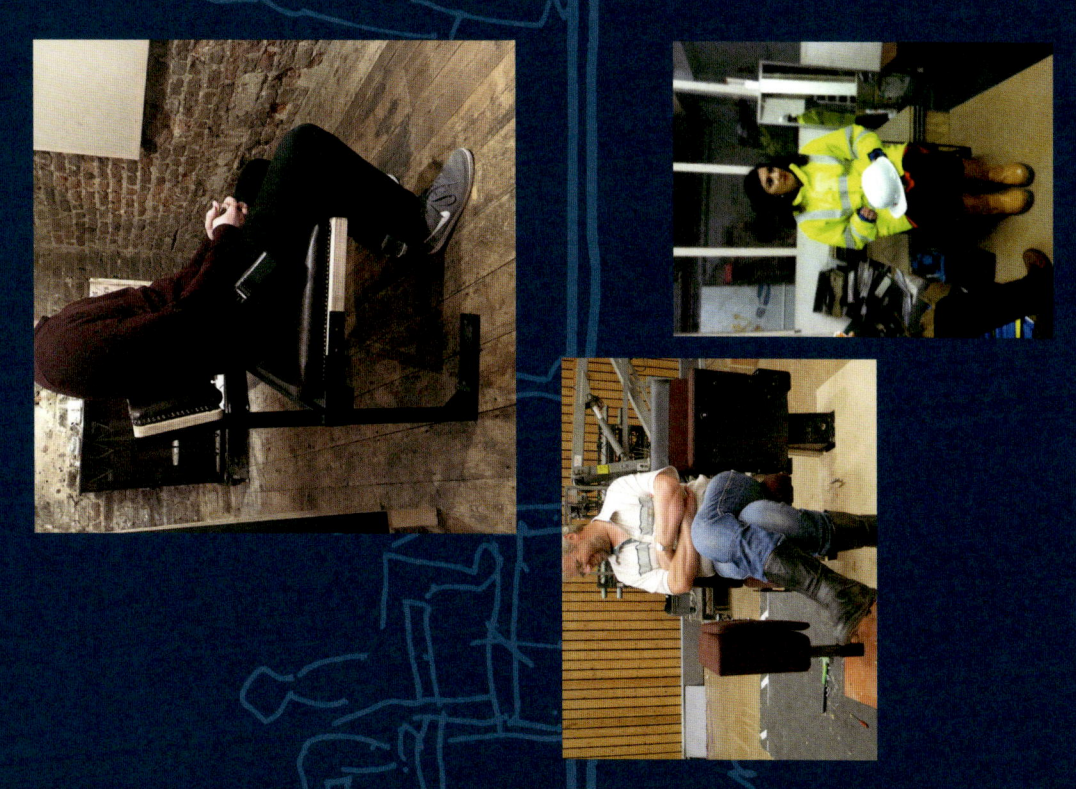

```
TOP Lucy Osbourne's prototype seat for
Wilton's Music Hall, London.
ABOVE National Theatre Dorfman prototypes:
strapitains, seats which fold into the aisles
and spring closed when not being used.
ABOVE RIGHT Seat prototyping with Gemma Bodinetz,
Liverpool Everyman's former Artistic Director.
```

Temporary Theatres

It is axiomatic that you can stage a show anywhere there's enough space for the actors and audience to interact. Particularly in 'immersive theatre', where there is complete intermingling to the extent that you become part of the action yourself. More conventionally, as the musical/movie trope from the late 1930s onwards had it, when push comes to shove, you can put on the show 'right here in the barn'.

The origins of theatre are not so different. The cart drawn up in the ancient Greek town square some two and a half millennia ago acted as a stage, while in late English medieval times the appropriating of the galleried courtyards of inns with their convenient vantage points provided enough of a theatre. The venerable tradition of the highly stylised Noh theatre in Japan dates back a millennium, and by the 14th century had assumed the form it takes today. The audience would have been outside, gathered around two sides of a rectangular roofed stage resembling an open-sided summerhouse. Today this arrangement is typically enclosed within a much larger purpose-built auditorium. The temporary has a tendency to become permanent.

A strong strand of Charcoalblue's work is in purpose-designed temporary theatres which can act as testbeds for permanent design ideas or simply be one-offs.

A strong strand of Charcoalblue's work is in purpose-designed temporary theatres which at times can act as test beds for design ideas to take forward for permanent ones; at others, they can simply be one-offs, fulfilling a function for a festival or for a few seasons, sometimes while work is being carried out on a permanent theatre space.

One particularly fertile strand began in 2005, courtesy of the RSC under Artistic Director Michael Boyd and Executive Director Vikki Heywood. She had previously had a similar role with Stephen Daldry in the remaking and expansion of London's Royal Court Theatre, a key project opening in 2000 that established the reputation of architects Haworth Tompkins (their first theatre) and was an early job for the equally youthful founders of Charcoalblue, then working for Theatre Projects Consultants. The upshot of this was that a good working relationship was already established by the time the RSC work began. And what work it was.

This series of collaborations spawned three separate temporary theatres, respectively in Stratford-upon-Avon, London and (at arm's length) New York City. All were aspects of the RSC's painstaking, hands-on research into how to make an ideal permanent theatre. The knowledge gained here fed directly into (and to some

Temporary Theatres

extent borrowed from) the culmination of all this R&D, namely the permanent Royal Shakespeare Theatre (RST), with architects Bennetts Associates (see p.86).

As so often with theatrical endeavour, the key determinants were money and public awareness. The company had to be kept busy and productive during the long closure needed for the rebuilding of its main house. This supported the repertory nature of the company, kept ticket sales healthy, maintained the tourist hinterland of Stratford-upon-Avon, and retained the good name of the RSC in front of the public in various places.

First up was the Courtyard in Stratford, opening in 2006, a 1,050-seat theatre with a deep thrust stage inside an industrial-scale oxidised-steel box: construction cost £6m. Architect Ian Ritchie used the entrance and foyers of the existing The Other Place studio theatre in the Stratford campus and grafted this new full-size theatre onto the back. Charcoalblue worked on the development of the prototype auditorium, done at full scale.

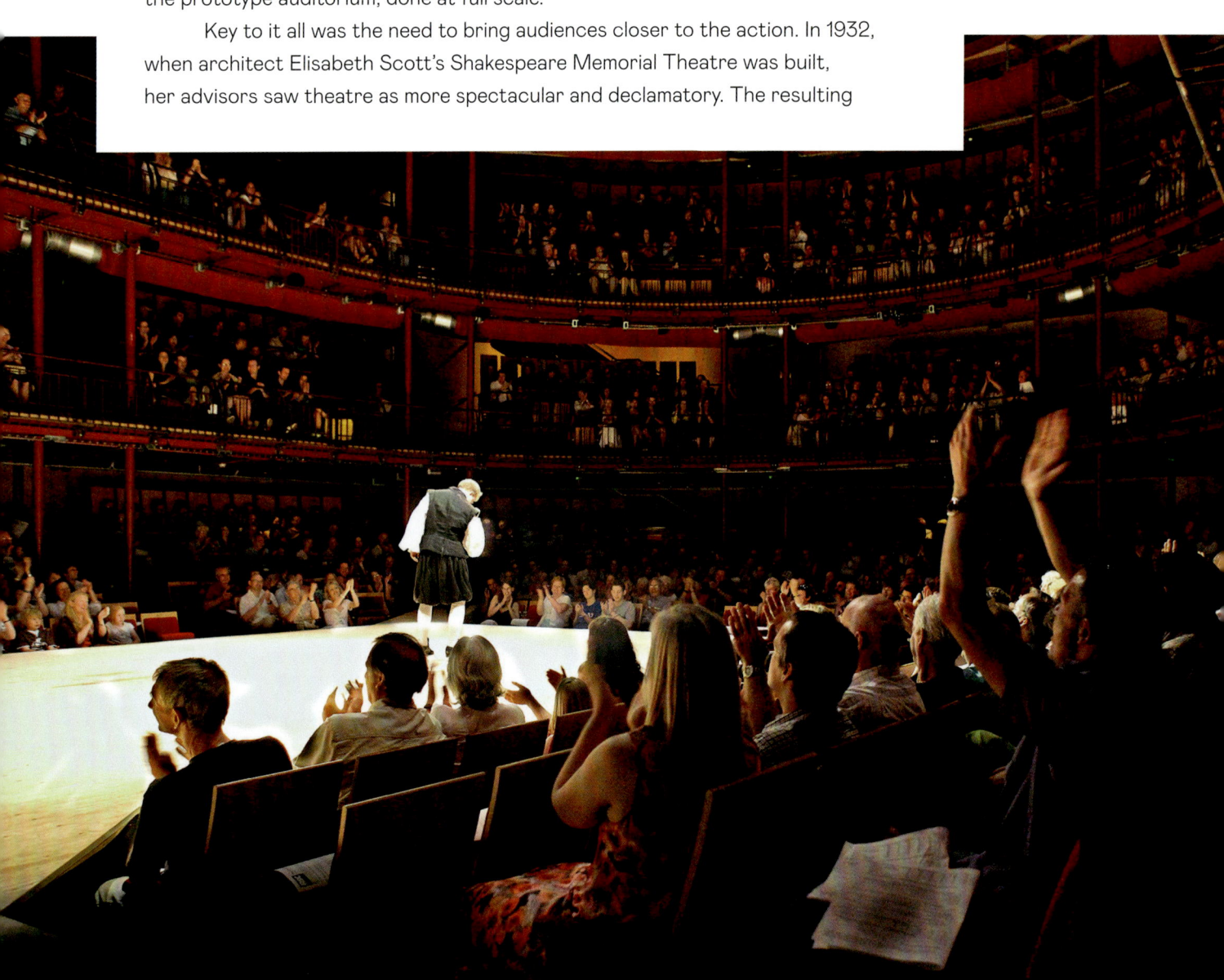

Key to it all was the need to bring audiences closer to the action. In 1932, when architect Elisabeth Scott's Shakespeare Memorial Theatre was built, her advisors saw theatre as more spectacular and declamatory. The resulting

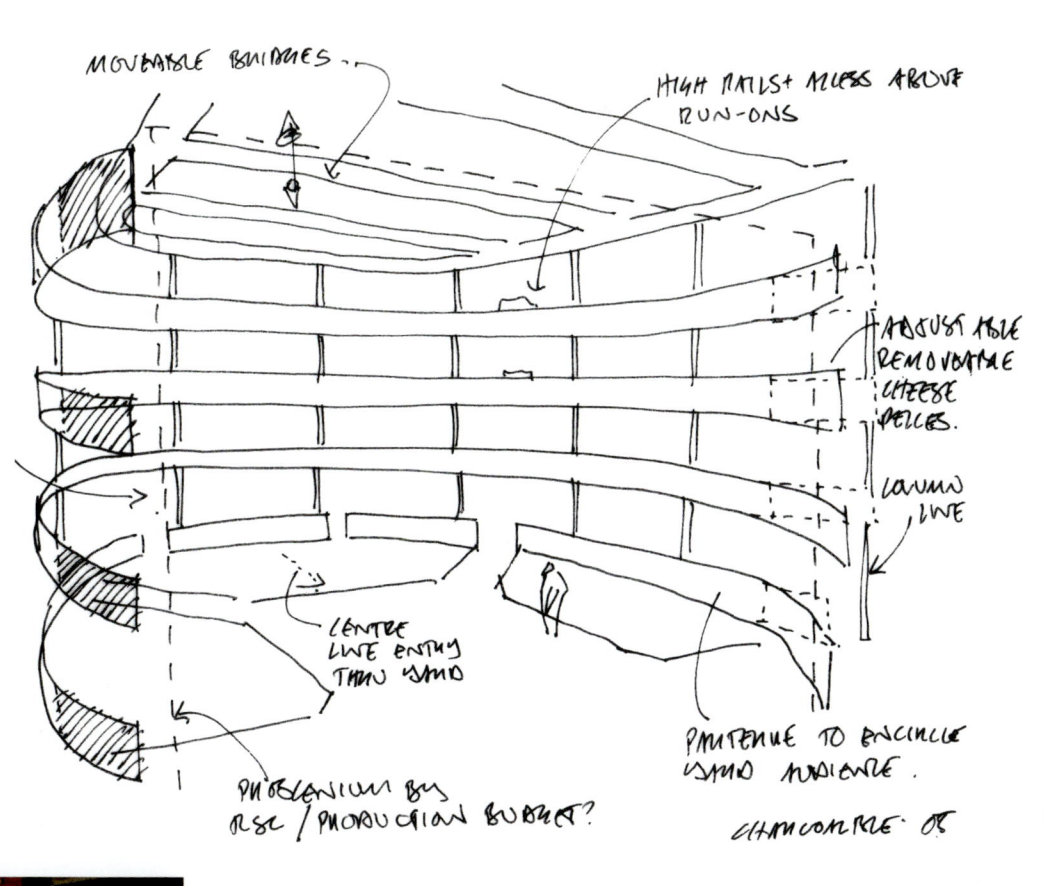

PAGES 68 Inside The Shed at the National Theatre.
LEFT Opening weekend in a tightly packed, intimate Courtyard auditorium.
TOP AND RIGHT Concept sketch by Charcoalblue's Gavin Green, with historical precedents.
ABOVE Charcoalblue at the Courtyard's opening night; Jack Tilbury, Jon Stevens, Nathalie Murray, Viv Murray, Gavin Green, Gavin Owen, Andy Hayles and Katy Winter.

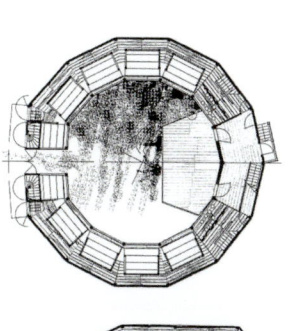

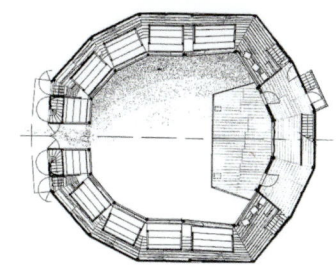

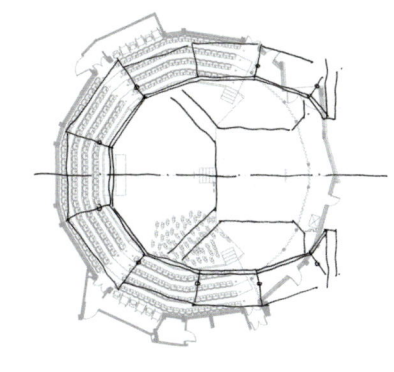

Temporary Theatres

fan-shaped cinema-style auditorium's geometry meant that most seats were towards the back, the furthest being 27m away from the stage. It was just too big and wide. Despite various attempts made down the years to improve the audience–actor relationship, such as extending galleries down the sides, this basic flaw remained. The 1,000-seat Courtyard almost halved that distance, bringing it down to 17m in a much more intimate, wrap-around galleried auditorium. The stage, a long-thrust design with actors' access from the corners as well as the rear, was surrounded by the audience on three sides at stalls level, with two further levels of galleries above. It was immediately regarded as a huge improvement over the old house and proved popular.

In terms of feel, the physical and spatial audience relationship with the actors was a revelation, the more so for being a first-time discovery for many at this scale. The actors felt the power of the space immediately. Chuk Iwuji, playing Henry VI at the opening, remarked: 'It's so high, like a cathedral of theatre, but then you notice how close the audience is. The space is big, but they're right there. It's a perfect example of marrying the epic with the domestic and personal.'

Few in the audience would have noticed the background tech that kept the budget low – such as the loose-laid sound, lighting and video cabling arrangement distributed around the auditorium and technical level in wire cable baskets, avoiding the need for the usual permanent installation. Indeed, virtually every part of the Courtyard could be taken to pieces and reused elsewhere. It succeeded in its mission (a quite incredible opportunity available to very few): to prototype at full scale in real life an auditorium design that would then, with tweaks, be made permanent in the RST itself.

LEFT Repurposed 'The Other Place' theatre at the RSC: now foyer for the new Courtyard Theatre.
RIGHT Charcoalblue's Andy Hayles at a test event.
BELOW Auditorium from the last row on centreline.

Temporary Theatres

The Roundyard, London

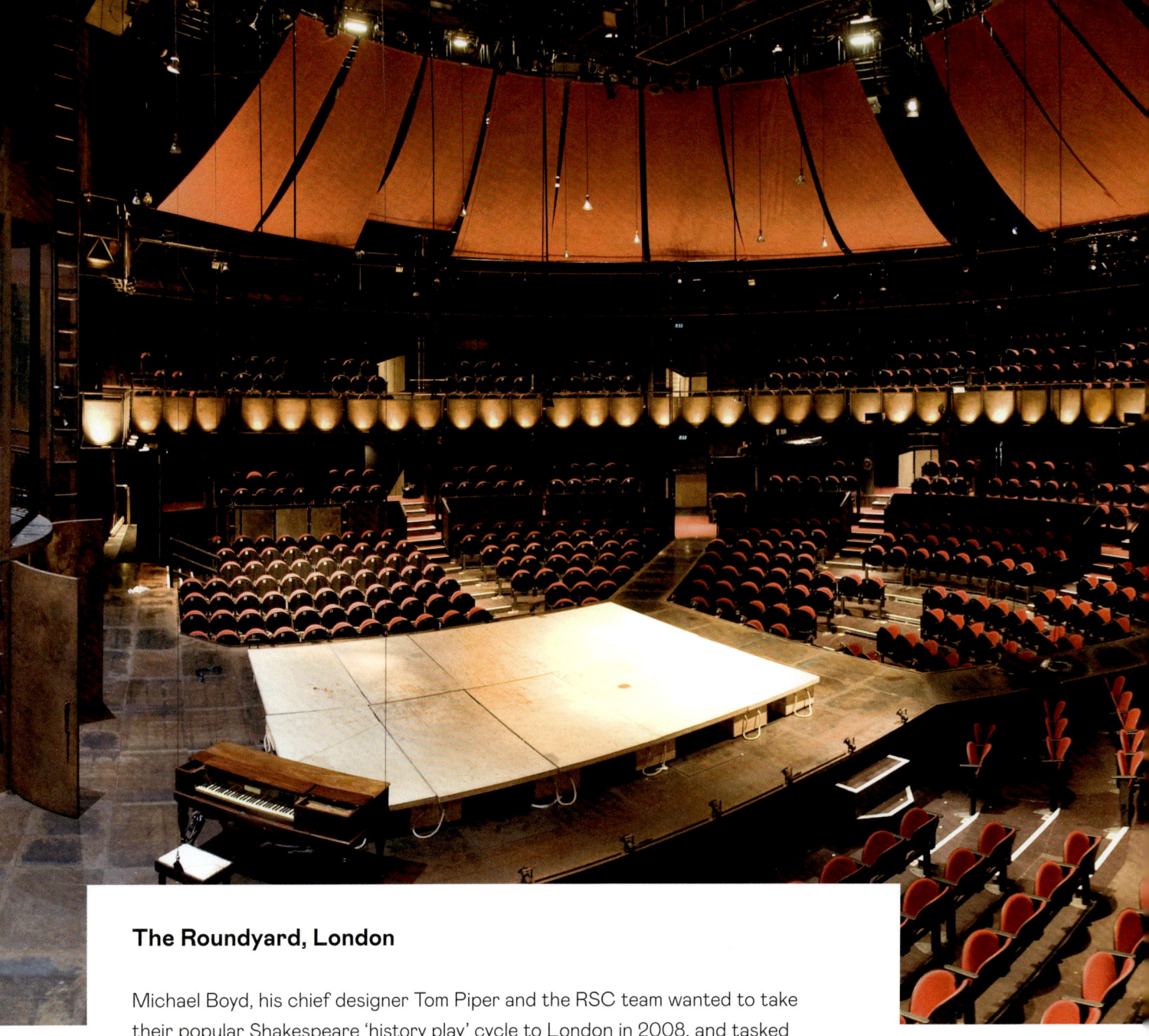

Michael Boyd, his chief designer Tom Piper and the RSC team wanted to take their popular Shakespeare 'history play' cycle to London in 2008, and tasked Charcoalblue with finding a venue to house it. Since the Courtyard was working so well, the initial idea was to replicate it inside the chosen host building in the capital. In the event, things could not work out like that because of the physical nature of the available buildings. But an elegant solution was found. Another recently completed project was the Roundhouse in Camden, a former railway engine turntable shed that had long enjoyed a second life as a performance venue and which had recently been comprehensively upgraded by architect John McAslan, working with Charcoalblue as technical consultants.

The geometry and structure of the Roundhouse could not contain a tight galleried theatre like the Courtyard — its more usual format is in-the-round — so instead Charcoalblue worked with what the building wanted to be, taking about half of its circumference to make a wrap-around thrust-stage arrangement that could receive the Stratford production with ease and keep up the seat numbers. Costs were kept low by reusing the Roundhouse's own seating, reconfigured. The necessary new components were made in the RSC workshops in Stratford and trucked down to London: not the last time that the technical and constructional abilities of the workshop team would be called upon.

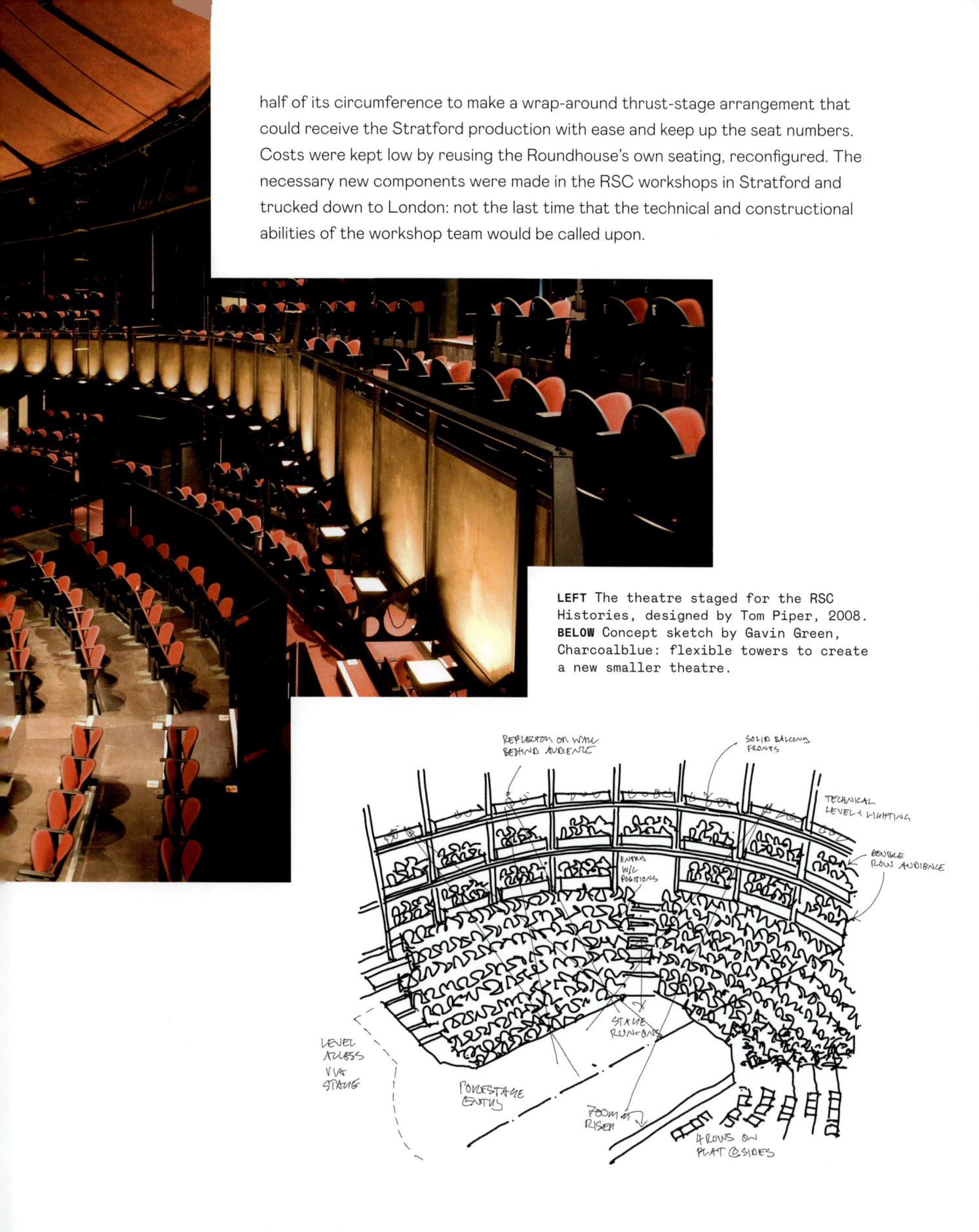

LEFT The theatre staged for the RSC Histories, designed by Tom Piper, 2008.
BELOW Concept sketch by Gavin Green, Charcoalblue: flexible towers to create a new smaller theatre.

Temporary Theatres

The Scarlet and Gray Stage at Park Avenue Armory, New York City

Having conducted a secret scouting mission in NYC to find a possible home for the RSC's history play cycle in the late noughties, in the summer of 2011 the third iteration of Courtyard thinking took the RSC to New York to perform the six-week season of five history plays in repertory as part of the Lincoln Center Festival.

The arrival of the troupe was something of a media sensation, because as well as themselves and their productions, played to perfection at the conclusion of a three-year cycle, they brought a complete 975-seat theatre with them. By then, this was based on the Charcoalblue/Bennetts final 'fully prototyped' RST auditorium in Stratford-upon-Avon, and the London Roundyard.

The theatre's component parts were again made in the Stratford workshops over nine months. Along with all the stage equipment, scenery and costumes, it was packed into 46 shipping containers for its transatlantic journey: around 350 tonnes of kit in all. On arrival at the Armory on Park Avenue, it was assembled over 12 days in the cavernous space of the Wade Thompson Drill Hall. 'We are bringing . . . a new theatre, a revolutionary new auditorium,' said Boyd. Bennetts and Charcoalblue were brought to NYC to explain the concept, so the whole affair was a kind of advertisement for the reborn Stratford. Charcoalblue's Gary Wright, then production manager for the RSC's build at the Armory, has the following recollection:

> We reused the containers that the theatre was shipped in to house the actors' dressing rooms under the auditorium that we built. We built the theatre on top of its storage system!

Its official name, the Scarlet and Gray Stage, had a Shakespearean ring to it, but this was coincidental: these are the colours of the Ohio State University Buckeyes football team, and philanthropist Leslie Wexner, who donated $1m to the project, was a graduate of that university.

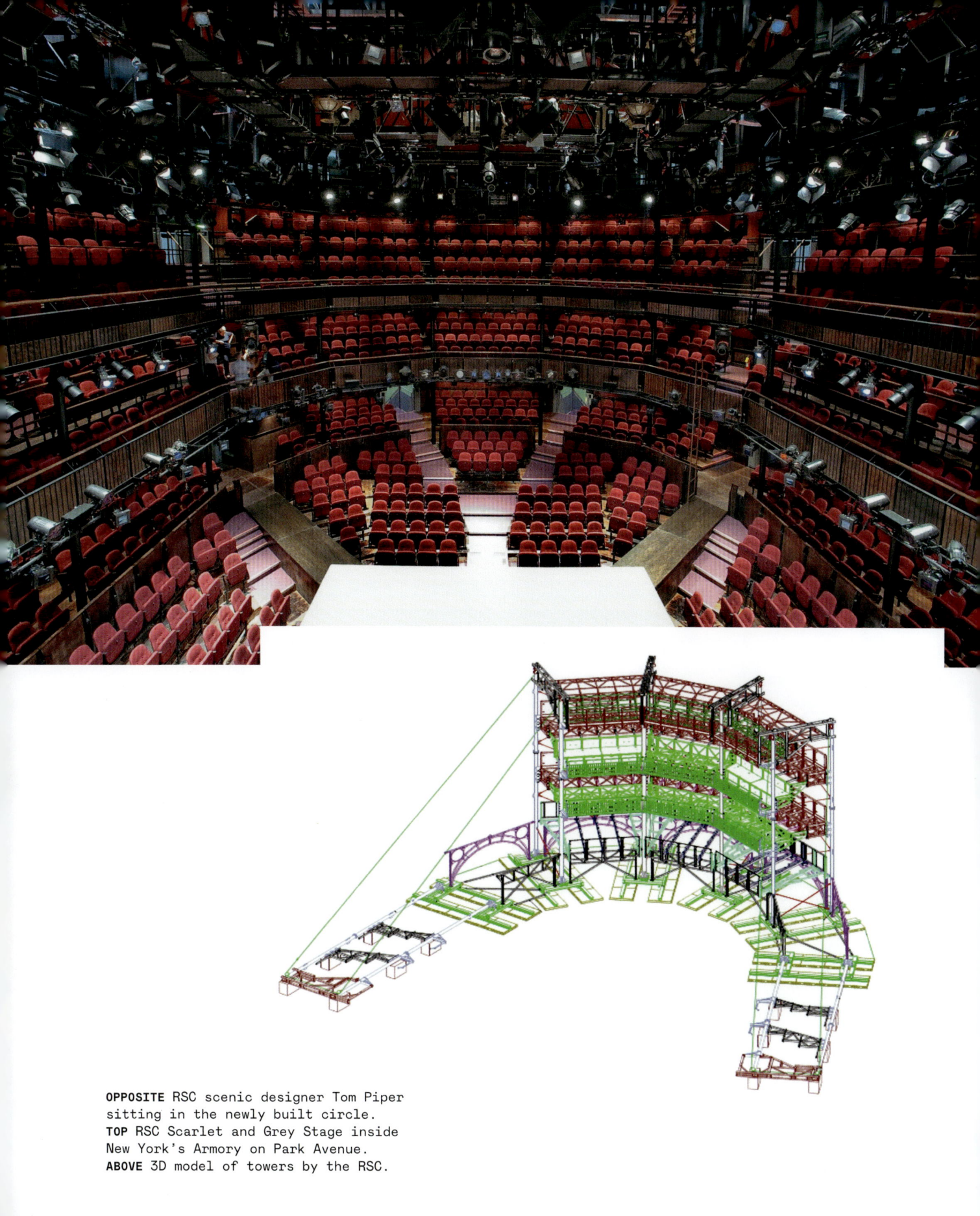

OPPOSITE RSC scenic designer Tom Piper sitting in the newly built circle.
TOP RSC Scarlet and Grey Stage inside New York's Armory on Park Avenue.
ABOVE 3D model of towers by the RSC.

Temporary Theatres

Theatre on the Fly, Chichester

This project was very much by way of 'a bit of advice'. People in the theatre world help each other out. While Charcoalblue was working on the big refurbishment of the original Chichester Festival Theatre (CFT) with Haworth Tompkins for artistic team Jonathan Church and Alan Finch, and the place was closed for rebuilding, the CFT ran two seasons in different temporary theatres. The first of these, in 2012, was 'Theatre on the Fly', an early project by one of the most inventive and socially engaged young practices of the period, Assemble. It was an ingenious timber-and-fabric structure – the fabric being a dirt-cheap fibrous translucent membrane, not a material usually put on show, inspired by flytowers (something the original theatre lacked). It had a charmingly rough-and-ready, barn-like quality, functioned as much outdoor as indoor and was built by volunteers.

In this spirit, Charcoalblue provided informal advice on the rake and spacing of the seating and the positioning of the stage, and then got back to work on the main house.

The Shed (Temporary Theatre), National Theatre, London

A vivid presence on London's South Bank from 2013 to 2017, the Shed was designed by architects Haworth Tompkins with Charcoalblue for the artistic team of Nicholas Hytner and Nick Starr, as a temporary replacement for the National's Cottesloe experimental theatre while the same team was transforming that into what is now called the Dorfman (see p.94). So successful was it that it lasted three years longer than its originally planned single year, meaning that for a while the National became a four-auditorium theatre. In a knowing contrast with the famous boardmarked concrete of Sir Denys Lasdun's 1976 building, the Shed was clad in real timber boards stained bright red. Its cubic form was marked at the corners by tall louvred natural-ventilation chimneys in the same material. Windowless and sculptural, it referenced the external protrusions of Lasdun's mothership.

LEFT Theatre on the Fly, scaffolding auditorium with chipboard bench seating and side musician gallery.
BELOW On-site at The Shed, NT: theatre and natural chimney towers wrapped up.

Temporary Theatres

Designed to be as sustainable and low-waste as possible, its interior was conceived by working closely with the National's team. It emerged as a very intense small auditorium, at 225 capacity roughly half the size of the Cottesloe, with raked seating (the old seats from the Cottesloe) set tightly around three sides of a flat-floor stage. Indeed the front row of the audience was effectively sitting on the stage, eye to eye with the actors. There was a small fixed audience gallery above. The deep thrust format could be converted into in-the-round simply by moving sections of seating.

Whereas the Courtyard in Stratford was a large theatre plugged into the existing facilities of a small one, here the reverse was true: all the many facilities of the National and its capacious foyers were there for the Shed, and part of one of its outdoor terraces was temporarily enclosed with translucent polycarbonate and mood lighting to lead through to its interior. Despite being placed on the riverside right in front of the older building in a space normally used for outdoor events, this connection felt strangely natural. Unlike the Cottesloe/Dorfman, with its separate side entrance, going to the Shed was part of the main theatre experience. Its attraction to young theatregoers and its production of riskier work than might have been presented in the 'grown-up' building was notable.

The sustainable agenda, aside from the use of renewable timber, was enhanced with LED stage lighting, reusable modular panel construction for the stage floor and galleries, minimal disturbance of the paved forecourt of the National and, of course, natural, stack-effect ventilation — normally a big expense and energy consumer. The Shed had no mechanical plant whatsoever. This was theatre unplugged. As much of an art event as a building, described by design and architecture magazine *Dezeen* as 'a startling and enigmatic presence', it could not stay forever, but it claimed the affections of Londoners and visitors alike.

RIGHT The Shed located in the National Theatre's 'Watch This Space' plaza.
OPPOSITE Concept sketch by Gavin Green, Charcoalblue.

Temporary Theatres

ABOVE Concept model by Charcoalblue's Ben Hanson.
RIGHT Flexible and compact auditorium from the gallery.
BELOW Auditorium in construction, all materials to be recycled in the future.

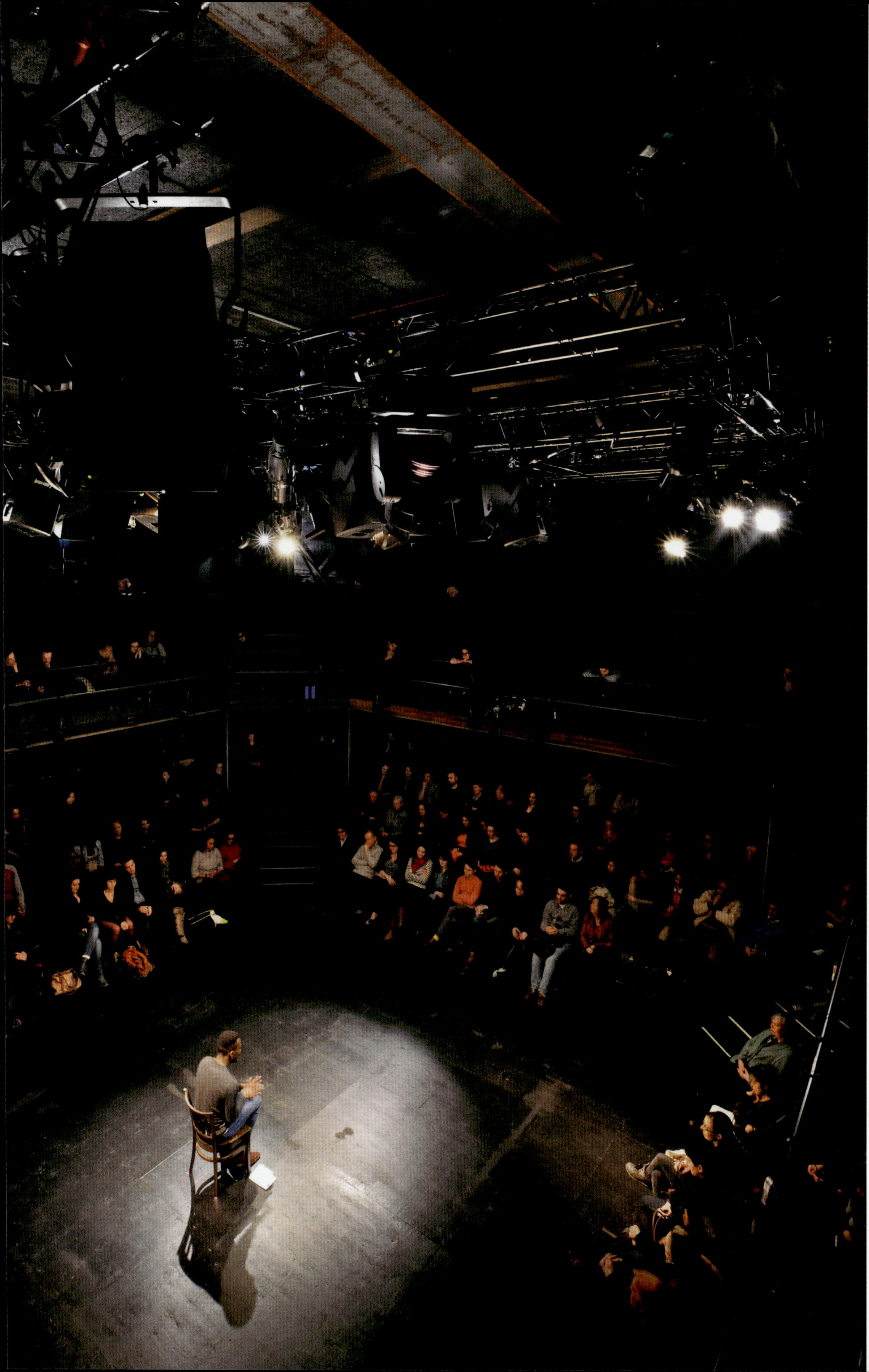

Against the Culture Palace

Something to be avoided: being over-specific in your design, tailoring a building so precisely to a specific stated set of needs that it becomes very difficult to change course later. This way of designing is perhaps less prevalent than it used to be, but the mantra of 'long life, loose fit, low energy' is only really starting to hit the mainstream now, more than 50 years after it was first uttered by architect and RIBA President Alex Gordon. It is especially applicable to theatre.

Two of the great UK cultural institutions, the Royal Shakespeare Company and the National Theatre, in their different ways both suffered from 'culture palace syndrome', the notion that their importance should be recognised by buildings that set out firmly and forever How Things Should Be Done. Even in repurposed spaces, such as the Wharf Theatres for the Sydney Theatre Company (STC), dating from a 1980s refurbishment of harbourside pier buildings, things can ossify over time.

The demands of the theatre community, from playwrights, audiences and actors to directors and producers, constantly evolve. It helps, then, if your building can be adaptable as well. Guess what? Many aren't, because back at the start people were chasing the idea of locking down the perfect permanent space. It is Charcoalblue's habit to pull these places gently apart and reassemble them to work better, in a variety of ways.

> **The demands of the theatre community constantly evolve; it then helps if your building can be adaptable as well.**

The Royal Shakespeare Theatre in Stratford-upon-Avon has already been mentioned several times because of its remarkable evolution from a temporary theatre, the Courtyard (see p.70), rapidly purpose-built at full scale to test its bold auditorium concept. That opened in 2006, while building work began on the permanent theatre in 2007. The auditorium, the team reckoned, could do with being a bit tighter than the Courtyard, and this was achieved by imagining a 12-sided geometrical plan opened out at one end. This plan wraps round the deep thrust stage more closely and brings the depth of the stage into play forward of the original proscenium arch, now left in raw industrial brick. At the same time, the geometry breaks up the run of the galleries vertically into discernible subsections.

The Courtyard taught another lesson: that in theatre, action can happen above and under the stage as well as on it. In the 2006 opening cycle of 'history plays', Michael Boyd and designer Tom Piper placed the French Court up high on trapezes and moved some of the mêlée of the Battle of Agincourt upwards too. Duly noted: for the RST the sightlines were adjusted to better allow for aerial acting, while the substage was deepened to ensure that the element of surprise was protected from steeper gallery sightlines too. Finally, there was a period of eight months when design elements from the final theatre could be tested with live audiences in the Courtyard to gauge their reactions: a pilot process that Charcoalblue had previously been able to undertake in their temporary home for St. Ann's Warehouse in Jay Street, Brooklyn, pending the move to its permanent new home at the Tobacco Warehouse on the banks of the East River (see p.14).

The new RST auditorium sits within the shell of Elisabeth Scott's 1930s theatre with its Art Deco foyers: the regained space extends those public areas, making things less of a crush. The foyers are also extended out towards the street in a glazed extension that serves to link the main theatre to the existing smaller Swan Theatre: the two theatres also now share backstage accommodation and equipment.

In 2006 I could compare and contrast. I went and sat in the furthest seat from the stage in both the legacy Scott main theatre and the then-new Courtyard.

OPPOSITE Taking a bow onstage at the RSC to a full house.
ABOVE RSC auditorium taking shape: view from stage.
BELOW Concept sketch by Gavin Green, Charcoalblue.

Against the Culture Palace

ABOVE Charcoalblue's Theatre Designers Ben Hanson and Sonya Baker.
LEFT Charcoalblue team on-site – left to right: Greg Allen, Nathalie Murray, Andy Hayles, Gavin Green and Gavin Owen.

BELOW Charcoalblue design development model by Greg Allen, including front-of-house technical levels, the 'wedding cake', substage and upstage rigging at the RSC.

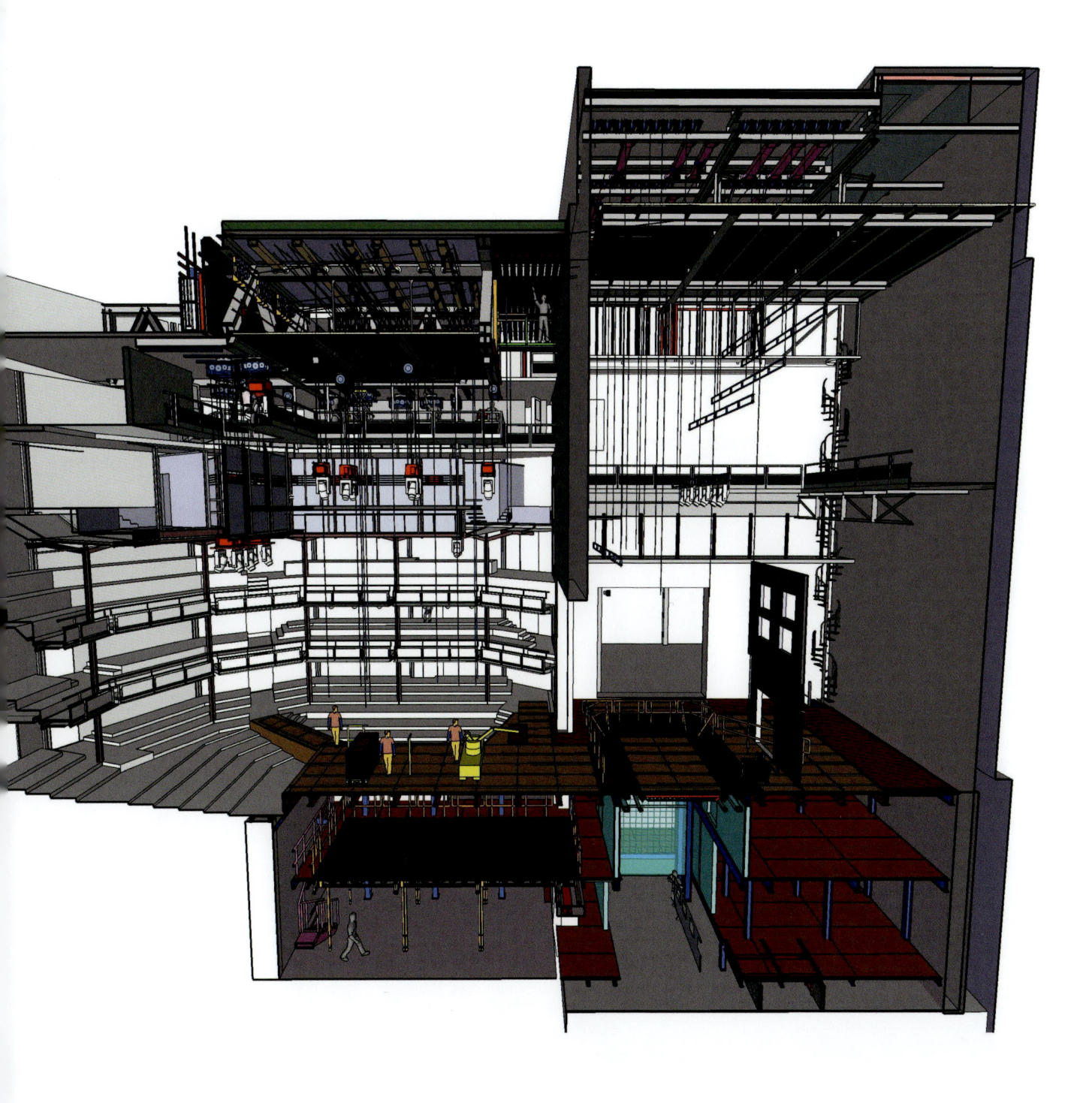

At the National Theatre in London, the 'set in stone' (or in this case concrete) nature of the listed 1976 Denys Lasdun building was even more pronounced. It is a masterly building but — except perhaps in the case of the late addition of the Cottesloe Theatre into the original programme — deliberately resistant to change. The Charcoalblue mantra of 'keeping the concrete to the edges', so allowing for future flexibility, is spectacularly hard to apply here, in a building that is almost geologically tectonic both outside and in. But the 'NT Future' programme in the time of Director Nicholas Hytner and his executive team, led by Nick Starr, managed to do it.

By working with rather than against the spirit of the building, frequent architect collaborators Haworth Tompkins subtly adapted the fabric of the complex in an invisible-mending kind of way throughout, upgrading it for present-day habits and needs, and adding a new scenic workshop building at the rear, the Max Rayne Centre, to free up space. Two main areas of what was a long programme involved Charcoalblue in particular, who were the theatre

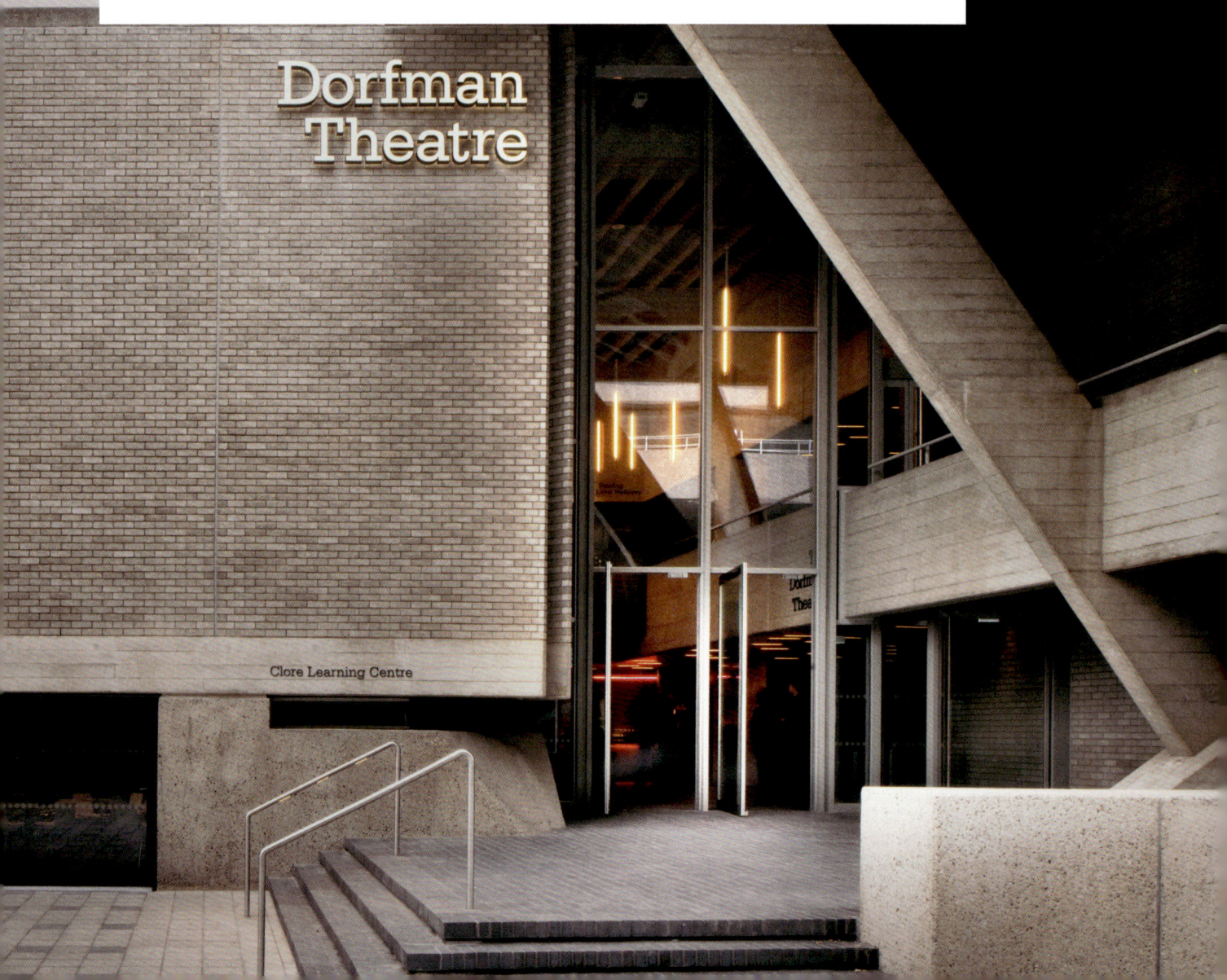

OPPOSITE Dorfman Theatre foyer entrance.
ABOVE Substage elevators for flexible stalls floor.

Against the Culture Palace

ABOVE Concept sketch by Gavin Green, Charcoalblue; flexible stalls lift to create both steep and shallow rakes at the Dorfman.
RIGHT Dorfman auditorium in steep rake from the side.

Against the Culture Palace

consultants for the entire NT Future project. These were the transformation of the original Cottesloe Theatre into the considerably more agile Dorfman, and the masterplanning of the technical facilities of the other two theatres, the Greek-amphitheatre-inspired Olivier and the conventional proscenium-arch Lyttelton. Plus the temporary theatre known as the Shed (see p.79).

The relationship with the NT had, however, started earlier, back in 2008, when Haworth Tompkins and Charcoalblue had restored and upgraded a fascinating separate building, the 1958 National Theatre Studio. This brick-Brutalist building had been designed by architects Lyons Israel Ellis to be the production workshop building for the NT in its original home of the Old Vic Theatre in Waterloo. The task was to restore the building (listed in 2005) and convert it into rehearsal and production development spaces where writers, actors and directors can brainstorm and refine new productions in a private space away from the bustle of the NT proper: a 'secret ideas laboratory', as architecture critic Ellis Woodman has called it. The building also contains the NT archives. For Charcoalblue as theatre consultant, an unusual aspect of the task was to keep the worlds of actors and technicians sufficiently distinct to allow for total concentration on the work in hand.

Back in Lasdun's main theatre complex, the Cottesloe, with its cramped separate entrance on the eastern flank of the building, had long been the place for more experimental productions on the 'courtyard' model, but it was due a considerable upgrade. It was stripped out and a new highly adaptable seating system was installed (see Aside: Developing Seats, p.66), and by pushing right out to the original structural walls of the space, more than a hundred extra, bigger seats and more circulation space were created.

Now the new Dorfman is part of a mini-complex of its own, its foyer also leading to a studio space and education centre, and a public route for the inquisitive running at a high level through the Max Rayne Centre – which has taken over and expanded the production capability historically housed in the NT Studio. Thus a previously off-limits part of the whole theatre's activities has been opened up to view. In itself, the Dorfman can now be configured in multiple ways, including shallow and steep seating rakes, flat-floor promenade, end-on stage and in-the-round. Whatever the director and producer envisions, the transformation can be made in under an hour.

OPPOSITE Seat commissioning – left to right: Charcoalblue's Gavin Green, Elena Giakoumaki, Ben Hanson, Peter Ruthven Hall and Alex Wardle.
BELOW Early prototype folding seat with Haworth Tompkins' Steve Tompkins and Paddy Dillon, and Charcoalblue's Alex Wardle, Andy Hayles and Elena Giakoumaki.
RIGHT Mock-up testing – second-row high seats with Haworth Tompkins' Jason McKay, NT's Chris McDougall and Charcoalblue's Peter Ruthven Hall and Gavin Green.

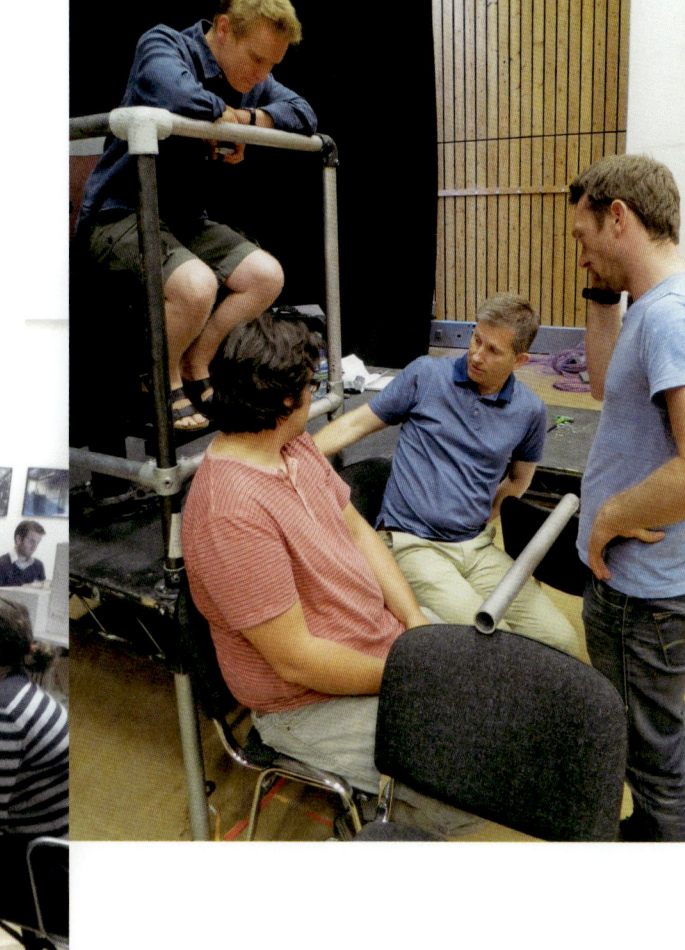

Against the Culture Palace

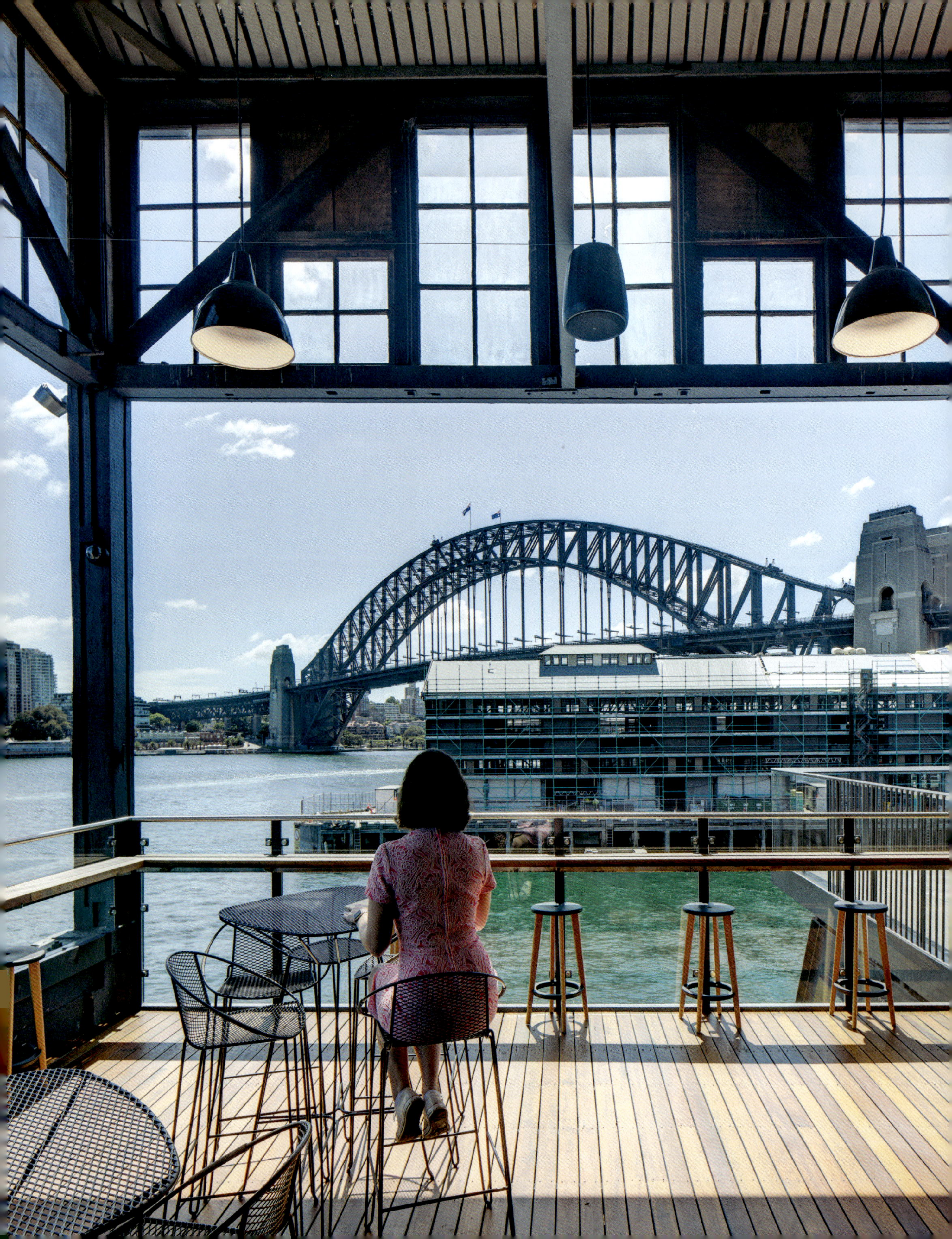

The 'anti culture palace' mantra applies at all levels: even the compact Tricycle Theatre in north-west London, a hotbed of creative and radical programming, had become a kind of institution, with its auditorium format hardly ever varied until its transformation into the Kiln, led by Indhu Rubasingham (see p.36).

It was a similar story in Sydney, Australia, where time had caught up with the Wharf Theatres at Miller's Point next to the Sydney Harbour Bridge. There, the Sydney Theatre Company had inhabited a range of early 1920s timber-framed pier buildings since 1985, somewhat frustrated that money was too tight at the outset to make the adaptable theatres its founders wanted. Some 35 years later, the company having grown hugely in stature and reach, the opportunity arose to put this right in a root-and-branch interior rebuild.

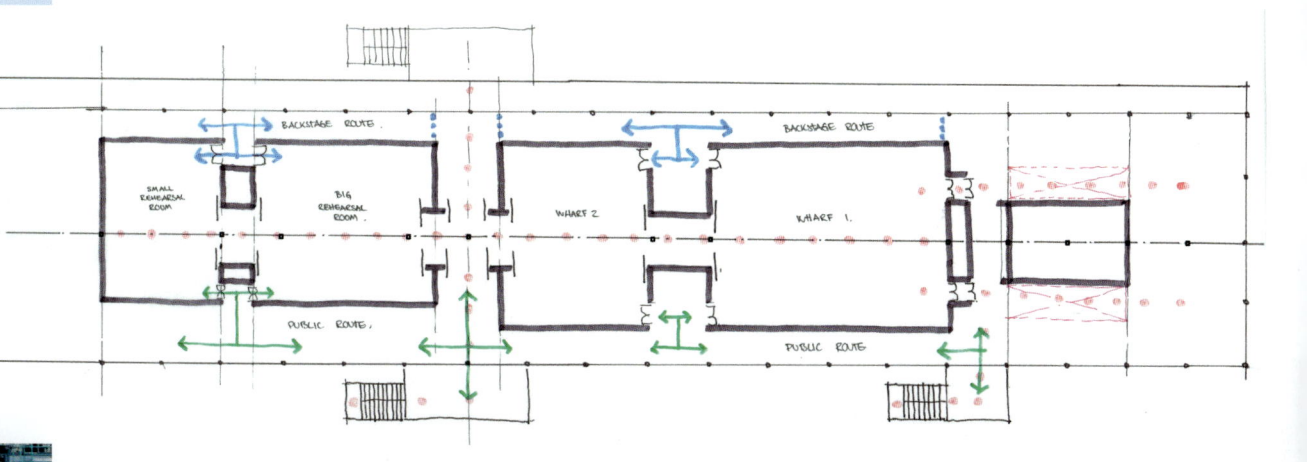

FAR LEFT Foyer and bar space overlooking Sydney Harbour.
ABOVE Concept sketch by Eric Lawrence, Charcoalblue: building organisation.
LEFT Design team meeting around concept theatre model with STC Project Director Julia Pucci, Charcoalblue's Eric Lawrence, TTW Engineers' David Carolan, Hassell Director Ken McBryde (architect) and STC Technical Director Jono Perry.

Against the Culture Palace

ABOVE Concept sketch by Eric Lawrence, Charcoalblue.
RIGHT Wharf 1 Theatre in construction.
BELOW Wharf 1 Theatre from stage in end-stage format.
BELOW RIGHT Charcoalblue's Pablo Romero inspecting the construction of the acoustic separation.
OPPOSITE The heart of the building: the rehearsal room.

Working with architects Hassell (based in a similar pier nearby) for artistic clients Kip Williams and Patrick McIntyre, Charcoalblue made the company's two theatres properly flexible in both configuration and the full range of stage and technical equipment plus acoustic design: no simple job in a timber heritage building with relatively low ceiling heights and no flytower. The result, which opened in 2021 despite the challenges of a global pandemic, is a much-improved pair of theatres. Wharf 1 seats 350 to 420 in three main formats (end-on, corner theatre and in-the-round), while the Wharf 2 studio theatre seats 160 on a retractable unit. In a very theatrical move, both can be combined into one large theatre by opening full-height doors, so becoming Wharf 3. In the process, the public areas of the building were opened up considerably, making the most of the original structure. Keeping the familiarity and uniqueness of the place was a key part of the brief: the watchword for the design team was 'wharfiness'.

For the Waikato Regional Theatre in Hamilton, North Island of Aotearoa, New Zealand, it was a matter of starting afresh. The existing 1962 Founders Theatre was big (with 1,250 seats) and successful, but its building was ageing and eventually closed by Hamilton City Council in 2016 following safety, fire and earthquake concerns. Charcoalblue were appointed by the Waikato Regional Theatre Governance Panel in 2016 to scope out the entire project and to lead the team, before a site had been chosen. There was extensive public consultation on the project, including careful, sincere collaboration with local Māori iwi, Tainui.

Construction was underway at the time of writing. The architects for the project are Jasmax. The theatre will form part of a new arts precinct, incorporating the facade of the historic Hamilton Hotel, on what is a very fine site overlooking the tree-lined banks of the Waikato River. A lyric theatre, it will have a 1,340-seat main auditorium capable of adjusting for drama, symphony orchestras and ballet, adaptable in scale for the local community's use while also appropriate for the country's national companies to visit. A new place for culture rather than a culture palace, it does its best to 'keep the concrete to the edges' and so allow future change to happen. It will certainly fulfil the role of a focus for the Waikato Region.

LEFT Architect's render: building the set into the landscape.
BELOW Architect Jasmax render, exploring auditorium finishes
RIGHT *Waikato Times* feature on the theatre.

Against the Culture Palace

105

106   Charcoalblue

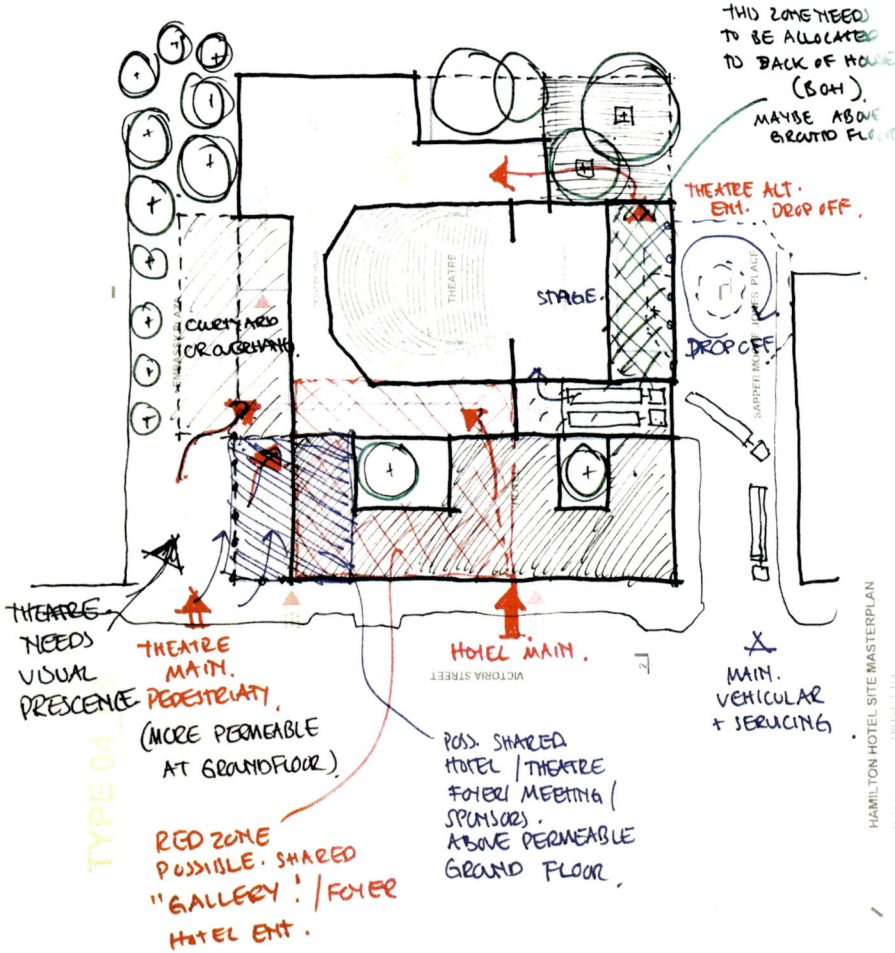

OPPOSITE ABOVE Charcoalblue's Eric Lawrence and Erin Shepherd meet New Zealand's former Prime Minister Jacinda Ardern.
OPPOSITE BELOW Concept sketch by Charcoalblue's Eric Lawrence: building organisation.
ABOVE Construction progress, April 2024.

Against the Culture Palace

Theatrical Transformations

While many of the projects in this book can be seen as radical interventions, reinventions and clean-slate fresh starts in the world of live performance, there is another folder in the Charcoalblue portfolio: theatres that are rescued and improved while broadly retaining their inherited formats. Often, though not always, with additions.

There is some prime theatrical real estate involved here – the Hudson Theatre in Manhattan, for instance, of which more later – but first up is a real curiosity: the original Victorian theatre in London's Alexandra Palace, the 'people's palace' on the hill dating from 1875. This was conceived as North London's answer to South London's Crystal Palace, originally home to the Great Exhibition of 1851 in Hyde Park.

Alexandra Palace was a 'destination', offering grand exhibitions, zoos and circuses, music recitals, restaurants and even balloon rides, boating and horse-racing in the park created around it. It had its own railway spur and dedicated tram shuttle. Its Great Hall could seat 12,000. In 1934 its south-eastern corner became the first home of BBC Television and its studios, the transmitter mast for which remains to this day.

The palace always struggled financially, however, and in 1980 it suffered a devastating fire in the western half of the building, after which it was partially rebuilt. But the eastern end, which escaped the fire, contained a singular relic: the large Victorian theatre in the north-east corner, complete with original stage machinery but in a semi-derelict state. Bringing this back to life was not just a matter of restoration: its original configuration was an elongated rectangle with much of the audience placed in three tiers towards the back of the room, allowing for an arena in front of the stage.

There is another folder in the Charcoalblue portfolio: theatres that are rescued and improved. Some prime theatrical real estate here.

This was the Victorian theatre of spectacle. It had later been converted into a cinema, and then just left to decay for 80 years. Bringing it back to life, something made possible by the Heritage Lottery Fund, was part of a sequence of works for the palace trust drawn up by architects Feilden Clegg Bradley Studios. It is an example of 'arrested decay', with its interior surfaces stabilised as found rather than recreated in the Victorian manner or replaced by modern equivalents.

However, the feeling of being in something of a steampunk ruin has been offset by the creation of new auditorium seating that can be arranged for 500

Theatrical Transformations

seats in-the-round or 1,000 seats in conventional format. Straightforward technical gantries are suspended from strong points in the void above the plaster ceiling. Acoustics are good. By 2018, the theatre was back in business and, beyond its role as a local London theatre, became familiar to many as home to Jools Holland's 'Later...' live music series for BBC TV, thus re-establishing the BBC's historical connection with the palace.

PAGE 108 Alexandra Palace theatre side auditorium walls with historical fabric preserved.
ABOVE Seat snagging with Charcoalblue's Peter Ruthven Hall.
RIGHT 'Arrested decay' in the auditorium from gallery to stage.
OPPOSITE Concept sketch by Gavin Green, Charcoalblue: flexible staging.

Theatrical Transformations

The Hudson Theatre, Manhattan

This was a matter of fettling a theatre that had lost its focus. When built in 1903, it had been a classic, confident 1,076-seat proscenium house, operated by the successful Broadway producer Henry B. Harris. Quite luxurious, designed in the Beaux-Arts manner, it had unusually large foyers at a time when the crush was more

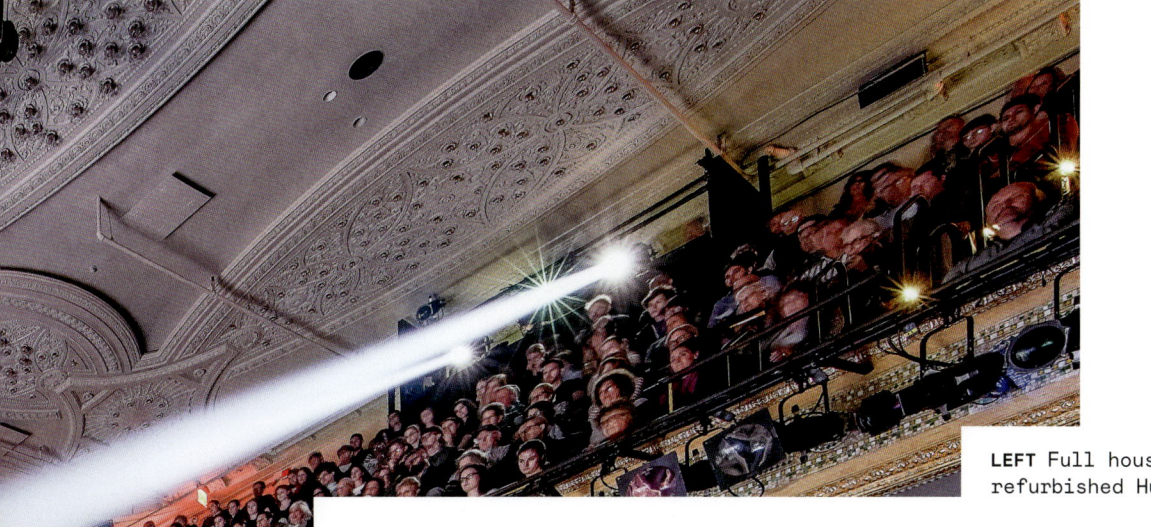

LEFT Full house in the newly refurbished Hudson Theatre.

the norm. Harris sadly perished with the *Titanic* in 1912, whereupon the theatre passed to his widow, Renee, who survived the sinking. She became the first female theatre manager and producer in the United States. Things went well until she lost everything in the Wall Street Crash of 1929 and the Great Depression that followed. The Hudson became at various times a radio theatre, television studios, a porn theatre, a cinema, a music venue and a conference centre auditorium. Through all this, its interiors, including its original Tiffany lobby bar survived remarkably well and it became a landmark building. Then, in 2016, new owner operators arrived: the Ambassador Theatre Group, now ATG Entertainment, who wanted to turn it back into a proper Broadway theatre, with up to 970 generously sized seats. Charcoalblue worked with Martinez + Johnson Architecture, now OTJ. The Hudson has naturally good acoustics and an intimate feel, and it was vital not to make any changes that might affect that. This was a relatively light-touch transformation, providing more and better seats, broadly reinstating the original profile of the auditorium for modern conditions and codes, and greatly upgrading the technical equipment in the stagehouse. The partnership with ATG Entertainment and their Group Property Development Director, Dave Andrews, continues across a number of other transformations in New York, Hamburg and London.

In this vein, Charcoalblue have also carried out refurbishment and improvement projects on a number of historic UK theatres, some of them Grade I listed. Take the **Bristol Old Vic**, first opened in 1766 and so the longest continuously operating theatre in the nation. Having originally been unlicensed and hidden away, in 1972 it was substantially rebuilt, incorporating the adjacent 1744 Coopers' Hall as the main facade and entrance. By the early years of the 21st century it was time for another rethink, and, following earlier interventions in the main auditorium which Charcoalblue and Andrzej Blonski Architects had collaborated on, the now well-rehearsed team of Haworth Tompkins architects and Charcoalblue got to work in 2014 on the front of house and a new studio theatre.

Theatrical Transformations

So this was a hybrid project: introducing a brand-new second auditorium as part of the general uplift of the oldest British theatre. It was built in the former basement barrel store of Coopers' Hall, with a reinstated grand public room at first-floor level above. Naturally ventilated and cooled, it is a simple space with the old granite walls revealed, and bench seating in both stalls and gallery. Meanwhile, the new foyer to the whole complex, a timber and glass structure built to the side of Coopers' Hall on the site of the former 1970s studio theatre, is itself highly theatrical. The original Georgian wall of the theatre is revealed and pierced with openings at various levels by the Haworth Tompkins team, with stairs and walkways enlivening the space. It is a meeting place for Bristol as much as a theatre lobby, opening up this once secretive theatre to the world.

The Perth Theatre in Scotland, dating from 1900, was a relatively recent manifestation of a performance venue in the town. Theatres of one kind or another had (somewhat sporadically, it must be said) been a part of life there since the flowering of drama in Elizabethan times. A performance by a travelling troupe in an open-air amphitheatre is recorded in 1589, though the church elders who ruled the roost at the time insisted on 'no swearing or any scurrility'.

Come 1900, things had loosened up somewhat, although, as was the custom of the time, the theatre was also grandly pronounced to be an opera house, often code for 'music hall' or variety. It staged everything, in fact. From the mid 1930s it became a successful repertory theatre, finally came into public ownership in the 1960s and physically expanded in the early 1980s with a not entirely successful three-storey extension. It presented largely blank brick facades to the streetscape.

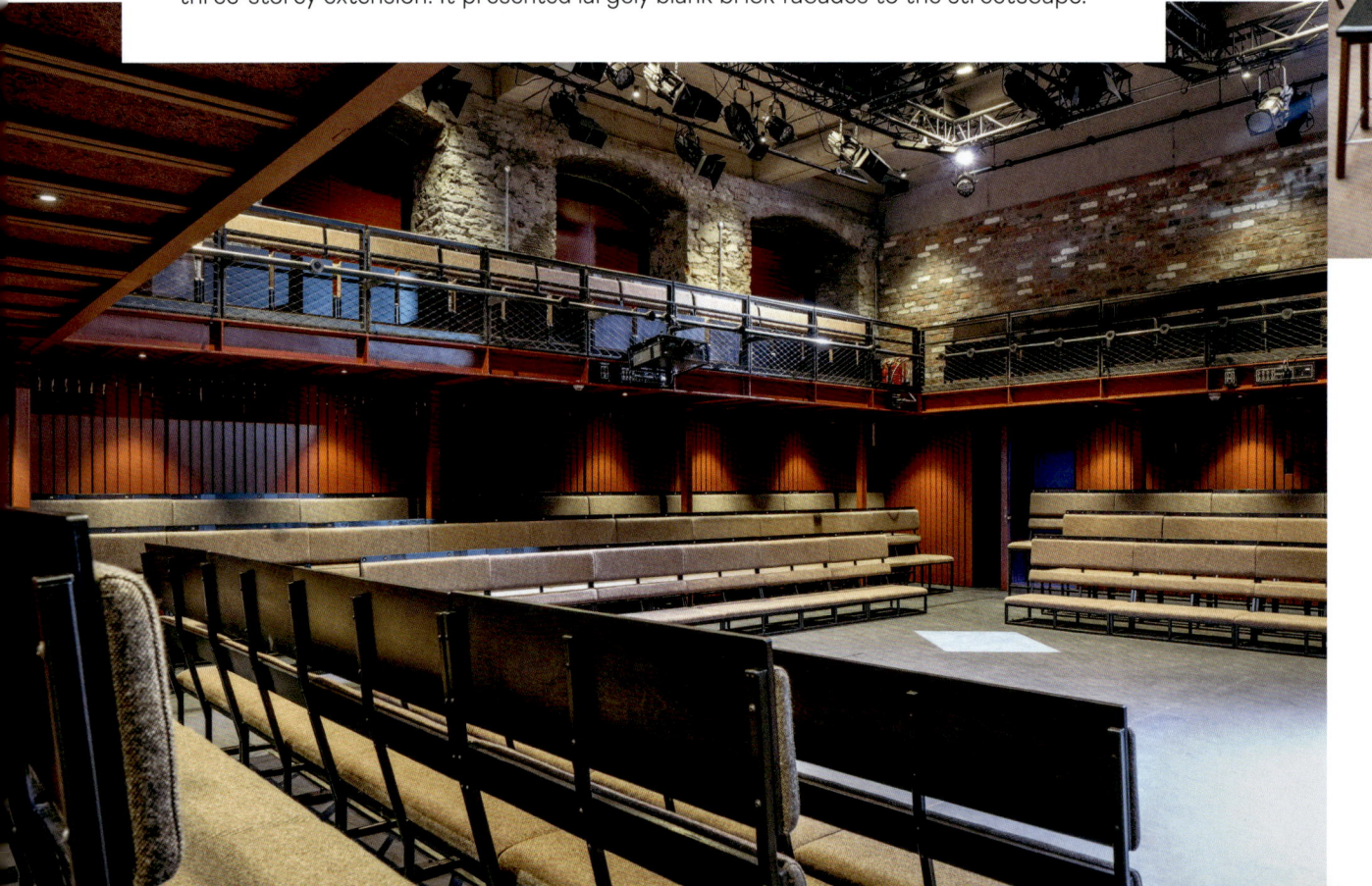

OPPOSITE Bristol Old Vic Studio – new highly flexible room inserted into the historic building.
ABOVE Bristol Old Vic, historic Georgian façade and dramatic new entrance lobby on King Street, the project includes a new intimate studio theatre.
LEFT Bristol Old Vic, vibrant new entrance lobby off King Street, architects Haworth Tompkins with Charcoalblue completing the public space acoustic design.

Thirty years later, it was time for a fresh start. Richard Murphy Architects and Charcoalblue restored the listed original auditorium, a fine red-plush proscenium house, to near-original appearance complete with gallery – which had been partitioned off to make offices previously. As with the Bristol Old Vic, the theatre's original external flank wall was revealed in the process via a full-height atrium. A new studio theatre was added alongside this at first-floor level, plus much more generous public foyers with a restaurant. In the manner of Murphy's cultural projects (indeed this is a characteristic of many of the architects and clients Charcoalblue works with), it throws its net wider than the ostensible task at hand, becoming a meeting place for the town.

It is never easy updating a historical auditorium for modern purposes technically, and here it is done more or less invisibly. Most systems were replaced, and some (such as the counterweight flying system) overhauled, with much greater flexibility of use built in. In the new section, the 200-seat studio theatre has a retractable seating system and a community room for the outreach and creative learning programme. Overall, this is a relatively compact theatre complex that, since completion in 2017, has had a renewed sense of civic importance and public engagement.

Theatrical Transformations

Aside: New York City venues

- Fordham High School for the Arts
- People's Theatre Project
- Classical Theatre of Harlem (study)
- Aaron Davis Hall (study)
- Victoria Theater
- National Black Theatre
- Apollo Theater
- Bloomingdale School of Music
- Dalton School

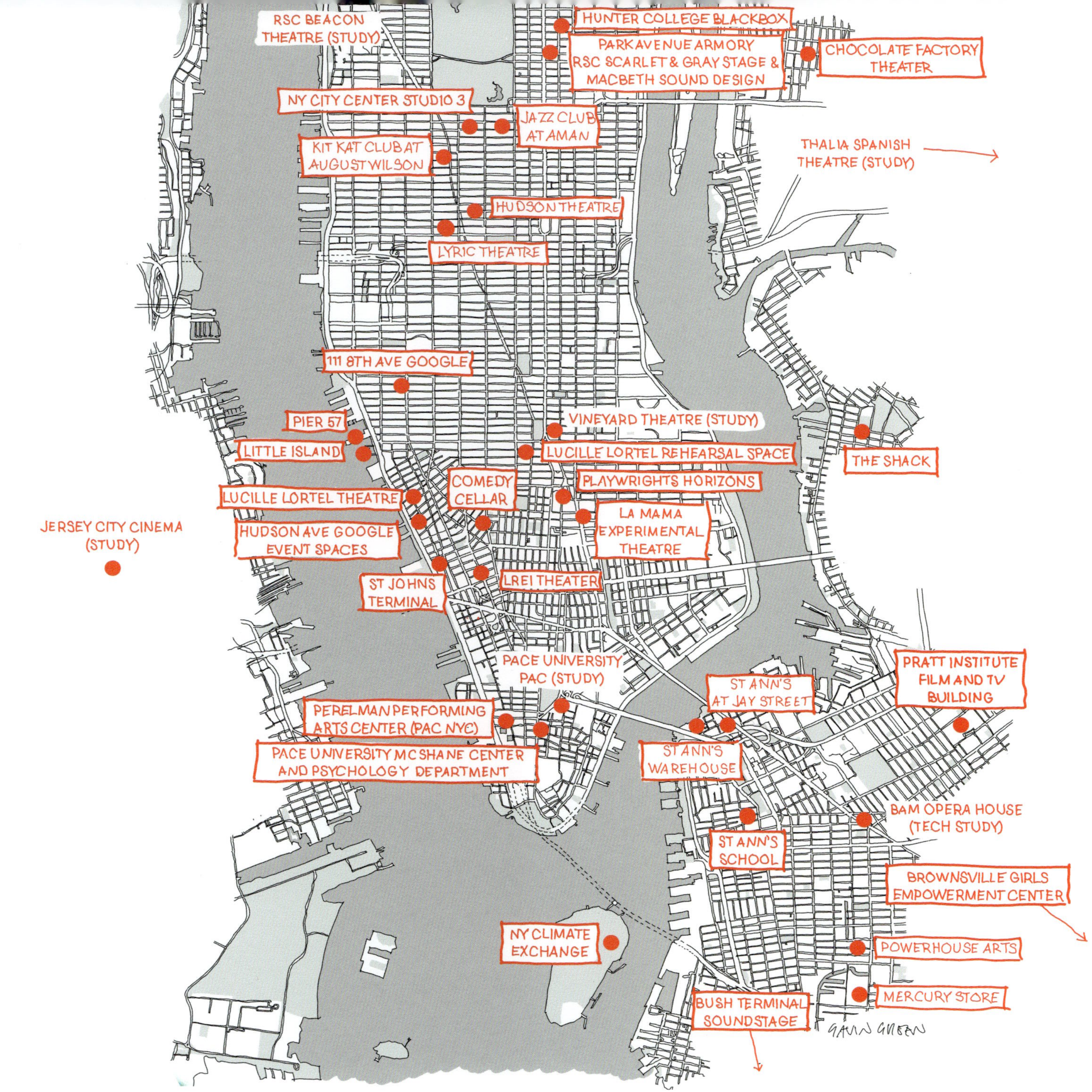

RSC BEACON THEATRE (STUDY)
HUNTER COLLEGE BLACKBOX
PARK AVENUE ARMORY RSC SCARLET & GRAY STAGE & MACBETH SOUND DESIGN
CHOCOLATE FACTORY THEATER
NY CITY CENTER STUDIO 3
JAZZ CLUB AT AMAN
KIT KAT CLUB AT AUGUST WILSON
THALIA SPANISH THEATRE (STUDY)
HUDSON THEATRE
LYRIC THEATRE
111 8TH AVE GOOGLE
PIER 57
VINEYARD THEATRE (STUDY)
LITTLE ISLAND
LUCILLE LORTEL REHEARSAL SPACE
THE SHACK
LUCILLE LORTEL THEATRE
COMEDY CELLAR
PLAYWRIGHTS HORIZONS
LA MAMA EXPERIMENTAL THEATRE
JERSEY CITY CINEMA (STUDY)
HUDSON AVE GOOGLE EVENT SPACES
ST JOHNS TERMINAL
LREI THEATER
PACE UNIVERSITY PAC (STUDY)
ST ANN'S AT JAY STREET
PRATT INSTITUTE FILM AND TV BUILDING
PERELMAN PERFORMING ARTS CENTER (PAC NYC)
PACE UNIVERSITY MC SHANE CENTER AND PSYCHOLOGY DEPARTMENT
ST ANN'S WAREHOUSE
BAM OPERA HOUSE (TECH STUDY)
ST ANN'S SCHOOL
BROWNSVILLE GIRLS EMPOWERMENT CENTER
NY CLIMATE EXCHANGE
POWERHOUSE ARTS
MERCURY STORE
BUSH TERMINAL SOUNDSTAGE
GAVIN GREEN

Hidden Gems

Although, as we've seen, Charcoalblue works with many of the famous names and prime venues of the theatre world, there is no discernible difference in attitude between these and the more fringe buildings and companies. Especially as those have their equally fascinating alternative histories and are often the crucibles of future theatre talent. Given Charcoalblue's own history as a once-precocious start-up parking its charabanc on the lawn of established consultancies, there would seem to be a natural affinity between what they do and what the more offbeat performance companies, in sometimes off-pitch locations and converted buildings, do.

So in New York City the La MaMa Experimental Theatre Club (La MaMa ETC) is proud of being the original 'Off-Off-Broadway' venue, started by its legendary founder Ellen 'Mama' Stewart in 1961 as 'a home for rebels and outsiders'. After some 5,000 productions in various locations, featuring 150,000 artists from 70 nations — all done on a defiantly non-commercial basis — its mission remains the same. It is obviously doing quite a lot right: art as a force for change, battling bigotry and intolerance, nurturing new talent wherever it is from. Many now-famous actors and playwrights began their careers here.

Given Charcoalblue's own history as a once-precocious start-up, there is a natural affinity between what they do and what the more offbeat performance companies do.

Since 1974, La MaMa ETC has been based on East 4th Street in the East Village in Lower Manhattan. This is a street of originally commercial buildings, still run down in parts but lifted by the exaggeratedly neoclassical frontage of its building at, coincidentally, No. 74. Annoyingly for numerologists, it dates from 1873. As found by Stewart, it was in a derelict state, and she set to restoring it — very successfully — but it and the adjoining La MaMa buildings needed a considerable refresh after nearly 50 years of theatre here.

Completed in 2023, this was a relatively large job in which Charcoalblue worked with architects Beyer Blinder Belle and legendary director Peter Brook's scenographer Jean-Guy Lecat to re-restore and upgrade the theatre and its facilities both spatially and technically. There are now two properly sound-separated auditoria — one a much-improved main theatre, the other a smaller studio, rehearsal and education space. Charcoalblue's role covered technical

Hidden Gems

theatre and acoustical consultancy for the project, overseeing the implementation of seating systems, stage lighting, audiovisual design and acoustics. It might be a 'hidden gem' in the order of magnitude of the projects in this book, but it is an almost sacred theatrical space in the cultural life of Manhattan, and deserved all the respect that entailed.

PAGE 118 La MaMa's narrow site in construction.
LEFT A newly renovated home for La MaMa on East 4th Street.
BELOW Charcoalblue team visit. Left to right: Clemeth Abercrombie, Ben Hanson, Chris Dales, Bruno Cardenas and Ollie Wade.

RIGHT Charcoalblue's Owen Hughes, Bruno Cardenas and Jerad Schomer at the ribbon cutting.
BELOW The Club at La MaMa, a highly flexible space.

Hidden Gems

That was one of the most recently completed projects at the time of writing. It's worth spooling back to the very first official Charcoalblue project as an independent consultancy, the **Siobhan Davies Studios**, which opened in 2006 but had been planned for a decade prior to that. It is in the district of South London known as Elephant and Castle, a somewhat ragged part of town which, despite endless redevelopment projects, is not yet the destination it wants to be. This building was a cultural advance guard. Sarah Wigglesworth Architects turned the sow's ear of a battered and derelict 1898 school building into the silk purse of a mecca for contemporary dance as practised by choreographer Siobhan Davies and her company. Davies had tired of taking productions on tour to conventional, usually proscenium, theatres, and wanted something more immersive. The result is a building composed around the rhythms and postures of dance in which every part can be used for performance or practice: even the meeting rooms have sprung floors.

The key move was the building of the main studio on the roof of the main school, composed as a series of linked asymmetrical plywood-lined arches rather than the usual rectilinear box. Charcoalblue's contribution was to fulfil the technical requirements of a hybrid building which could work for both public performance and intense experiment and rehearsal. A separate administration wing at the rear links through to the main building.

I visited it when it was newly complete and was impressed at how such a visually, aurally and tangibly rich building could arise on such a low budget from the base material of an old school. My report in *The Sunday Times* said: 'It's hard to describe what is so good about this building except to say that it is fully alive . . . Money was tight, but it's seldom I've seen it better, or more joyfully, spent.'

OPPOSITE Roof steelwork in construction at Siobhan Davies Studios.
ABOVE Rehearsal room and flowing ceiling with integrated lighting bars.

Hidden Gems

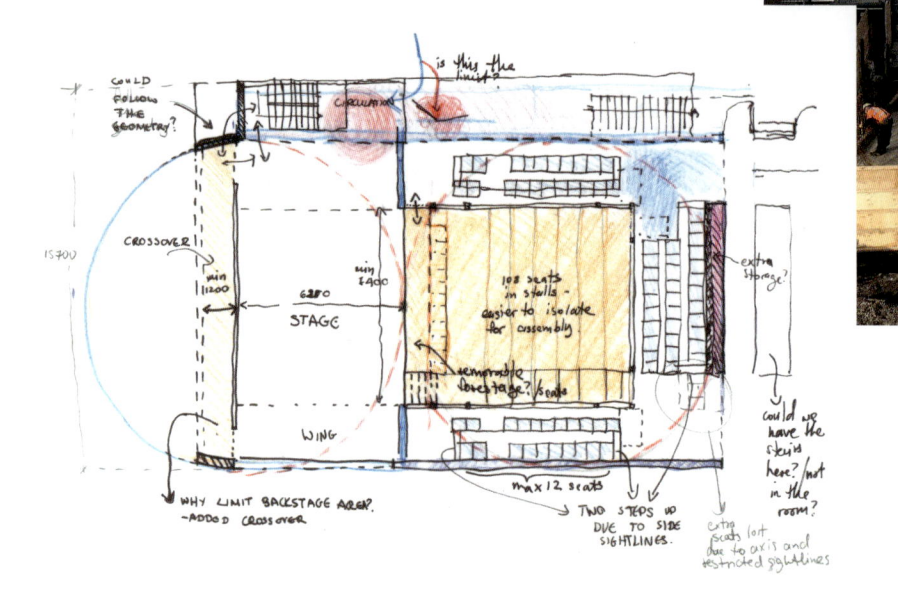

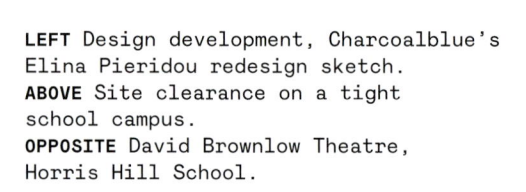

LEFT Design development, Charcoalblue's Elina Pieridou redesign sketch.
ABOVE Site clearance on a tight school campus.
OPPOSITE David Brownlow Theatre, Horris Hill School.

It has a slightly indeterminate quality which is quite appealing — is this a public or a private place? Answer: both. The same could be said of another 'hidden gem' in the rural context of the David Brownlow Theatre at Horris Hill School outside Newbury, Berkshire. This independent prep school, like many others, sets great score by the performing arts: such schools are in a very competitive sector — performance is a great boost to pupils' confidence and all-round abilities, so it is important for schools to have the best facilities to show. Charcoalblue has worked on well-known examples such as the theatres at the Perse and Leys schools in Cambridge, England (respectively with Haworth Tompkins and bb+c architects); the 350-seat music recital hall in the Cedars Hall complex by architect Eric Parry for Wells Cathedral School, Somerset; ArtsEd in Chiswick with De Matos Ryan, and the Old Malthouse Theatre for the King's School, Canterbury, with Tim Ronalds Architects.

The Horris Hill example, however, is an unusual case. It is certainly well hidden. More austere than the norm (a result of its very modest budget), it is a naturally ventilated and well-daylit building made of cross-laminated timber (CLT), distinctly barn-like, clad in a red cementitious wood-panel finish and sited on what was previously an open car park so as to help define a new car-free square. Its 350-seat auditorium is used for everything from school assemblies to performances; its design also includes an outdoor auditorium. As part of the school's outreach to its hinterland, it is also used by local drama and music groups. Jonathan Tuckey Design succeeded in designing a very different kind of performance building here in two overlapping volumes, the taller part marking the stagehouse.

Charcoalblue provided theatre, technical and acoustics consultancy for this very sustainable building, something that feeds through to the architecture in the form of the double-swooping polished ply underside to the auditorium roof which provides an optimal acoustic response. This is part of the integration of acoustics and architecture: for instance, the patterns of the timber-lined interior walls are scaled to the wavelengths found in the spoken word. The auditorium is tuned to the pitch and volume of young voices, while the simplicity and robustness of the technical equipment is itself seen as a learning resource, providing valuable experience in theatre operation. As Gavin Green remarks, 'It's a lovely example of small scale done well'.

Crazy Adventures

Increasingly, Charcoalblue are called on to redesign theatres to accommodate a specific long-running production, with changes that go considerably beyond the temporary adaptations that theatres habitually make for relatively short runs. These are the productions that require completely new environments in order to immerse audiences in the worlds being created. If not quite full-scale rebuilds, they are nonetheless transformative in much the same way. The production runs in such places may be anticipated to be long, but the design and construction work to achieve them is usually on an intense, rapid programme – normal for theatre, where nobody likes the house to be 'dark' for too long.

And so, willkommen, bienvenue, welcome to the Kit Kat Club at the Playhouse Theatre at the bottom of London's Northumberland Avenue, wedged right next to the trains clanking and screeching into Charing Cross station. Despite its Edwardian neoclassical exterior, this turned out to be a fitting place for an all-star revival of the 1966 Kander and Ebb dark musical *Cabaret* in a setting intended to evoke the Weimar-era Berlin of Sally Bowles and her manipulative Emcee.

Willkommen, bienvenue, welcome to the Kit Kat Club at the Playhouse Theatre wedged next to the trains clanking into Charing Cross station.

You can't evoke a seedy cabaret too well in an unaltered conventional proscenium-arch theatre such as the Playhouse previously was. Radical alterations were needed which shrank the auditorium down to 550 seats, arranged in-the-round, with some of that seating set on two levels on what had been the rear stage, while the new circular stage was surrounded by appropriately nightclubby bar tables and chairs.

It began with a request in early 2021 from the theatre owners, ATG Entertainment, at the time led by Mark Cornell with a bold vision to give a lift to the theatre industry coming out of the pandemic. Could the Playhouse work as an in-the-round space? The whole design team was led by Charcoalblue, employing architects Carmody Groarke and production specialist Gary Beestone, who managed the production/building interfaces giving director Rebecca Fretnall and designer Tom Scutt time to develop the production's aesthetic. Three months of design work were followed by seven months of building to create this new, intimate space where architecture and production overlap. You enter the theatre via the stage door, along an authentically grotty corridor: no bourgeois foyer nonsense. A lost opening was unearthed that was perfect for wheelchair access.

Crazy Adventures

PAGE 126 New in-the-round stage in construction.
RIGHT The Playhouse Theatre exterior transformed into the Kit Kat Club.
BELOW Initial concept plan sketch by Gavin Green, Charcoalblue
BOTTOM Concept sketch by Gavin Green, Charcoalblue.
OPPOSITE New in-the-round theatre with existing levels re-tiered to maximise sightlines.

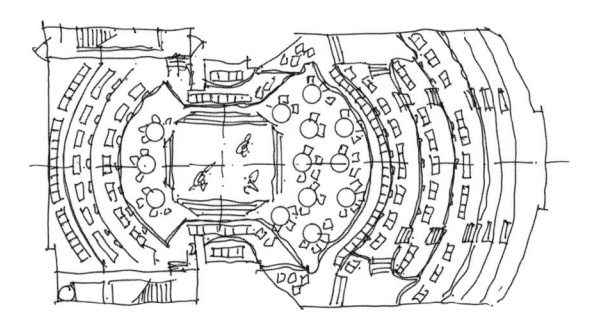

Charcoalblue

The public areas share in the overall theming of the place. The addition of a professional kitchen means that meals can be served along with the action. It all feels a bit transgressive. The interventions are entirely reversible – nothing has been lost and the old Playhouse can return – but this reconfiguration has a design life of 15 to 20 years if need be, allowing for other future in-the-round productions.

On Broadway, ahead of the 2024 TONY awards, the August Wilson Theatre was given a similar treatment for *Cabaret* with a new on-stage gallery redefining the room with a similar in-the-round stage for the Kit Kat Club. ATG Entertainment, Kostow Greenwood Architects, Gary Beestone, Tom Scutt and Charcoalblue reinvigorated their collaboration.

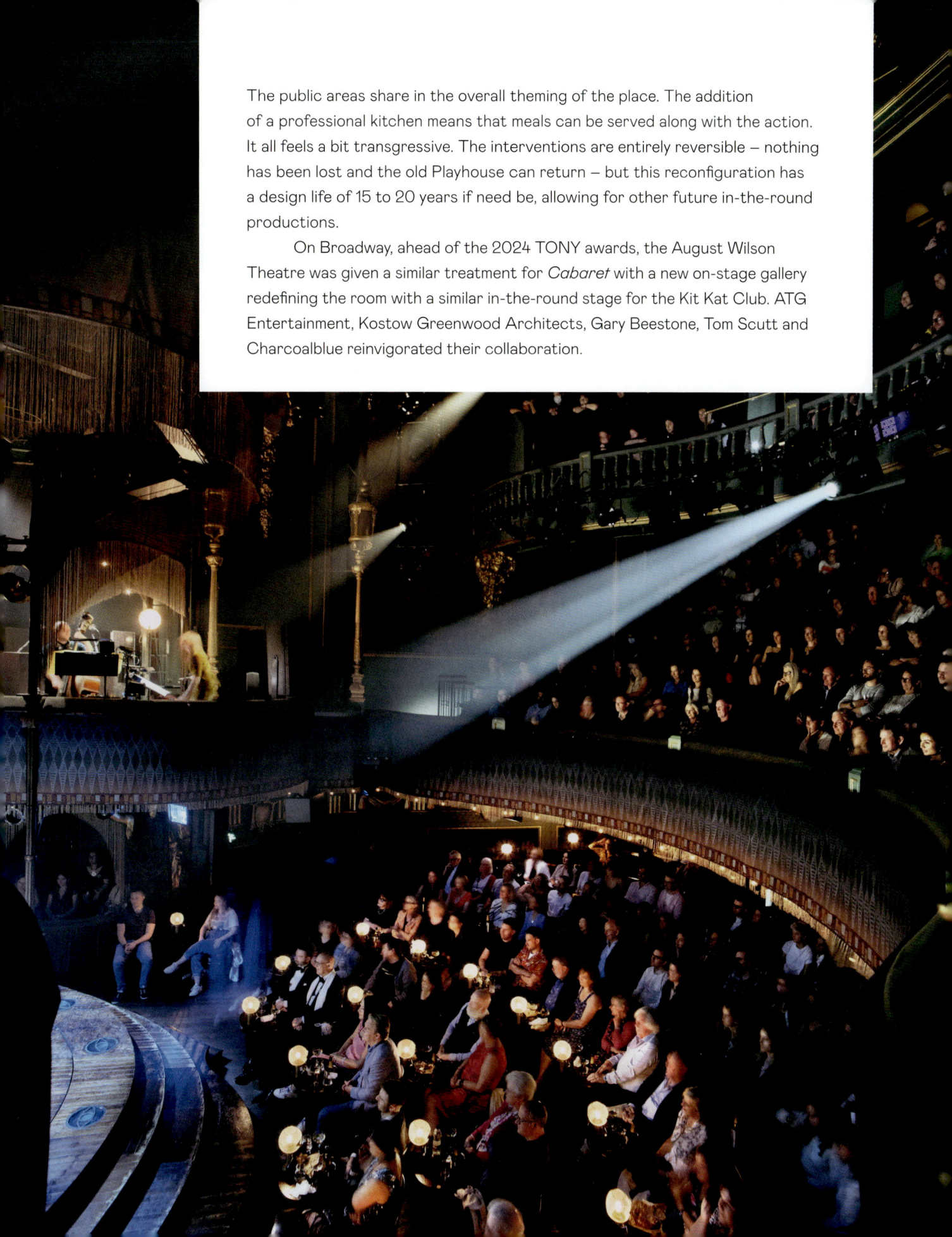

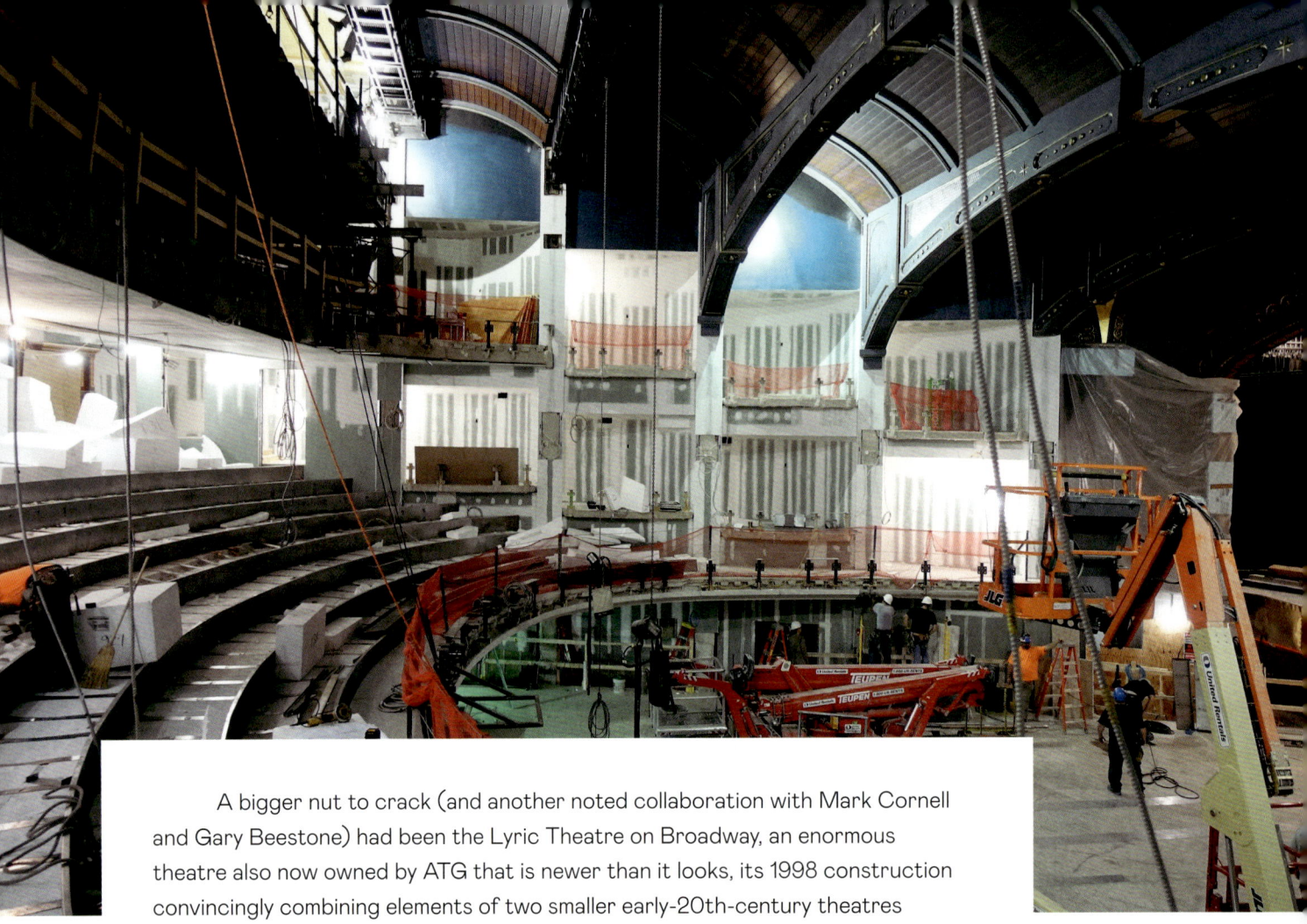

A bigger nut to crack (and another noted collaboration with Mark Cornell and Gary Beestone) had been the Lyric Theatre on Broadway, an enormous theatre also now owned by ATG that is newer than it looks, its 1998 construction convincingly combining elements of two smaller early-20th-century theatres on the site. At more than 1,900 seats, it was, however, considered by many to be too big for an intimate theatrical experience, and had previously acquired an unfortunate reputation as 'the theatre where shows went to die' after some famous flops prior to ATG's ownership. *Harry Potter and the Cursed Child*, however, originally opening in 2018 as a two-parter following its London success, was emphatically not one of those, because – apart from the global appeal of the Potter franchise – it was housed in what is effectively a new smaller, more focused Charcoalblue theatre built within the shell of the old Lyric – which is still there, dormant and out of sight.

The theatre was entirely reshaped by means of new sidewalls (constructed off the Manhattan bedrock) and a lower arched ceiling. The dress circle was extended forwards, boxes were added and the whole medieval-gothic vibe of Potterdom became the decorative palette. This was a major reconstruction project, in which Charcoalblue again led the team, employing long-term collaborators Lissa So and Jonathan Marvel at Marvel Architects. Scenic designers Christine Jones and Brett Banakis, the duo who designed the original London production completed the team. The risk was rewarded, as the intimacy and good acoustics of the reborn theatre and the sense of being in Potter World from the moment you enter the building, enhanced what was already an excellent production.

OPPOSITE New sidewalls and ceiling in construction.
ABOVE Charcoalblue's Bruno Cardenas and Holly Burnell on-site.
RIGHT Concept sketch by Gavin Green, Charcoalblue - new theatre inserted inside the old Lyric.
BELOW new Lyric Theatre auditorium.

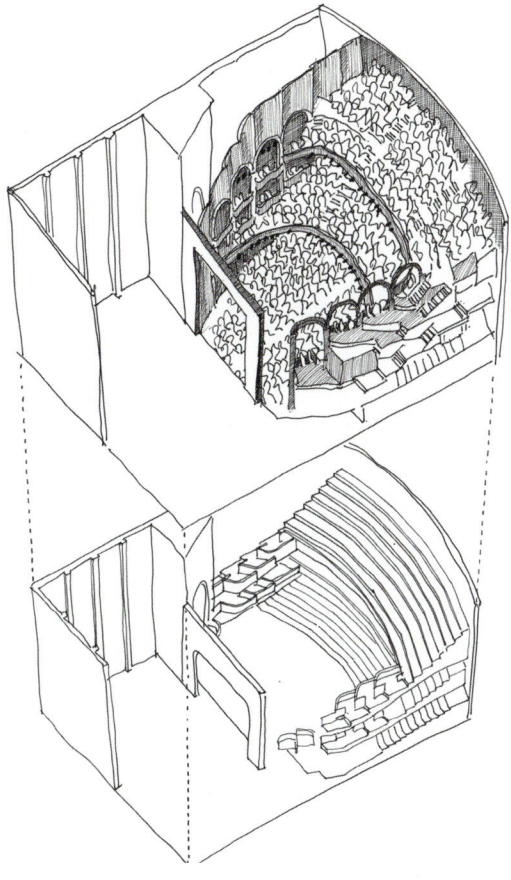

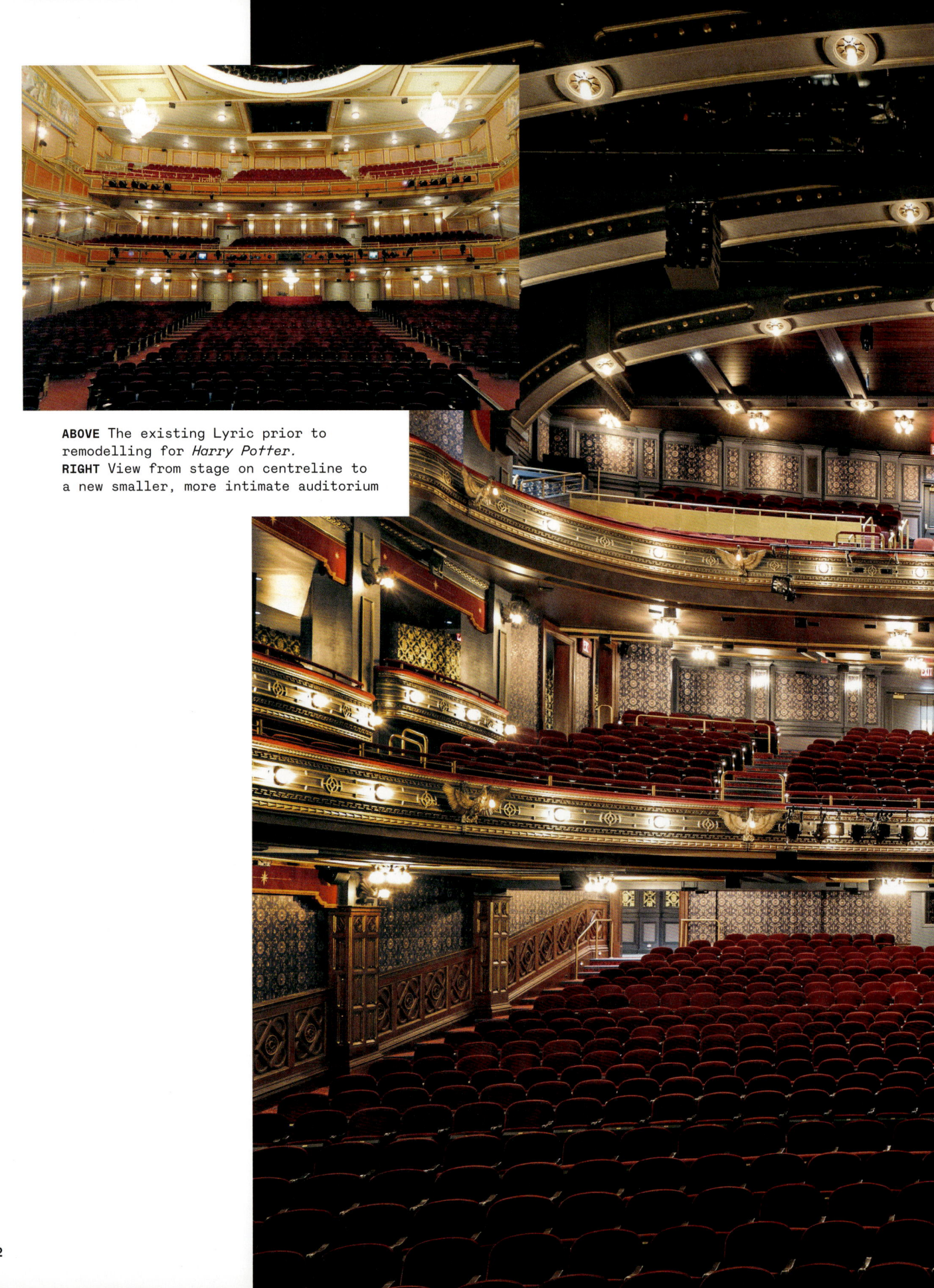

ABOVE The existing Lyric prior to remodelling for *Harry Potter*.
RIGHT View from stage on centreline to a new smaller, more intimate auditorium

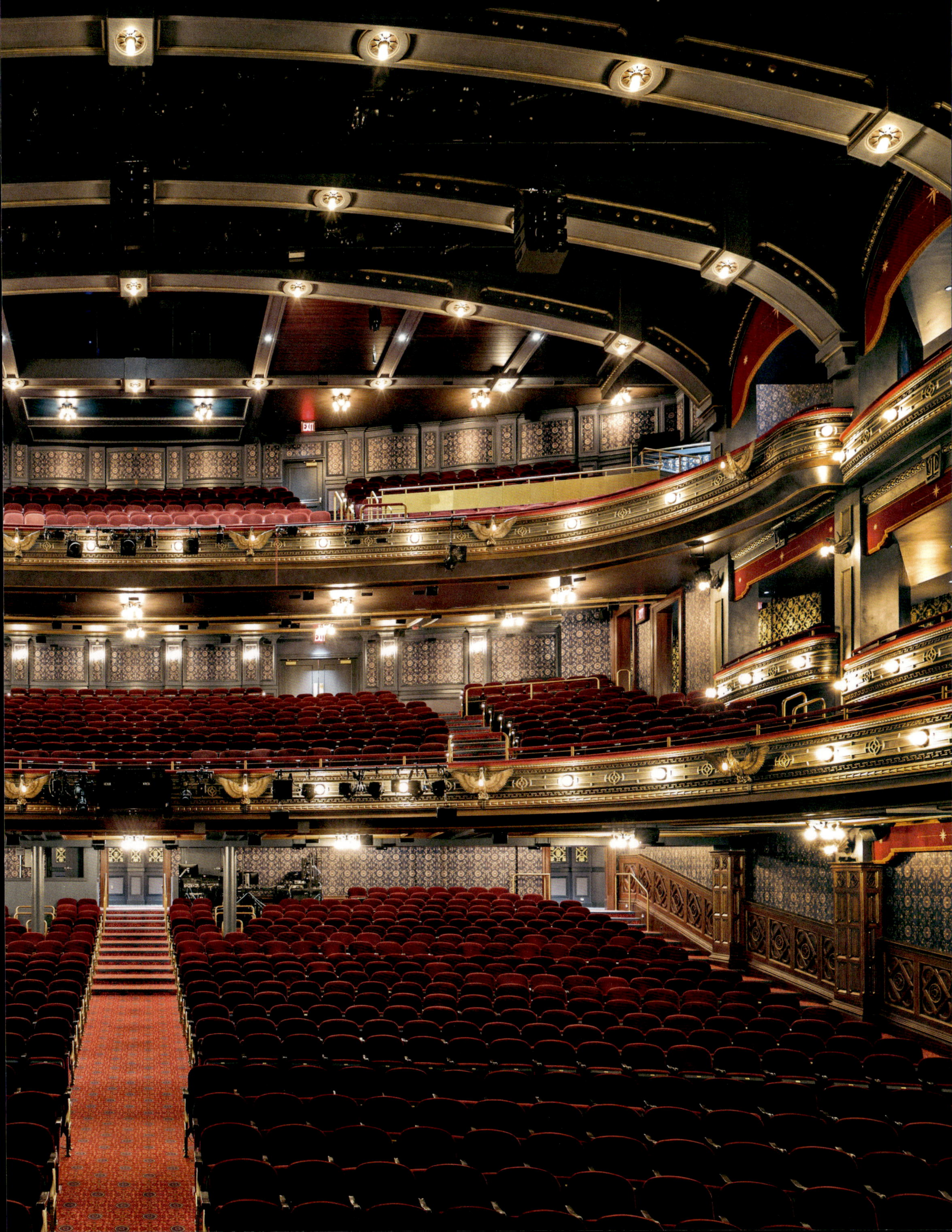
EXIT

Two Grandes Dames

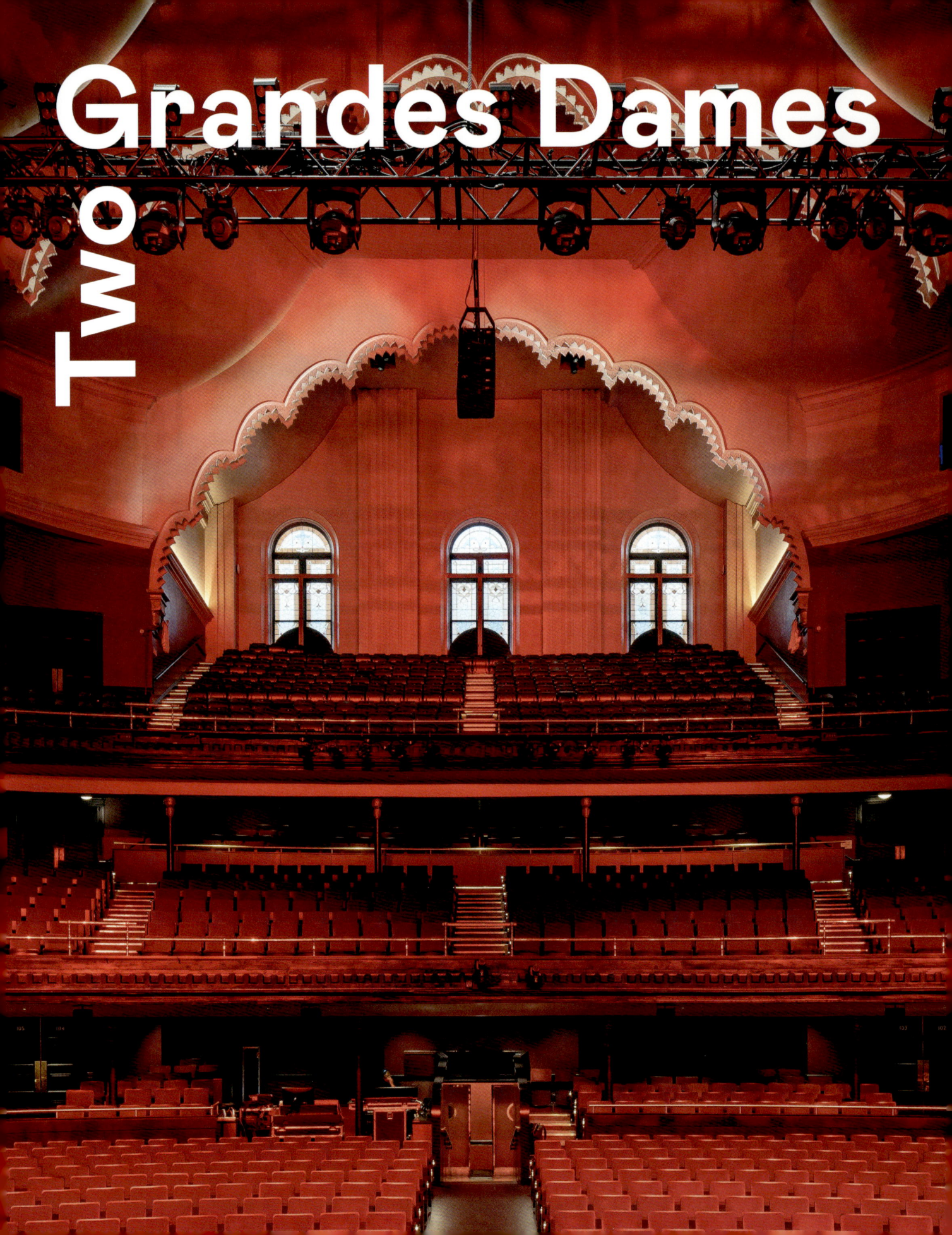

Some theatres and concert halls have a presence, history and civic importance that sets them apart from the run of performance spaces. They have a larger-than-life thespian character of their own, perhaps best conjured up by the thought of Sir Ian McKellen in panto. Just going to such buildings is an occasion, irrespective of what happens to be on there. These are the Grandes Dames.

Take the Theatre Royal, Drury Lane, one of the London West End's most enduring institutions. Everybody agreed that the Lane was old, important, and very big. But it had its awkward side. Despite its success as a home for blockbuster musicals (*Miss Saigon* ran for a decade from first opening in 1989), it was a tough place to play.

Theatres can have a larger-than-life thespian character of their own. These are the Grandes Dames.

A lot of that came down to the fact that, despite its Regency origins — the 1812 neoclassical playhouse by architect Benjamin Dean Wyatt replacing an earlier, even larger one destroyed by fire, as all previous theatres on the site had been, back to 1663 — the auditorium dated from an internal revamp in the 1920s. That was a time when (as with the Shakespeare Memorial Theatre in Stratford-upon-Avon, see p.70) some theatre architects and designers were over-influenced by the different, more remote seating layouts of cinemas. The sense of connection between actors and audience had thus become strained, but it had existed well enough in the original theatre, despite its 3,060-seat capacity on four levels. Owner Andrew Lloyd Webber wanted to regain that atmosphere and bring the technical capabilities of Drury Lane right up to date so as to stand comparison with another theatre of his, Frank Matcham's even larger London Palladium.

Today the Lane has a still-mighty 2,200-seat capacity, still presents performers with a wall of faces on four levels and retains its legendarily vast stage. With new lifts, restored foyers and accessible street-level entrances, it is in better shape than it has been for years, none of which is easy to achieve in a Grade I listed building which with its bars and restaurants is now an all-day place to visit.

Part of the job — by the auld alliance of Charcoalblue and architects Haworth Tompkins — was intangible: they were tasked with stewarding a sense of history. This is a famous site, synonymous with English theatre from back when comic actor Eleanor (Nell) Gwyn played at the first theatre here and attracted the long-term attention of the restored King Charles II, who had coincidentally legalised acting as a profession for women. Restoration drama was made here,

Two Grandes Dames

and later actor/manager Richard Brinsley Sheridan ran the third iteration of the playhouse.

Bringing the 1812 house back into focus was a technically demanding job. In the auditorium much work was done on improving sightlines and comfort, and gently tightening the geometry. All seats were replaced and reconfigured. Two existing boxes were reconfigured into technical positions and the overall acoustical quality improved such that it has attracted Decca Records to record live orchestral music in the theatre.

This is a multi-functional house, accustomed to staging TV shows (comedian Michael McIntyre recorded his prime-time show here at the time of writing), one-off concerts, events and of course musicals: following its £60m overhaul, the theatre reopened in 2021 with the musical of Disney's *Frozen*, replete with special effects. Unsurprisingly, the complete overhaul of backstage facilities and technical equipment was a key part of Charcoalblue's work in collaboration with Unusual Rigging, not least in making the quick changes between a great variety of incoming shows much easier without disrupting the resident productions. Removing legacy stage elevators freed up a usefully large substage basement. Low-energy LED lighting – including stage lights – helped reduce the overall energy consumption of the theatre by 40 per cent.

The Lane is a classic example of a building which (as with opera houses) is part public social space, part performance and backstage space, and part industrial, with full-height scenery workshops. Getting this sprawling historical complex fit and agile for our times was a considerable achievement.

PAGE 134 Massey Hall, Toronto.
RIGHT On stage at TRDL, orchestra recording with Andrew Loyd Webber.
LEFT On-site at TRDL, view from stagehouse to the auditorium birdcage.
BELOW Theatre Royal, Dury Lane (TRDL). Completed top to bottom renovation with remodelled circle and proscenium boxes.

Two Grandes Dames

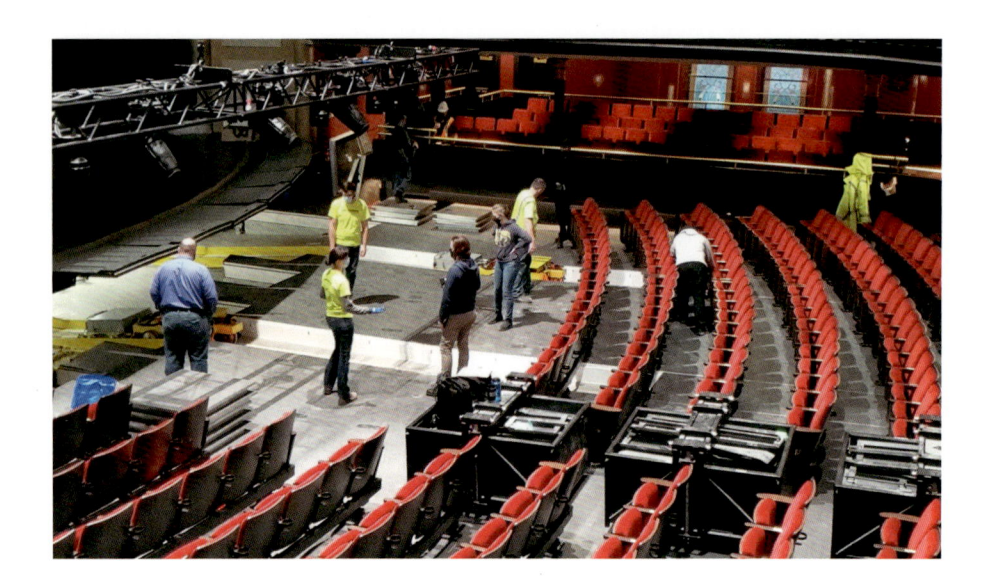

ABOVE Robotic seat installation.
BELOW Seating and sightline discussion – left to right: KPMB Architects' Marianne McKenna, MHRTC's Deane Cameron, KPMB's Meika McCunn, Charcoalblue's Clemeth Abercrombie, KPMB's Chris Couse and Charcoalblue's Ben Hanson.
OPPOSITE Flat floor audience inside the completed Massey Hall renovation for one of the first times in its 130-year history.

Massey Hall in Toronto is a Grande Dame of theatre if ever there was one: an imposing brick and terracotta pile like a rectilinear version of London's Royal Albert Hall, and fulfilling much the same role. Built in 1894 to the design of architect Sidney Badgley and funded by agriculture-machinery industrialist Hart Massey, it seats 2,700 people (originally 3,500) with many of those arranged in a double-decker U-shaped sweep of galleries. It could almost be an enormous nonconformist church of the kind Badgley turned out by the dozen in Canada and the United States, but for the fact that above your head is an extraordinary swooping ceiling of serrated plasterwork arches, inspired by the Andalusian Islamic architecture of the Alhambra in Spain. In stark aesthetic contrast to the sternly neoclassical frontage, these contribute to the excellent orchestral acoustics of the place, which also achieves a sense of intimacy despite its size.

The longest continuously operating performance space in Canada, Massey Hall has hosted everyone of musical note, from national orchestras through jazz (the Charlie Parker/Dizzy Gillespie/Bud Powell/Charles Mingus concert of 1953 is a legendary 'Live at Massey' album) to rock bands. Royalty has visited, as did Winston Churchill. The place is an important part of Canadian cultural life.

Canadian impresario Deane Cameron (who sadly died before the project was completed) was the driving force. He identified that the building had reached the point of needing a considerable upgrade for modern conditions, plus extending to provide a 200-to-500-seat flexible performance space. This is housed in a new 'tower' building behind. The architects were KPMB, a regular partner for Charcoalblue's North American work, such as the David Geffen School of Drama (see p.146).

The task was to improve circulation – especially access to and from the gallery levels – and to connect through to a new foyer building behind, something done with external enclosed walkways or 'passerelles'. But the treasured favourite-jumper feel of the place had to remain. Charcoalblue carried out theatre planning, stage lighting and stage engineering for the project. As part of this, a new concept for flexible 'robot' auditorium seating parks the chairs beneath the stage. This allows large-crowd standing events, thus expanding the Hall's appeal and adaptability for its varied programme well into the future.

OPPOSITE Charcoalblue's Phil Hampton on stage.
ABOVE The finished renovation of the historic Massey Hall: the restored auditorium with new seating and technical infastructure.

Two Grandes Dames

Academic Powerhouses

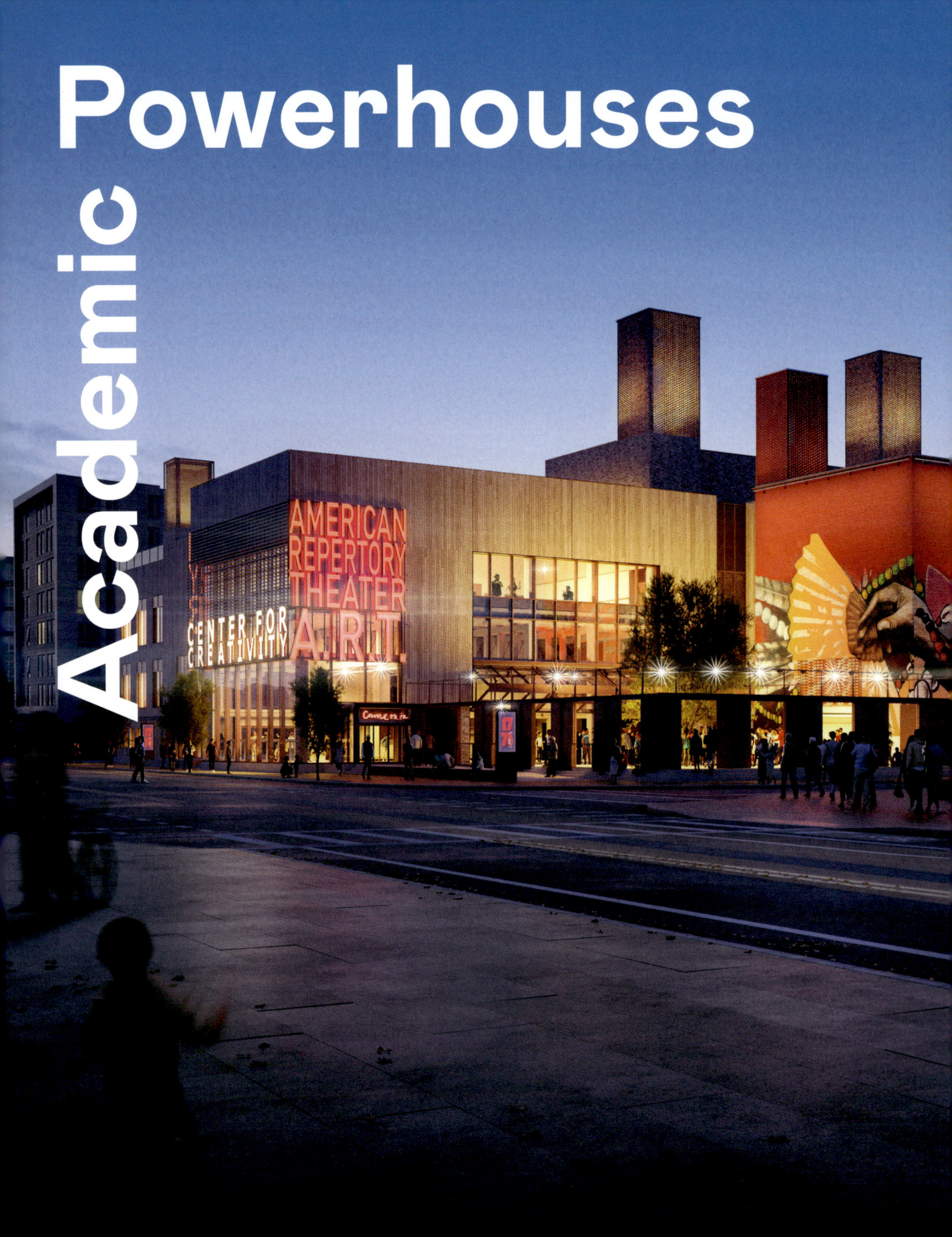

Harvard's American Repertory Theater, or ART, is an unusual institution, a place devoted to theatrical excellence, innovation and equality that exists as part of an august Ivy League university. Founded in 1980, it is a bridge between the university – where it provides a resource for undergraduate courses in theatre, dance, media and other disciplines including public health – and the Greater Boston community.

It originates and transfers productions, revives others, wins awards. But its main theatre, the 1960 Loeb Drama Center by architect Hugh Stubbins, was shared with other organisations, while ART's leased second auditorium, the Oberon, was a distance away. Artistic Director Diane Paulus, Producer Diane Borger and CEO Diane Quinn commissioned Charcoalblue at first to investigate the possibilities of thoroughly renovating the Loeb. After a series of studies, it became clear that it would make more sense to wipe the slate clean and start afresh, with both auditoria under the one roof. The new theatre will be in Allston, just across the Charles River from the main Harvard campus. It will strengthen the cultural element of an academic district also featuring the business school, sports facilities, applied sciences, engineering and a new arrival, the interdisciplinary studio spaces of the 'ArtLab'.

A place devoted to theatrical excellence, innovation and equality; a bridge between the university and the community.

Although Charcoalblue are accustomed to working in North America, this is the first time they have done so with their frequent UK architect colleagues Haworth Tompkins. With such a prestigious client and location for an all-new theatre complex, this is a singular honour. Design was being finalised as this book was being written, with the building emerging as a tough, simple and highly sustainable, naturally ventilated timber-truss structure which presents itself to the public as a matrix for changing displays of public art.

Inside, the usual distinction between front and back of house is blurred through the concept of 'rooms with no names', open to all, offering a range of uses. The overarching idea is to provide a future-proofed facility – an adaptable barn, if you like. While every project is different, Charcoalblue's role as theatre and acoustics consultants here is informed by their earlier work on ultra-adaptable auditoria ranging from St. Ann's Warehouse in Brooklyn (p.14) via Chicago Shakespeare Theater (p.24) to The Factory International in Manchester (p.56) – and by Haworth Tompkins' experience on the Bridge Theatre next to Tower Bridge in London.

Academic Powerhouses

For ART, for so long housed in a theatre that was a good example of its kind but not designed for their purposes, here is the opportunity to define and inhabit a building not only thoroughly attuned to the requirements of the present generation of theatrical innovators, but open to the ideas of the future. The best form of sustainability is longevity and 'loose fit'.

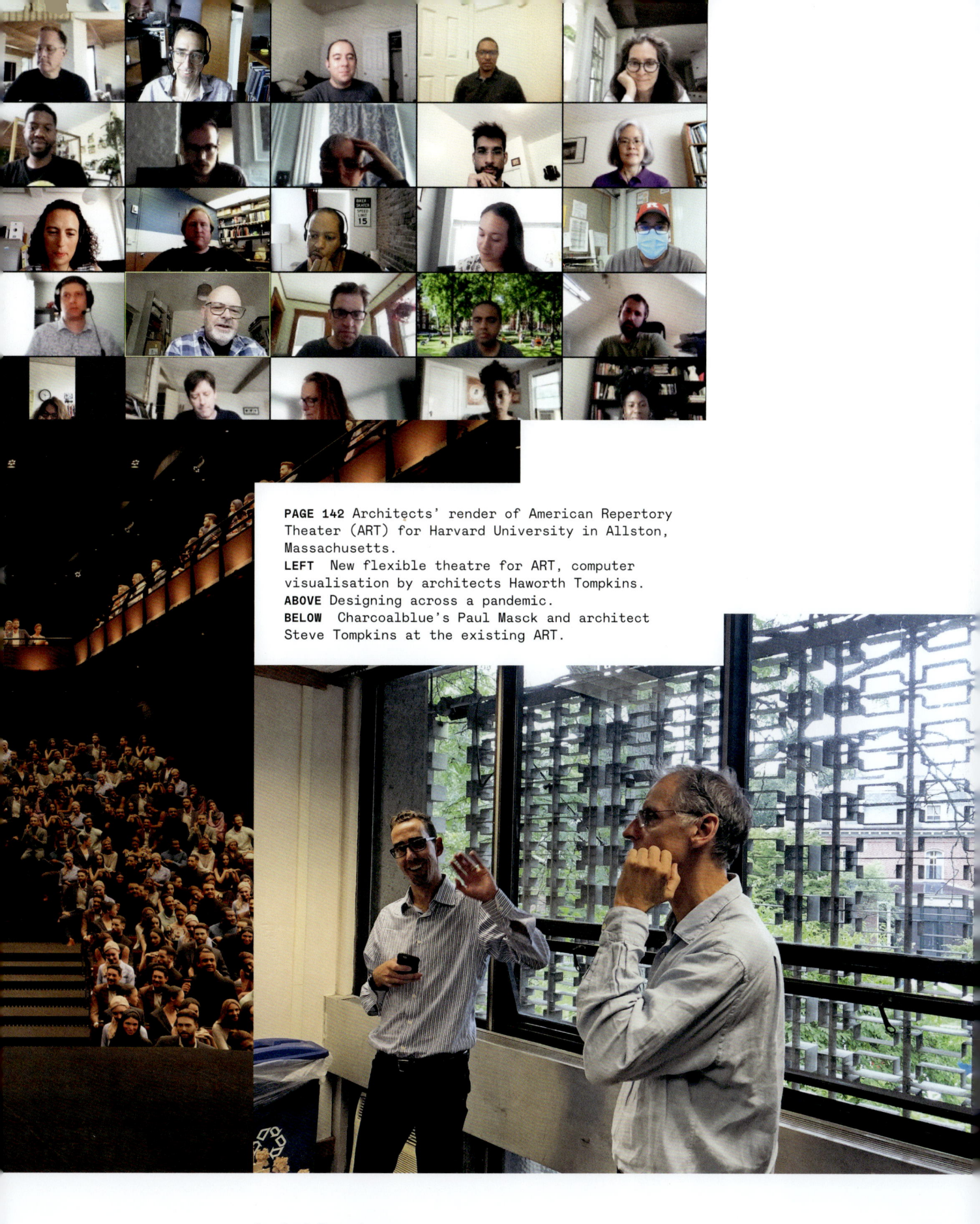

PAGE 142 Architects' render of American Repertory Theater (ART) for Harvard University in Allston, Massachusetts.
LEFT New flexible theatre for ART, computer visualisation by architects Haworth Tompkins.
ABOVE Designing across a pandemic.
BELOW Charcoalblue's Paul Masck and architect Steve Tompkins at the existing ART.

Academic Powerhouses

145

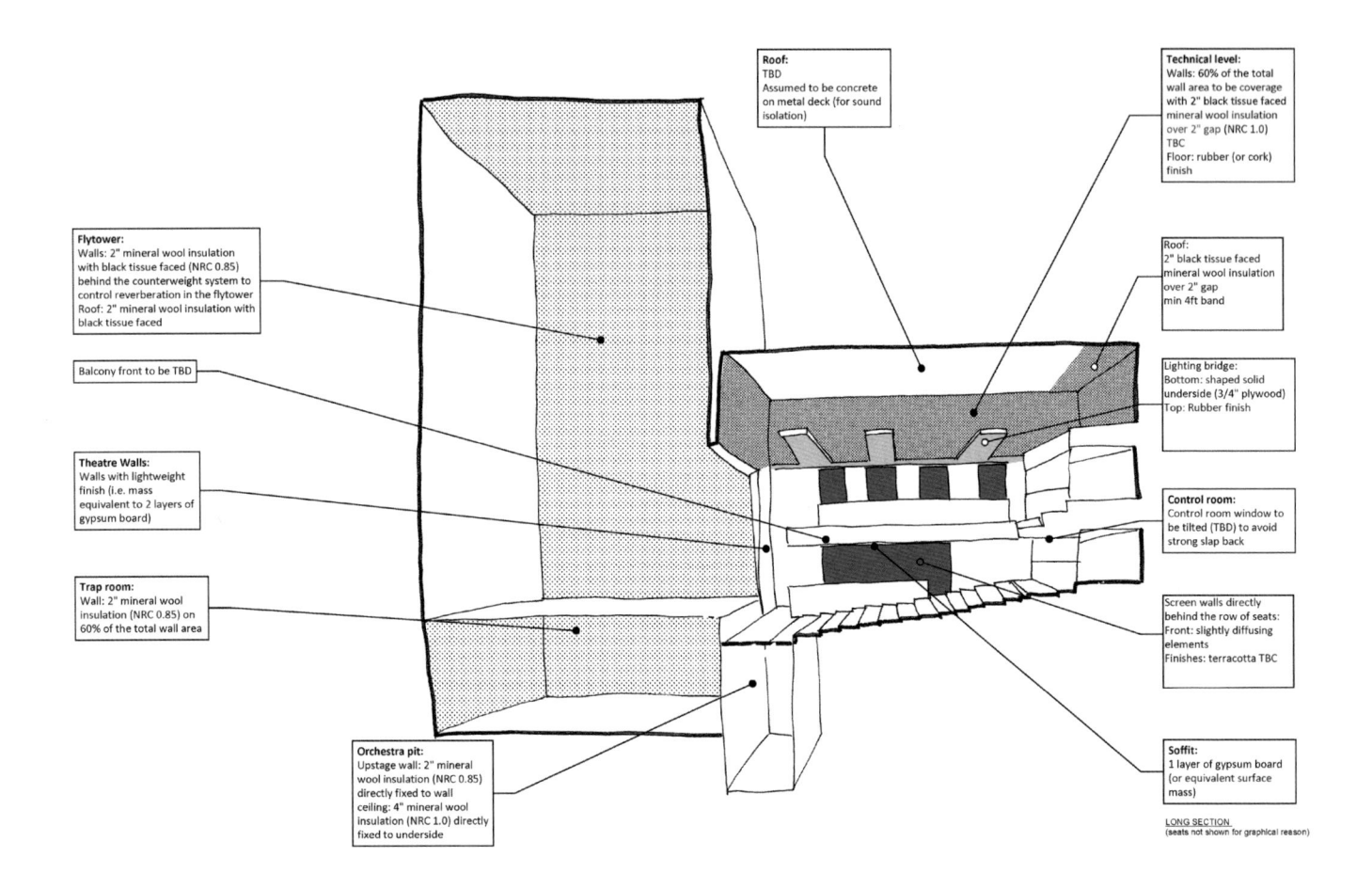

Roof:
TBD
Assumed to be concrete on metal deck (for sound isolation)

Technical level:
Walls: 60% of the total wall area to be coverage with 2" black tissue faced mineral wool insulation over 2" gap (NRC 1.0) TBC
Floor: rubber (or cork) finish

Flytower:
Walls: 2" mineral wool insulation with black tissue faced (NRC 0.85) behind the counterweight system to control reverberation in the flytower
Roof: 2" mineral wool insulation with black tissue faced

Roof:
2" black tissue faced mineral wool insulation over 2" gap
min 4ft band

Balcony front to be TBD

Lighting bridge:
Bottom: shaped solid underside (3/4" plywood)
Top: Rubber finish

Theatre Walls:
Walls with lightweight finish (i.e. mass equivalent to 2 layers of gypsum board)

Control room:
Control room window to be tilted (TBD) to avoid strong slap back

Trap room:
Wall: 2" mineral wool insulation (NRC 0.85) on 60% of the total wall area

Screen walls directly behind the row of seats:
Front: slightly diffusing elements
Finishes: terracotta TBC

Orchestra pit:
Upstage wall: 2" mineral wool insulation (NRC 0.85) directly fixed to wall
Ceiling: 4" mineral wool insulation (NRC 1.0) directly fixed to underside

Soffit:
1 layer of gypsum board (or equivalent surface mass)

LONG SECTION
(seats not shown for graphical reason)

Yale University Dramatic Arts Building

Always a rival to Harvard as Oxford is to Cambridge in the UK system, Yale has the performing arts well represented, with many courses — especially postgraduate — on offer from its David Geffen School of Drama, which operates out of ten buildings across the campus. The separate Yale Repertory Theatre (YRT) is housed in a converted church building, while the Yale Dramatic Society, or Dramat, dating back to 1900 and with Cole Porter as an alumnus, uses the school's 'Collegiate Gothic' University Theatre.

It's a familiar story of piecemeal expansion and rising ambition over the years, resulting in a variety of steadily less appropriate premises for present-day requirements. As is often the way, a better, combined centre for these scattered activities had long been discussed — for decades in fact — but resulted in no real progress. All this changed in October 2022, when Yale's President Peter Salovey announced plans to build a new theatre.

The two strands of activity are melded into one building, providing for both the school and the YRT. There's a clear connection between the two, bridging the gap between theory and professional practice, which has been likened by Dean of

Drama, James Bundy, to the relationship between a medical school and a teaching hospital. More than that, the new building will also house the undergraduate Theater and Performance Studies programme and the venerable Dramat. With the various rehearsal spaces, production workshops, classrooms and drama laboratories involved, this really is going to be a centre of theatrical excellence, a theatre within a university department. None too soon, according to the students vox-popped by the Yale newspaper, who want better acoustics, stages and dance facilities.

That, at the time of writing and with a site yet to be confirmed, is pretty much all that can be said. Charcoalblue has been working with Yale since 2017 on studies for the new facility, and was duly signed up for the design phase in 2022, working with Canada's KPMB Architects, who have previous experience at Yale. Another multi-project collaboration to note: Charcoalblue had most recently worked with KPMB on the renovation of the Eric Harvie Theatre (now the Jenny Belzberg Theatre) at the Banff Centre for Arts and Creativity in British Columbia, and before that on Toronto's famed Massey Hall (see p.139).

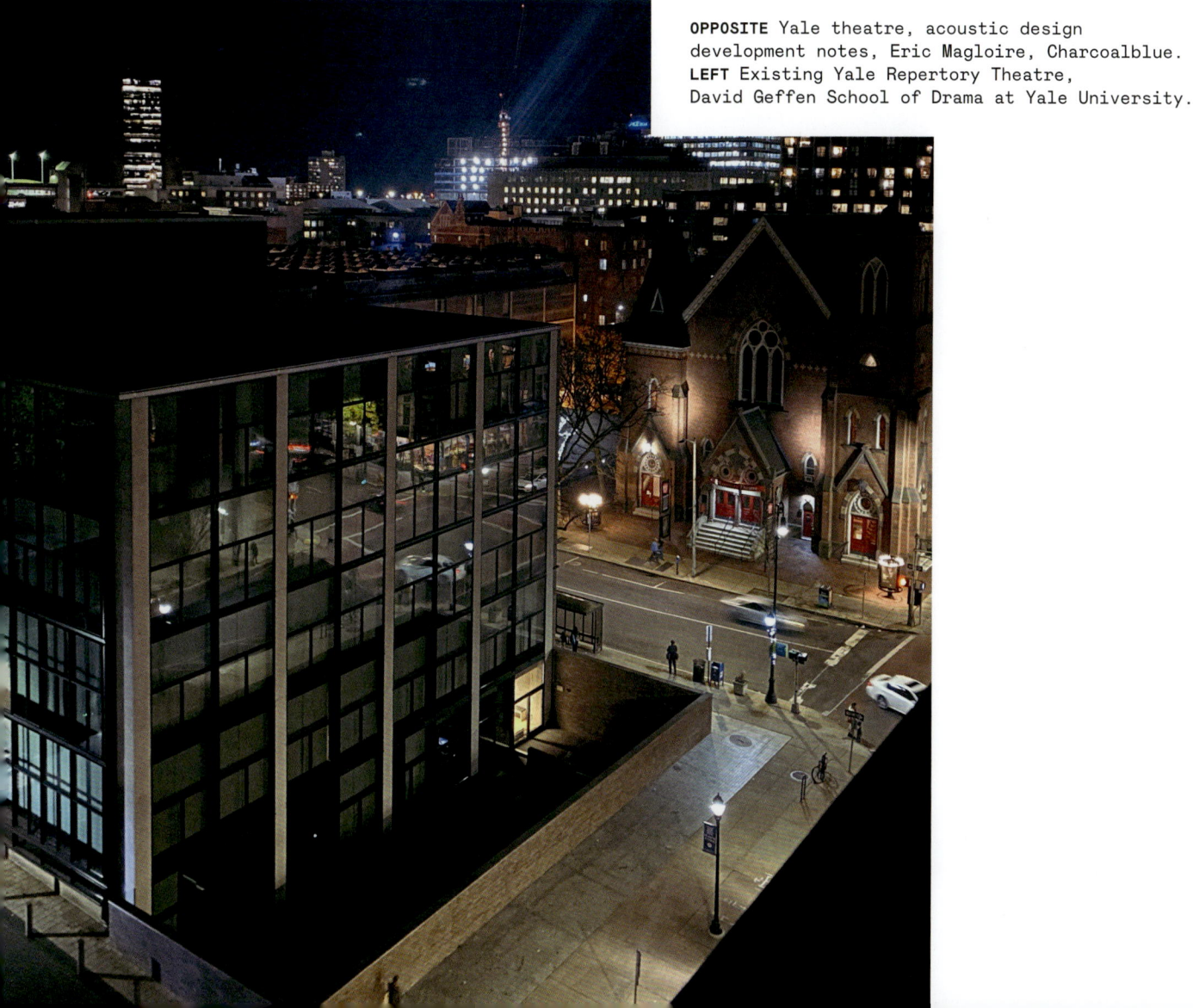

OPPOSITE Yale theatre, acoustic design development notes, Eric Magloire, Charcoalblue.
LEFT Existing Yale Repertory Theatre, David Geffen School of Drama at Yale University.

University of Oxford's Schwarzman Centre for the Humanities

'Oxford to receive biggest single donation since the Renaissance', went the *Guardian* headline in June 2019. The £150m in question was from Stephen A. Schwarzman, American financial power-player and a philanthropist committed to giving away most of his extraordinary wealth. This donation was all the more remarkable for the fact that Schwarzman has no particular connection to Oxford, being an alumnus of Yale, where he is also very generous. The money, which Schwarzman soon topped up to £175m, allowed building to start on the University of Oxford's long-delayed new centre for the humanities in what is called the Radcliffe Observatory Quarter, ten acres of former hospital site next to the eponymous Georgian observatory which is now part of Green Templeton College. It is rare to find such a large site so relatively close to the centre of town.

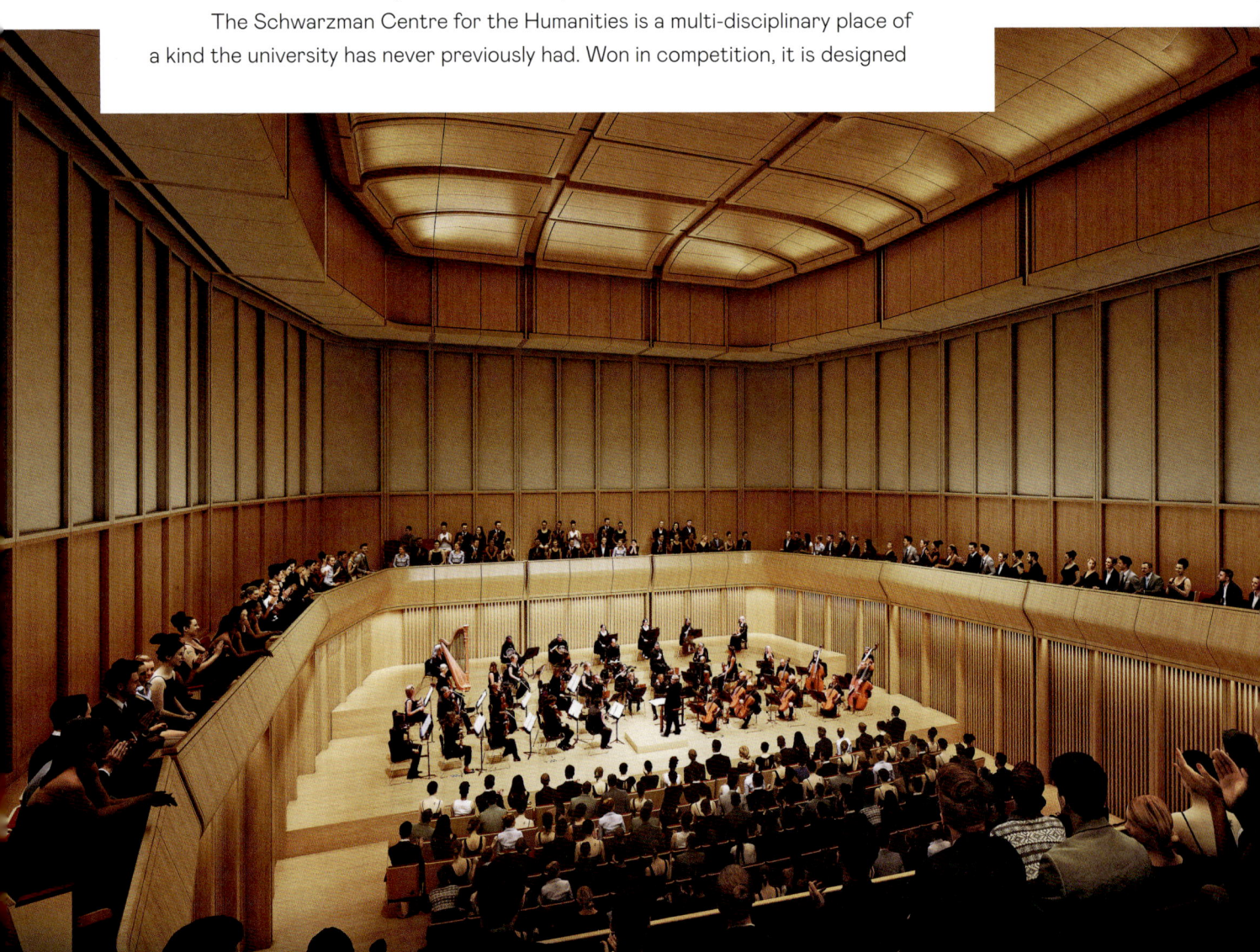

The Schwarzman Centre for the Humanities is a multi-disciplinary place of a kind the university has never previously had. Won in competition, it is designed

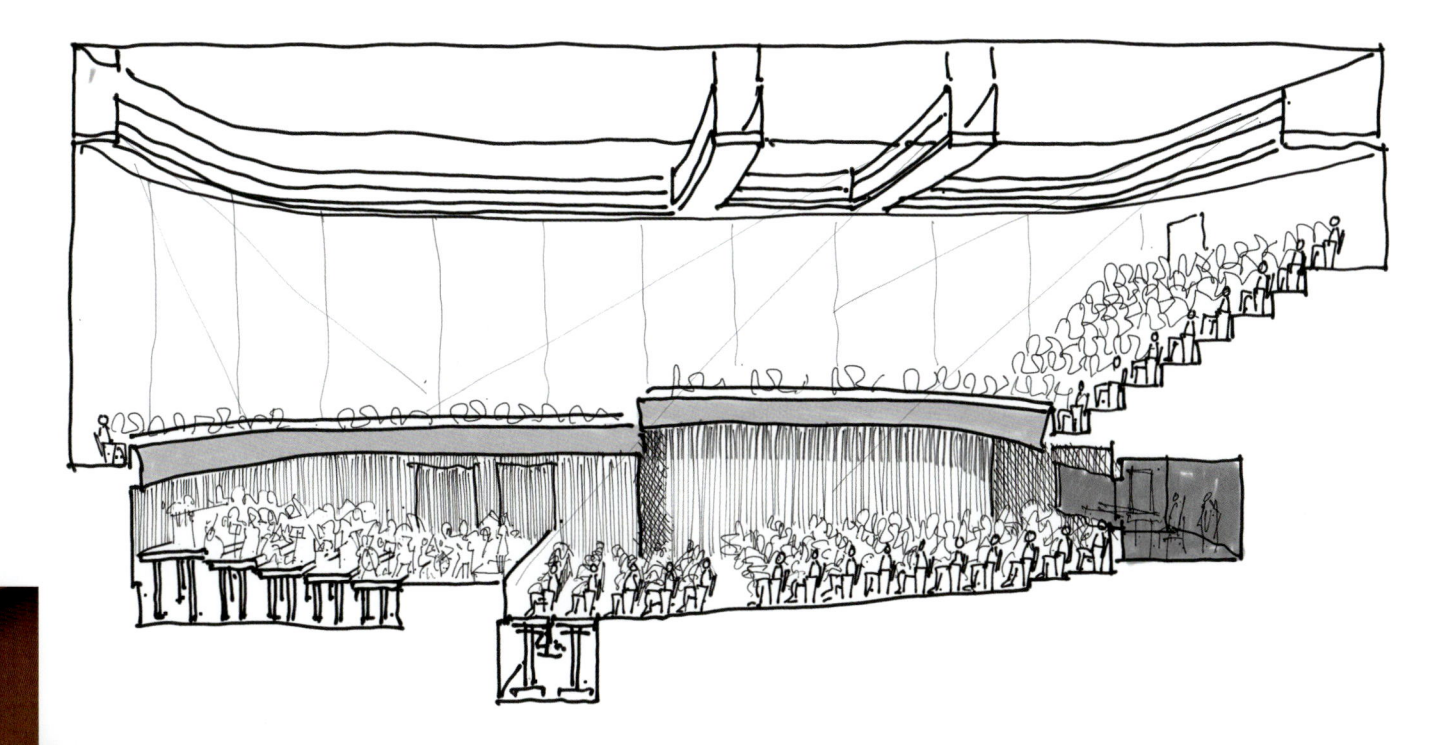

OPPOSITE Visualisation of the recital hall at the Schwarzman Centre for the Humanities by Hopkins.
ABOVE Concept sketch for the recital hall by Charcoalblue's Gavin Green.

by Hopkins Architects in an externally conservative stripped-classical style using the honey-coloured local sandstone. The university and donor regard it as a modern reinterpretation of a traditional Oxford building and set great store by its inclusivity, open to the public from the start, in contrast to the closed-gate exclusivity more usually associated with such buildings. Hopkins has also had experience building in Yale, Harvard and Princeton, including the Smith Campus Center for Harvard, where the design meetings for the new ART are held, which brings a satisfying circularity to this section.

In common with the examples above, the Schwarzman Centre mixes pedagogy with performance. The university expresses it thus:

> For the first time in the university's history, Oxford's programmes in English, history, linguistics, philology & phonetics, medieval & modern languages, music, philosophy, and theology & religion will be housed together in a space designed to encourage experiential learning and bold experimentation through cross-disciplinary and collaborative study . . . The building will include performing arts and exhibition venues designed to engage the Oxford community and the public at large.

Academic Powerhouses

That is not all: it will also house an Institute for Ethics in Artificial Intelligence, attached to the School of Philosophy.

It is a radical departure for Oxford, a university where subjects have traditionally been kept separate, much teaching takes place in the individual colleges, and Town and Gown seldom mix. At the heart of all this is a set of three auditoria: a 500-seat concert hall, a 250-seat theatre and a 100-seat 'black box' experimental music venue, the first of its kind in the UK. There will also be rehearsal spaces and music studios.

Its raison d'être is to be a cultural centre powered by research, set in a peaceful landscape. Charcoalblue is working with Hopkins and the university on all aspects of performance and operation of this trad-progressive complex, from the design of the official performance spaces to the layout of the dressing rooms and loading bay. But this building – ultra low-carbon in use, being built to Passivhaus standards – has a theatrical quality throughout, not least in its vaulted central atrium surrounded by galleries. It is likely to generate 'unofficial' modes of performance and learning, as intended.

While the above universities are venerable names, they have competition from a relative newcomer in the southern hemisphere: Edith Cowan University (ECU) in Perth, the capital of Western Australia. It may have been a designated university only since 1991, the result of the mergers of various higher-education institutes going back to 1901, but it is in expansionist mode, and is making a cultural hub in its ambitious new 'vertical campus' in the heart of Perth. Key to this is its Western Australian Academy of Performing Arts (WAAPA), which was established in 1980.

This is a large, multiple-venue project in which Charcoalblue is working alongside the new campus's Melbourne-based architects Lyons Architects, Perth firm Silver Thomas Hanley and long-time UK colleagues Haworth Tompkins Architects. There are five main performance venues of all types for drama, music and dance. Beyond those, the brief has expanded to include facilities for other faculties, such as screen, sound and broadcast-based activities, with full-scale studios to match. At the other end of the scale, WAAPA owns an internationally important collection of early keyboard instruments. It all amounts to a creative industries precinct.

If the word 'campus' suggests something out of town, think again: ECU City, as it is called, is an educational and cultural regeneration project for some 11,500 students right next to Perth's central business district and woven into it, comprising two large linked buildings on 11 levels. The performing arts elements at WAAPA are in the northern of the two blocks, adjacent to the city's existing cultural quarter. This new campus rises above a transportation hub.

It is emphatically not the Ivy League/Oxbridge idea of a university overall, but there are precedents, such as the multi-level 1960s Kensington Gore building of London's Royal College of Art. And, as we have seen at the Schwarzman

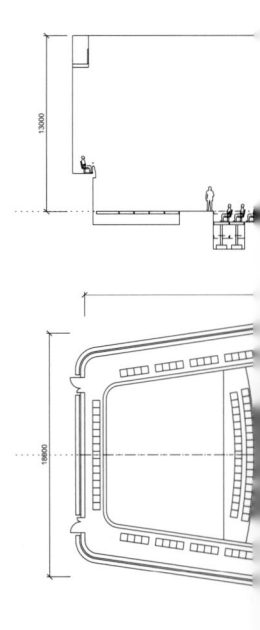

LEFT Charcoalblue's Team Leader, Paul Franklin at the topping out ceremony.
BELOW Design development drawings by Charcoalblue: suite of cultural spaces.

Centre in Oxford, there is an international trend towards large interdisciplinary buildings. ECU City gleefully breaks the mould with its digital display facades and aspirations to be the high-density urban university of the future, but the demands of proper performance spaces remain the same wherever they happen to find themselves, hence the ongoing involvement of Charcoalblue and its colleagues.

The largest venue, the full-scale proscenium-stage playhouse with ground-level entrance, includes a three-storey flytower wrapped round with other auditoria and facilities within the building, each with its own character. The overall aim of the project is urban regeneration through education and culture, with all the activities that implies. Given its location, ECU houses a business school as well, so cross-discipline working is not only possible but positively encouraged. It is scheduled to open in 2025.

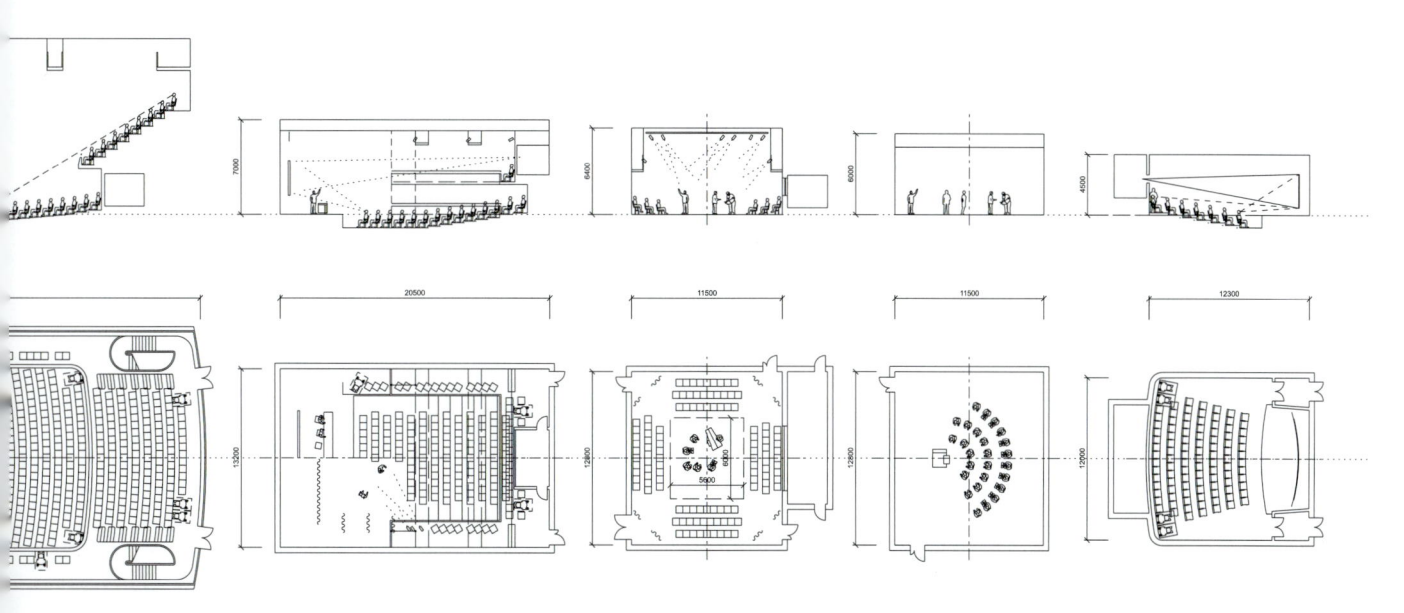

Academic Powerhouses

Aside: The Liverpool Everyman Theatre

This was a vital project during the early years of Charcoalblue, and it won the RIBA Stirling Prize, the first theatre ever to do so. Having got to know architects Haworth Tompkins from London's Royal Court Theatre rebuild and subsequently on the 2006 Young Vic in London's Waterloo, the Everyman – won in competition in 2007 – presented a particularly sensitive new challenge. From first enquiry, it was to take nearly a decade to achieve: plenty of time to refine the details.

The pre-existing theatre, founded in 1964 in the former Hope Hall, a dissenters' chapel dating from 1837 that went on to become a cinema, was a nationally renowned hotbed of theatrical talent. This included not only a whole generation of actors who were to become famous, but also one of its founding directors, Terry Hands, who led the Royal Shakespeare Company for 13 years in the 1980s and 1990s.

It was also a much-loved meeting place at the north end of Hope Street, an elevated thoroughfare bookended by the city's two great cathedrals. It had a downstairs bistro that was popular not only with audiences but also with academics and students from the nearby university quarter. But behind the scenes it was time-expired, leaky and inflexible, with poor accessibility and cramped backstage and front-of-house facilities. Nonetheless the task in hand – to demolish the lot and start again on the same site with an entirely new, much-improved Everyman – was always going to need very careful handling if its cherished character and reputation were not to be jeopardised.

My first impression, on arriving at the new theatre in early 2014 and sitting in the foyer, was to wonder how much of it was retained structure from the old place. Even the concrete beams spanning the space looked as if they could have been from some repurposed industrial structure. But no: this was all part of the design aesthetic.

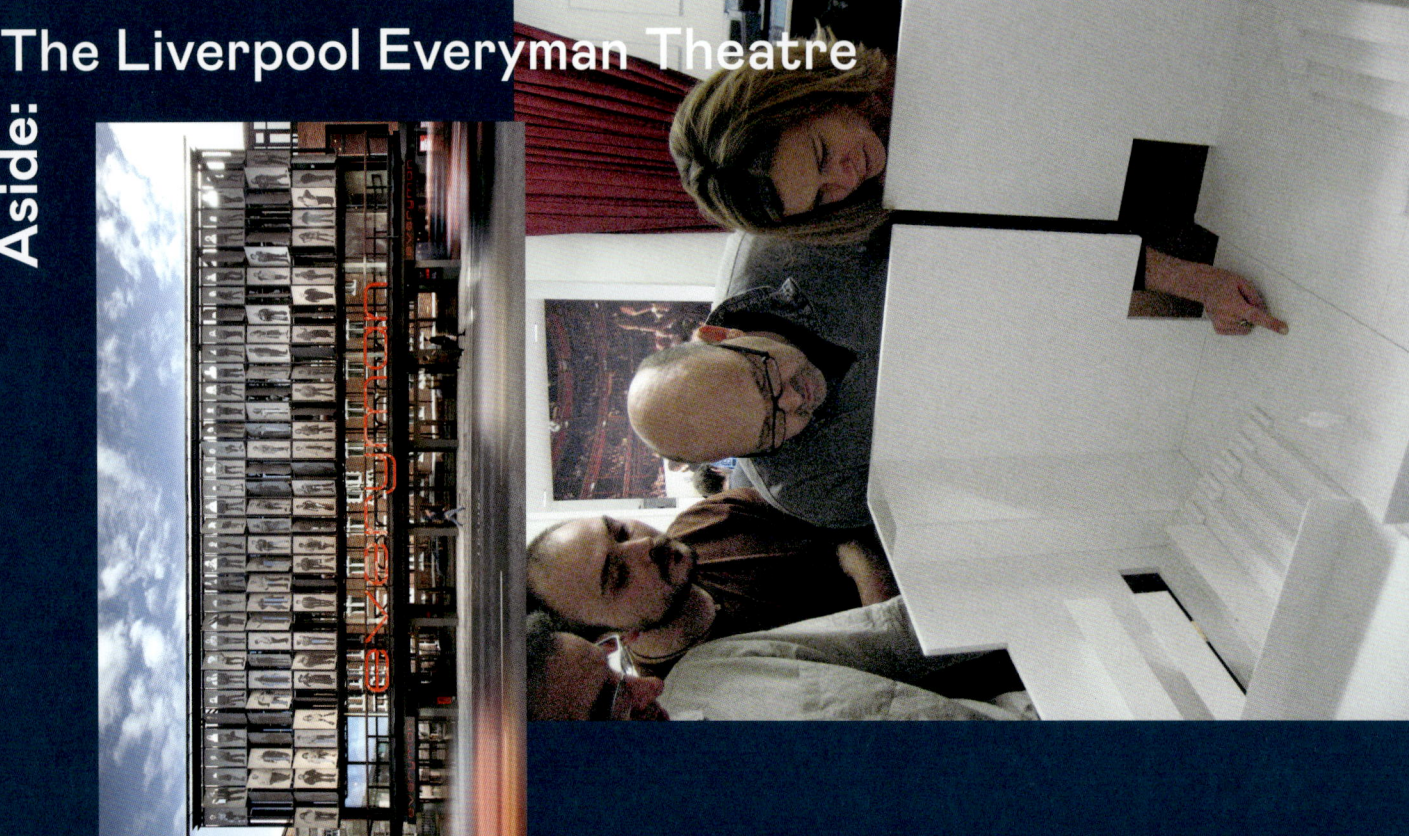

The previous theatre had not been posh – as its name suggests, it was for everyone – so nor should this one be. And although the (low-carbon) concrete was new, various materials were recycled, such as the timber shuttering used to cast the concrete and, most notably, 25,000 late Georgian bricks, reclaimed from the carcass of what had been Hope Hall and now lining the new auditorium.

The original stage configuration, unusual for its time in being a (very) wide-thrust configuration, was replicated with the addition of a seating gallery and over-stage technical bridges. But it does not have to stay like that: it is made of removable modular sections to allow a variety of configurations (end-on, in-the-round and traverse among them), while above, both manual and powered flying systems allow for maximum production creativity. Cabling connections run throughout the theatre so performances can happen anywhere.

As important were the new daylit dressing rooms backstage, a proper scene dock and equipment get-in, rehearsal room, separate studio space and a dedicated writers' studio. A new seat type, inspired by the old cinema seats which had comprised a large part of the former auditorium, was painstakingly designed, prototyped and tweaked (see 'Aside: Developing Seats', p.66).

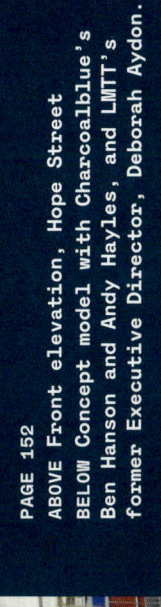

PAGE 152
ABOVE Front elevation, Hope Street
BELOW Concept model with Charcoalblue's
Ben Hanson and Andy Hayles, and LMTT's
former Executive Director, Deborah Aydon.

TOP Concept sketch by Gavin Green, Charcoalblue.
ABOVE LEFT Charcoalblue's Steve Roberts on-site.
RIGHT Charcoalblue's Ian Stickland, Team Leader
for the Everyman project, outside the finished
facade.
LEFT Balcony front and lighting bar mock-up.

TOP The original Everyman Theatre.
BELOW In construction: auditorium taking shape.

As the design progressed, the lighting strategy moved from conventional tungsten to all-LED, while a key low-energy strategy for the building was built in: natural ventilation, not unknown but by no means common at the time, especially on tight city-centre sites like this. The National Theatre Shed (see p.79) was a helpful prototype. Like the Shed, this natural ventilation is expressed in the architecture, with a row of cylindrical brick chimneys apparent at high level on the frontage. Not unlike ships' funnels: appropriate for a great port city.

Finally the main facade is itself a low-tech, low-energy affair. Facing west, it is shaded by more than 100 rotatable water-cut stainless-steel panels featuring portraits of Liverpool's citizens who volunteered. These might be regarded as the 'Everyfolk'.

Stirling Prize night 2014 was quite a moment for the theatre, its leaders — Artistic Director Gemma Bodinetz and Chief Exec Deborah Aydon of Liverpool and Merseyside Theatres Trust (LMTT) — its designers and the Everyfolk. Charcoalblue was getting used to winning and being nominated for awards with its architect colleagues and had already been on teams nominated for the Stirling four times — for the Young Vic in 2007, the Hepworth Gallery in Wakefield with David Chipperfield in 2012, the Royal Shakespeare Theatre in 2011 and the Library of Birmingham with Mecanoo in 2014 (a second nomination alongside the Everyman in a rich year). Both the Library of Birmingham and the Everyman represented a resurgence of civic pride in their respective cities, but the people of Liverpool had got right behind their new Everyman and were enthusiastic supporters. Plus, it was a delight for an inaugural theatre to win.

ABOVE Stirling Prize – left to right: Charcoalblue's Ian Stickland, LMTT's Robert Longthorne, and Charcoalblue's Andy Hayles, Ben Hanson and Gavin Green
RIGHT Intimate auditorium.

Of Sound Mind: The acoustics sto

Evidently enough, the way an auditorium sounds is crucial. It can look a million dollars, but if you can't hear clearly what's going on or are distracted by extraneous noise, it has failed (one famous West End theatre, for instance, was plagued for a while by the noise of high-speed hand dryers from its toilets, while in another you must try to ignore the rumble of an Underground train line beneath your feet).

Some historic auditoria just seem to get the basics right, while others have always been problematic and take a lot of adjusting. Certain composers take into account the acoustic quality of the place their music is to be performed in – Monteverdi and St Mark's in Venice, for example, are a perfect acoustic fit, while the direct actor–audience rapport of Elizabethan playhouses explains aspects of Shakespeare's dialogue – but such direct causal links are comparatively rare. Productions have always moved from place to place.

> **Some historic auditoria just seem to get the basics right, while others have always been problematic and take a lot of adjusting.**

Meanwhile, the vogue for performing in 'found spaces', often post-industrial, brings its own set of interesting challenges. The quality of sound transmitted within a building is one thing; so too is the level of damping-down of unwelcome external noise – trains, planes and automobiles usually, including vibration as well as air-transmitted sound. The St. Ann's Warehouse theatre in Brooklyn (see p.14), so close to the Brooklyn Bridge and with its suite of spaces set within an unusually open interior, shows what can be done. Variable acoustics – for instance, to suit both the spoken word and amplified music depending on circumstance – need to be as straightforward as possible: over-complexity is the enemy of flexibility.

Acoustic expertise is thus intrinsic to the overall design of the performance venue. Everything that is built or modified, along with the surroundings, has a bearing. Charcoalblue is fortunate in having Byron Harrison lead its global team of acousticians.

One of his early acoustics projects was the Elizabethan Theatre at the Château d'Hardelot in Normandy, an intriguing building that synthesises much research into the circular and polygonal theatres of Shakespeare and his contemporaries, but with a Japanese delicacy. Designed by Paris-based architect Andrew Todd, it sits in the grounds of the château, which acts as a cultural centre for the entente cordiale, specifically the cross-Channel relationship between the département of the Pas-de-Calais and the County of Kent. The château

Of Sound Mind: the acoustics story

had developed its own outdoor summer arts festival of British and French drama, opera, music and comedy. A new theatre offered its first opportunity for year-round performance. It sits among forests a little way inland just south of Boulogne and was opened in 2016 by Queen Elizabeth II as the only Elizabethan-plan example in France.

It is a timber (specifically cross-laminated timber) drum containing a thrust-stage auditorium to seat 388 people. Its exterior consists of a veil of vertical bamboo poles that help to dematerialise it, keeping something of the festival-structure feel. Todd knows theatre and its intimate workings, having previously worked with famed director Peter Brook and with Charcoalblue at the Young Vic. Meanwhile, Charcoalblue had all the experience of working on the thrust-stage auditoria at Stratford-upon-Avon to draw on. At Hardelot, it provided advice on acoustic design, designing technical performance systems and assisting with the wider building planning.

As built, the theatre is deceptively sophisticated: for instance, the six motorised flying bars double as mounts for timber reflectors to change the acoustics, closing off a layer of sound-absorbing material above the grid. Thus equipped, it can stage a wide range of performances with different acoustic requirements. Indeed, it can change character entirely, becoming an intimate opera house complete with orchestra pit and side wings.

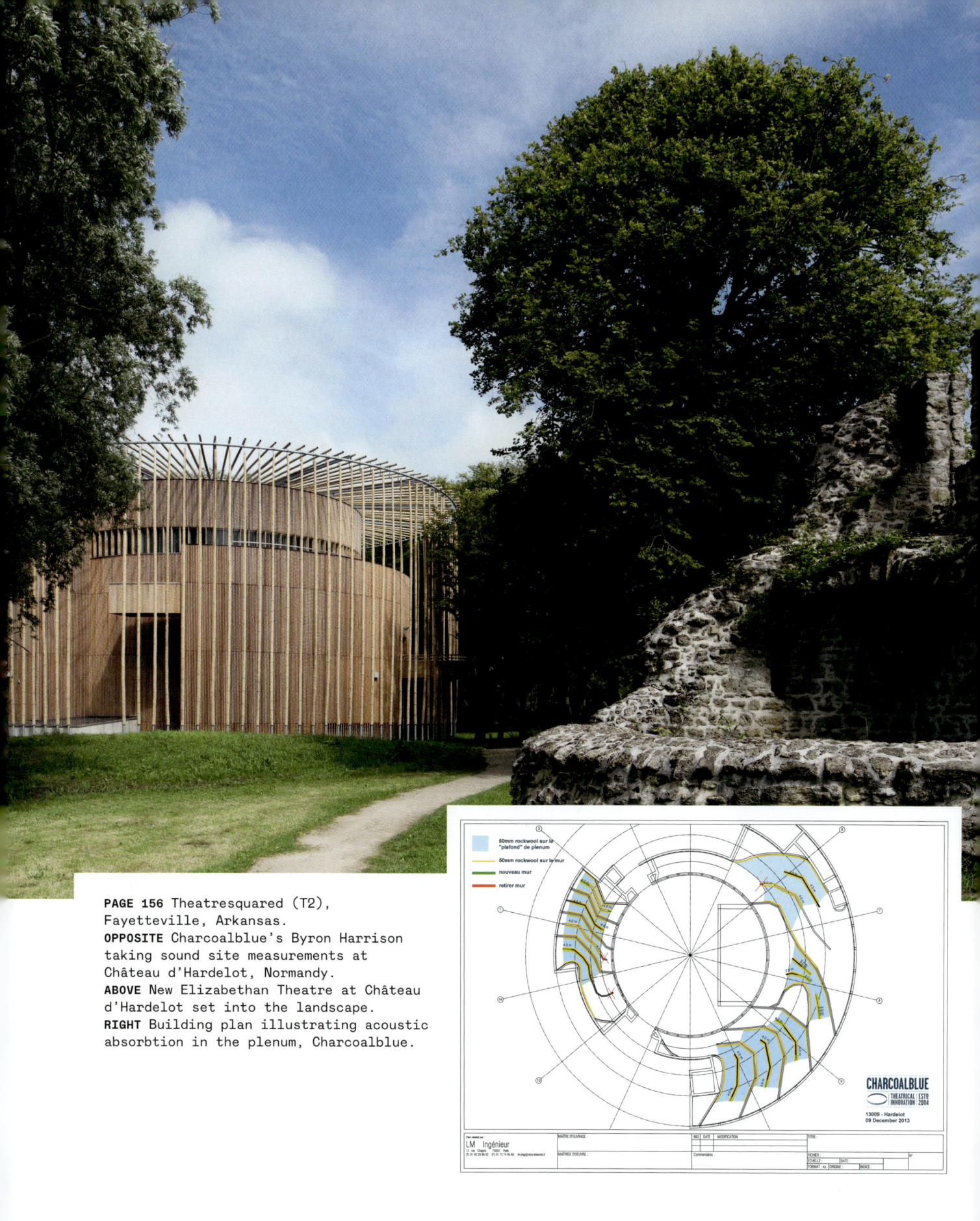

PAGE 156 Theatresquared (T2), Fayetteville, Arkansas.
OPPOSITE Charcoalblue's Byron Harrison taking sound site measurements at Château d'Hardelot, Normandy.
ABOVE New Elizabethan Theatre at Château d'Hardelot set into the landscape.
RIGHT Building plan illustrating acoustic absorbtion in the plenum, Charcoalblue.

Of Sound Mind: the acoustics story

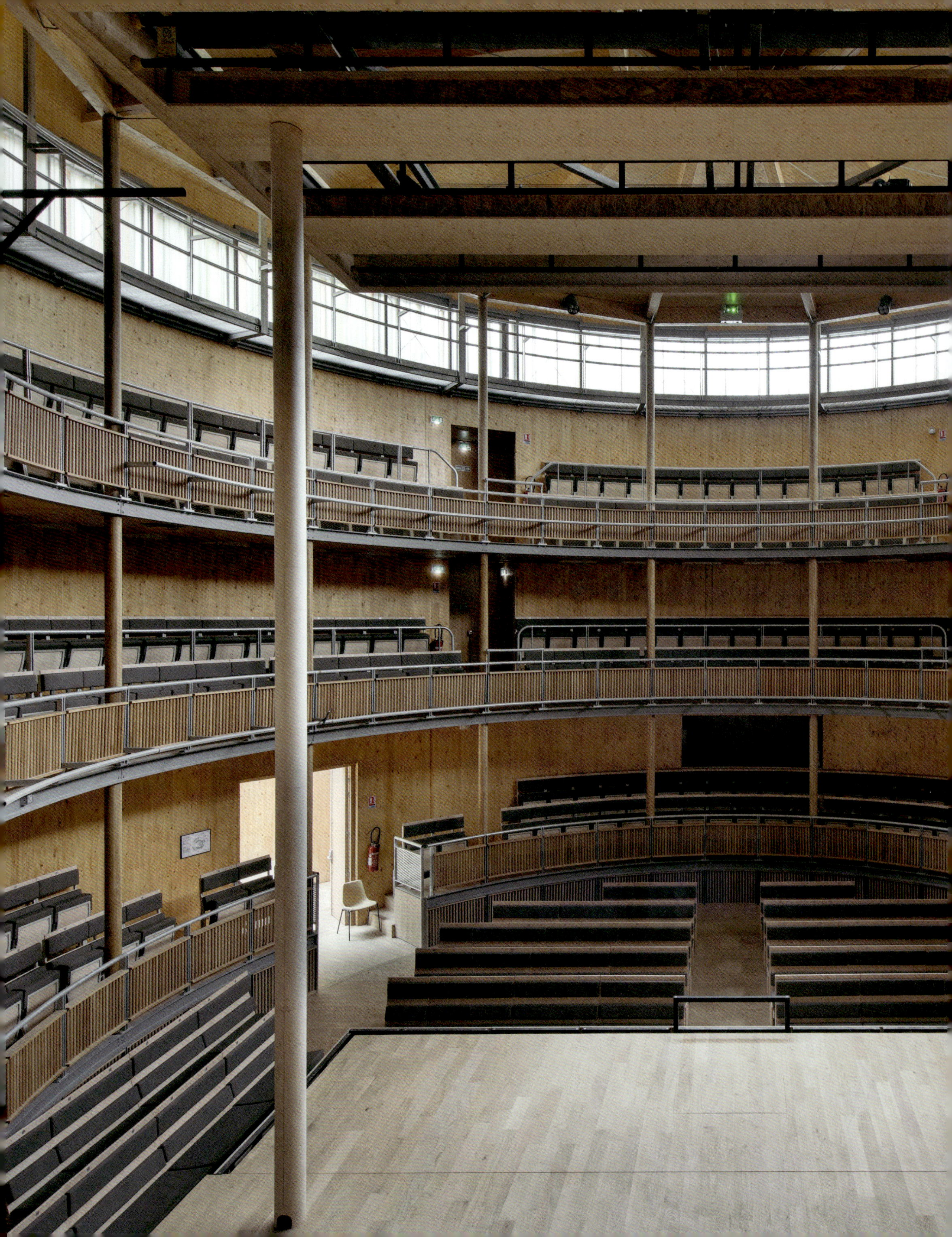

24.0 ms

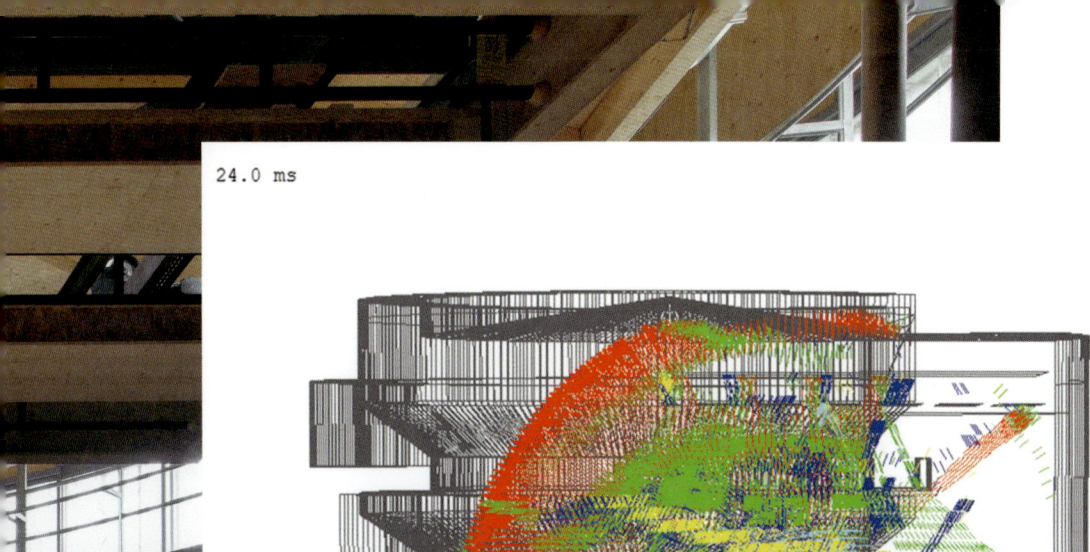

No of rays: 29810
Band   :   1 kHz
Max time : 75.0 ms
Time step : 1.0 ms
Max order :   4
Min level : -30.0 dB
Lost rays : shown

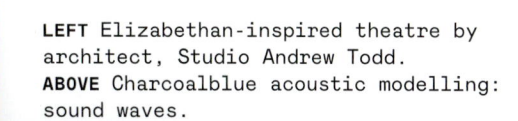

Order
0
1
2
3
4

LEFT Elizabethan-inspired theatre by architect, Studio Andrew Todd.
ABOVE Charcoalblue acoustic modelling: sound waves.

161

'A premier national theatre in north-west Arkansas' is how Robert Ford, playwright and Artistic Director of TheatreSquared (T2 for short), sees his building, and he is not wrong. Its hometown is Fayetteville, roughly equidistant from Oklahoma City to its west, Memphis to its east, Kansas City to its north and Dallas to its south. So this is heartland southern-states America, a grid-plan university city in the Ozark uplands. Not necessarily a place where you'd expect to find a leading progressive theatre company, perhaps, but Fayetteville has always been an individualistic kind of place.

T2 was founded only in 2005, found a ready audience and has grown steadily, largely on the basis of new work and diligent community outreach. Soon it had outgrown its 175-seat rented studio theatre and was in a position to commission a building of its own, helped greatly by the environmentally conscious Walton Family Foundation based in the town, set up by the family who founded Walmart, the world's largest retail chain.

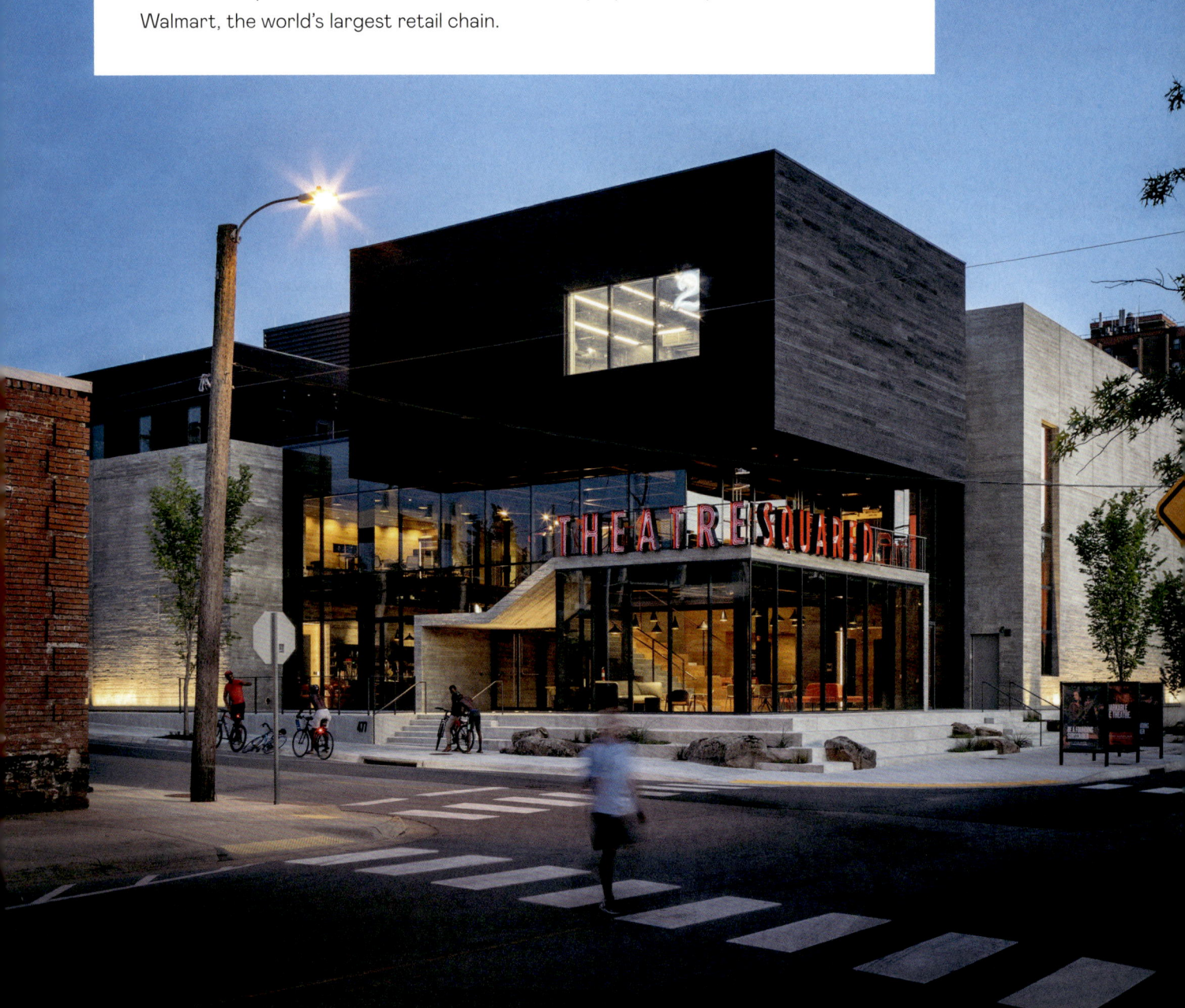

LEFT Welcoming new theatre in downtown Fayetteville.
ABOVE Client workshop on the old stage with Charcoalblue's Andy Hayles and John Owens, and TheatreSquared's Artistic Director Robert Ford, Executive Director Martin Miller alongside members of the T2 team.
RIGHT Orchestra-level mock-up with T2 Artistic Director Robert Ford, Executive Director Martin Miller, Associate Artistic Director Amy Herzberg and members of the T2 team.
BELOW Client workshop on the old stage with Charcoalblue's Andy Hayles, John Owens, T2 Artistic Director Robert Ford, former Executive Director Martin Miller, Associate Artistic Director Amy Herzberg and members of the T2 team.

Of Sound Mind: the acoustics story 163

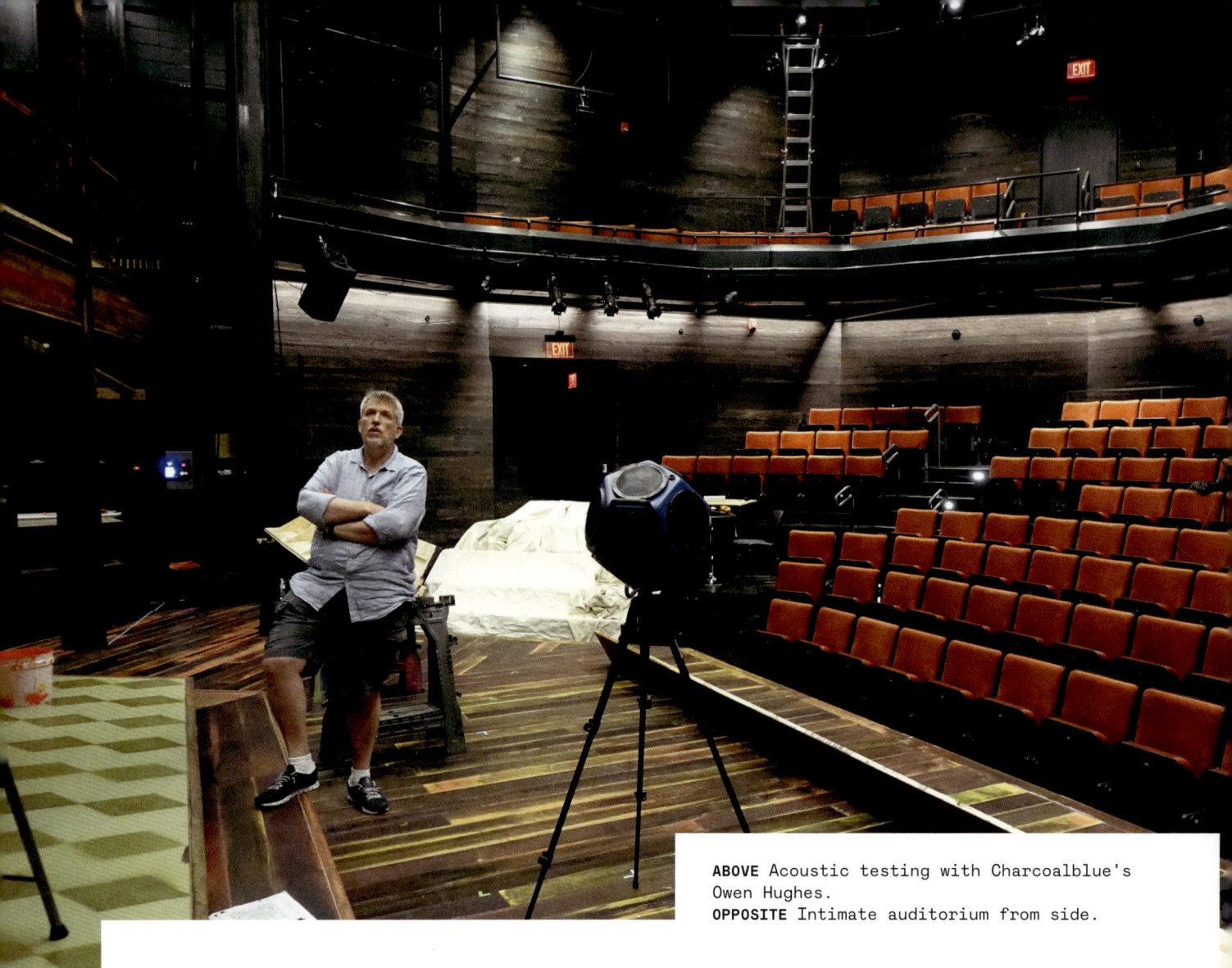

ABOVE Acoustic testing with Charcoalblue's Owen Hughes.
OPPOSITE Intimate auditorium from side.

Charcoalblue was the lead consultant for the project and brought in its frequent American collaborators Marvel Architects. The aim was nothing less than a multi-auditorium theatre and public meeting place with perfect acoustics and sightlines. Acoustically, the main challenge was the noise from the railroad track just one block away, a corridor for the region's long, slow, rumbling freight trains with their mournful, piercing sirens.

What emerged was a building where the three main theatre spaces – the main auditorium, studio theatre and rehearsal/occasional performance room – are expressed and elevated externally, with what Ford calls the 'theatre commons', the all-day meeting place/foyer, separating them at ground level.

The design and client team (including Executive Director Martin Miller, who had come from the earlier incarnation of the Chicago Shakespeare Theater (p.22)) travelled the world studying best practice in theatre design. It's remarkable to find National Theatre-style boardmarked concrete here as one of the construction materials, and delightful to find the actual boards in which the concrete was poured cleaned up and reused as an interior lining material.

Working collaboratively from the inside out, as is their way, Charcoalblue tackled theatre design, stage lighting, stage engineering, acoustics and audiovisual elements. As so often, those recalling the project later found it hard to pin down exactly who – client, architect, acoustician, designer – came up with a particular good idea. But what everyone points out is that the process helped to define what T2 was, what it wanted to achieve in the future, and that it wanted to make what it did clearly visible and immediate, both inside and outside the auditoria. Once opened, the visual and acoustic intimacy of the spaces and the lived-in familiarity of the whole building were immediately apparent, and the awards came thick and fast.

Of Sound Mind: the acoustics story

In the Esplanade Theatres district on Marina Bay in Singapore, the Singtel Waterfront Theatre was commissioned as a multi-purpose, medium-sized venue. It is a significant addition to what is the country's national performing arts centre. It already had its famous armadillo-like pairing of large concert hall and theatre dating from the mid 1990s, plus small studio spaces. In contrast with those, the Singtel caters for audiences of 600 to 700 depending on which configuration is selected (including proscenium, in-the-round, traverse and flat-floor).

The Esplanade Co Ltd called in Charcoalblue to devise the initial concept for the new waterfront theatre: Charcoalblue then led a multi-disciplinary team to establish the project brief and move on to detail design. Developed with long-established Singapore practice Architects 61, the building emerged as a four-storey-high theatre of a scale that could visually make a group with the existing buildings on this highly visible site.

A large sheltering roof overhang forms the main entrance, and a space-frame elevation facing the bay is articulated to resemble scaled-up Chinese domestic shelving, an unexpectedly good way to activate what would otherwise be a blank side facade. Other elevations use corrugated cement-fibre panels, and this functional aesthetic, itself designed to reflect external sound, carries through to the interior for acoustic purposes.

Varying in their sound-absorption and reflective qualities, with changing sinusoidal rhythms, the panels on the interior can move around along with the auditorium configuration to suit the production in question. They form part of an interior ambience that the architects call 'raw and casual . . . functional, accessible and welcoming'. It is essentially the ultimate 'black box' adaptable theatre, but it does this with considerable civic élan.

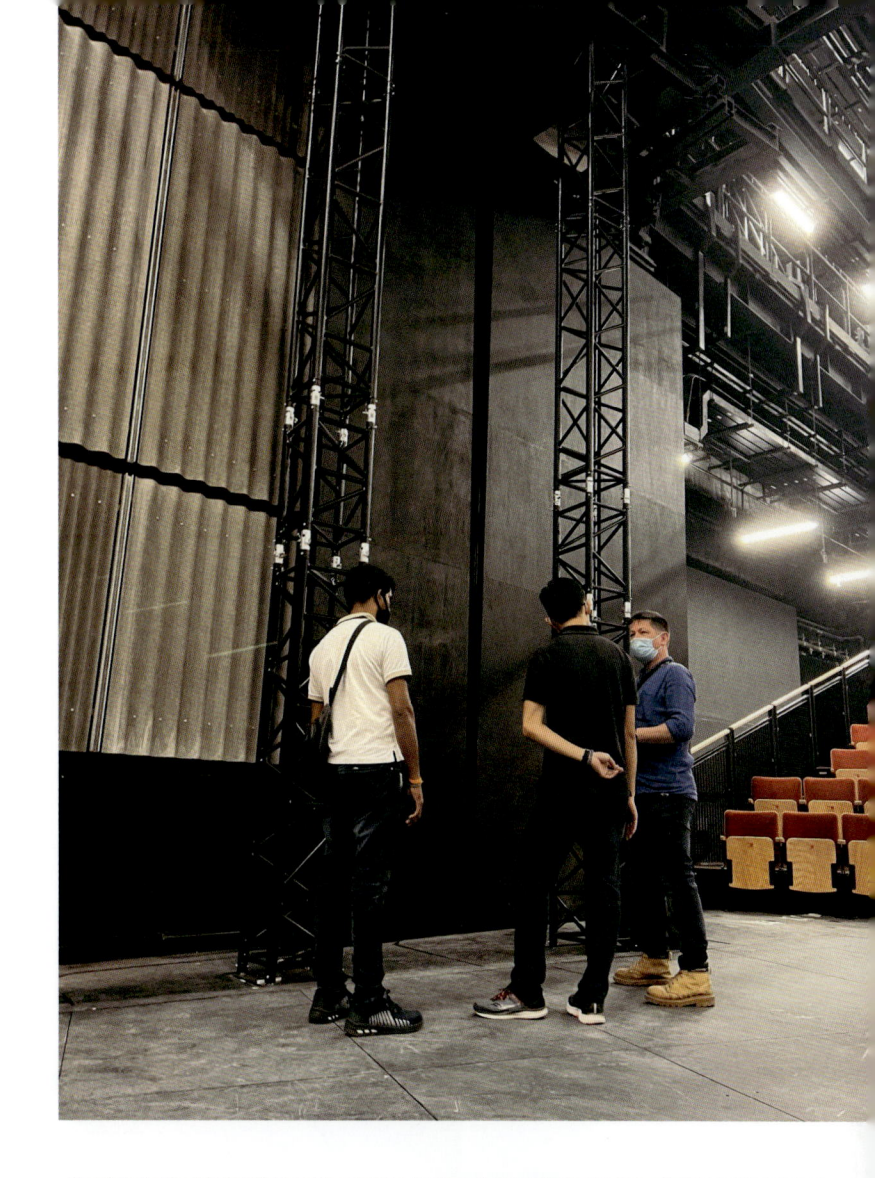

OPPOSITE Auditorium in construction: concrete stalls rake.
ABOVE RIGHT Inspection of the acoustic doors with Charcoalblue's Paul Halter.
ABOVE Sound measurements illustrated on a section drawing reflecting a stepped ceiling profile.
RIGHT Acoustic modelling, Charcoalblue.

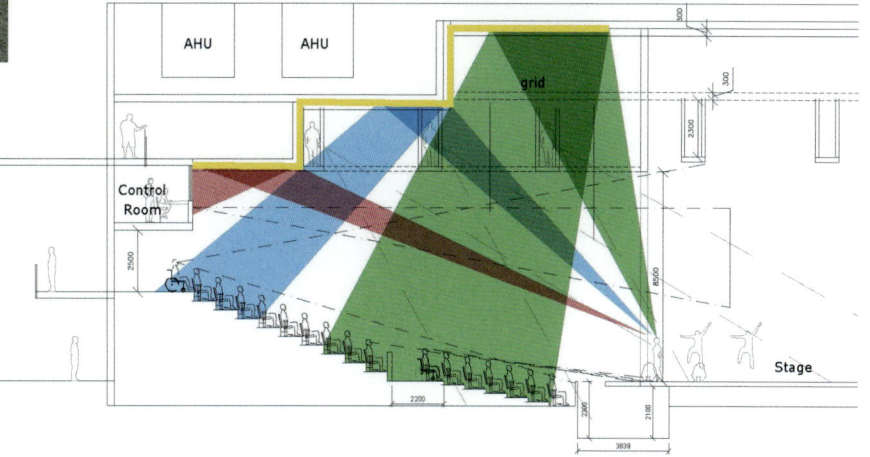

Of Sound Mind: the acoustics story

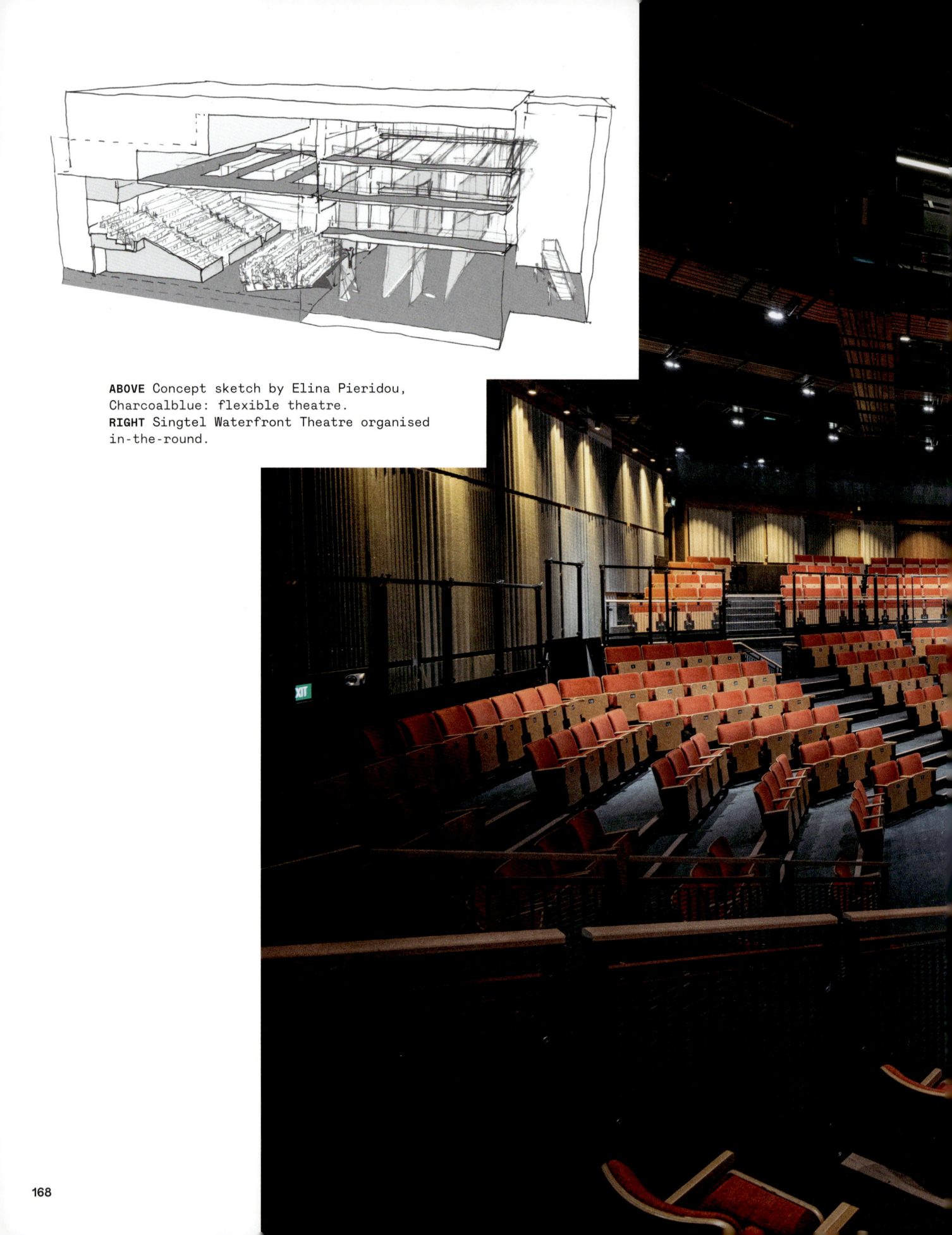

ABOVE Concept sketch by Elina Pieridou, Charcoalblue: flexible theatre.
RIGHT Singtel Waterfront Theatre organised in-the-round.

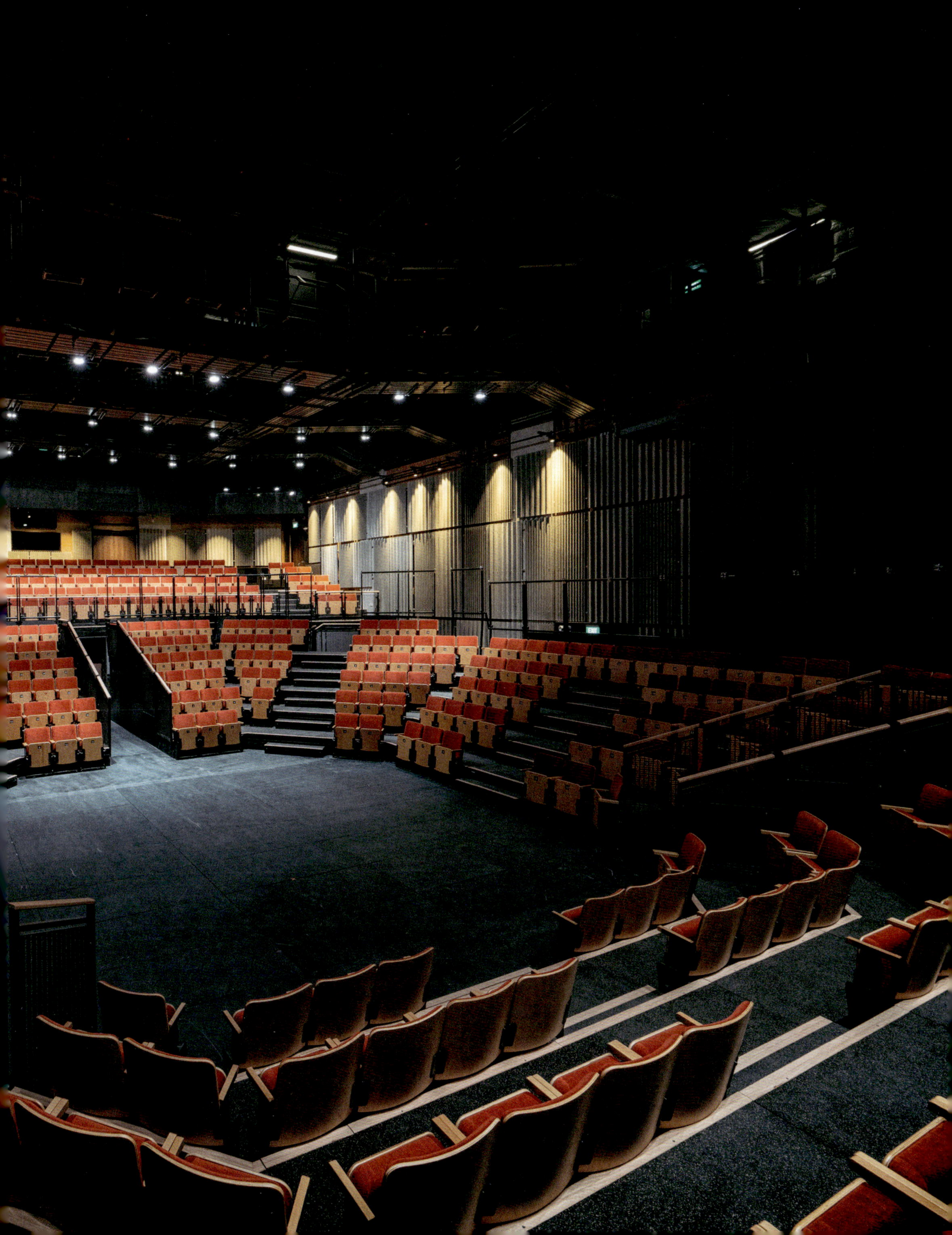

CBX: The Parallel Universe

After a while, you realise that the name Charcoalblue gives no clue as to the activities of the company, and that this is quite deliberate. For those who don't already know, the name tends to come with a subtitle, typically 'theatre, acoustics and experience'. This descriptor changes over time as new disciplines get added and existing ones develop, but the jazz-inspired name over the door remains the same: it's about creating an atmosphere and trading on Theatrical Innovation.

'Experience' is one of those catch-all words, but in reality what it describes in this context is very simple. The matter of telling a story visually and aurally to an audience is absolutely not confined to theatres, cinemas and other spaces co-opted for the purpose. Anyone with any kind of screen communication with other people, let alone those who give, say, TED Talks, finds themselves in the same world. Scale this up to corporate level, and then further still to worldwide company communications, and you have innumerable performance spaces, many as large as any theatre. Most of us are used to rooms retrofitted with videoconferencing kit, but they can be a lot better than that. They now form an intrinsic part of the design of new buildings.

A considerable string to Charcoalblue's bow – these are not places normally in the public eye...

Charcoalblue Experience or CBX was established in 2021. It grew out of the growing demand for audiovisual expertise across all areas of its work, theatres included, and the increasingly specialist knowledge required to deliver it. As CBX Managing Director Ian Stickland observes, theatre has always borrowed from the technologies available at the time: first the rigging and pulley systems of sailing ships, then the steam engines and hydraulic power of industrialisation, then gas and electric lighting and power, now the technologies of the digital age. For most consumers, these first manifested as live broadcasts to cinemas from the likes of the Metropolitan Opera in New York and the National Theatre in London. No surprise there, but what about beyond the acting world?

Knowing Charcoalblue's theatre work, I was at first surprised to find that it has this other considerable string to its bow: CBX is close to being a brand in itself. But then, with certain exceptions, these are not places normally in the public eye. A large client, for instance, is Google, at its various campuses around the world, such as its immense new HQ at King's Cross in London by architects/designers BIG and Heatherwick Studio, or equivalent campuses by various hands in San Francisco, New York, Gurgaon outside New Delhi in India, and Sydney. Google is one of the biggest users of videoconferencing in the world: effectively

CBX: the parallel universe

all its campuses can become one. Given this, obviously the optimum design and technology of what you might call its 'talking buildings' is essential.

Commercial confidentiality applies here – CBX employees tend to work in and alongside the host companies and are bound by their rules. As with anything building-related, the work divides the three main phases of research into what's needed and desirable, design and delivery. The latter, in this technological realm, is highly specialised, and so CBX fields teams of project and design managers who implement the designs. But buildings must adapt, and so on another level there is planning work that clients can do for themselves with the right tools: CBX has developed a web app for Google Cloud that enables the optimum design of meeting rooms and the videoconferencing technology powering them.

The same approach applies to sports venues – an example there is the new International Press interview room for the All England Club in Wimbledon,

PAGE 170 BAFTA'S Ray Dolby Room.
LEFT Google Bay View, Silicon Valley.
ABOVE Digital image mapping.
BELOW Charcoalblue Room Design Guide website.

CBX: the parallel universe

173

which went live in 2023 – there's an app for the best use of that; and education spaces such as the transformation of the Brutalist National Archives building at Kew, West London. This used to be a somewhat aloof place, but now, as internally redesigned in several phases by AOC Architecture, it is a public visitor destination incorporating a great deal of digital display technology alongside its priceless collection of documents gathered over a millennium. These are increasingly shared digitally with the world.

RIGHT Google Bay View and Charcoalblue's John Owens.
BELOW All England Club, Wimbledon Media Centre.

Earlier work in digital cinemas in a variety of buildings including performing arts centres led to a fascinating job for BAFTA (the British Academy of Film and Television Arts) on London's Piccadilly. Its new HQ opened in 2022. There CBX worked with Benedetti Architects. There are two cinemas but a great deal more of what the RIBA Awards jury called 'a dazzlingly sophisticated array of audiovisual technology'. This being a historic building, the technology is largely concealed. 'We had to weave a narrative into the spaces', says Stickland. 'It's a new type of consultancy.'

OPPOSITE ABOVE BAFTA, 195 Piccadilly.
OPPOSITE BELOW Concept sketch by Charcoalblue's Kate Nolan.
BELOW BAFTA'S Ray Dolby Room with immersive projection.
PAGES 178-179 Princess Anne Theatre.

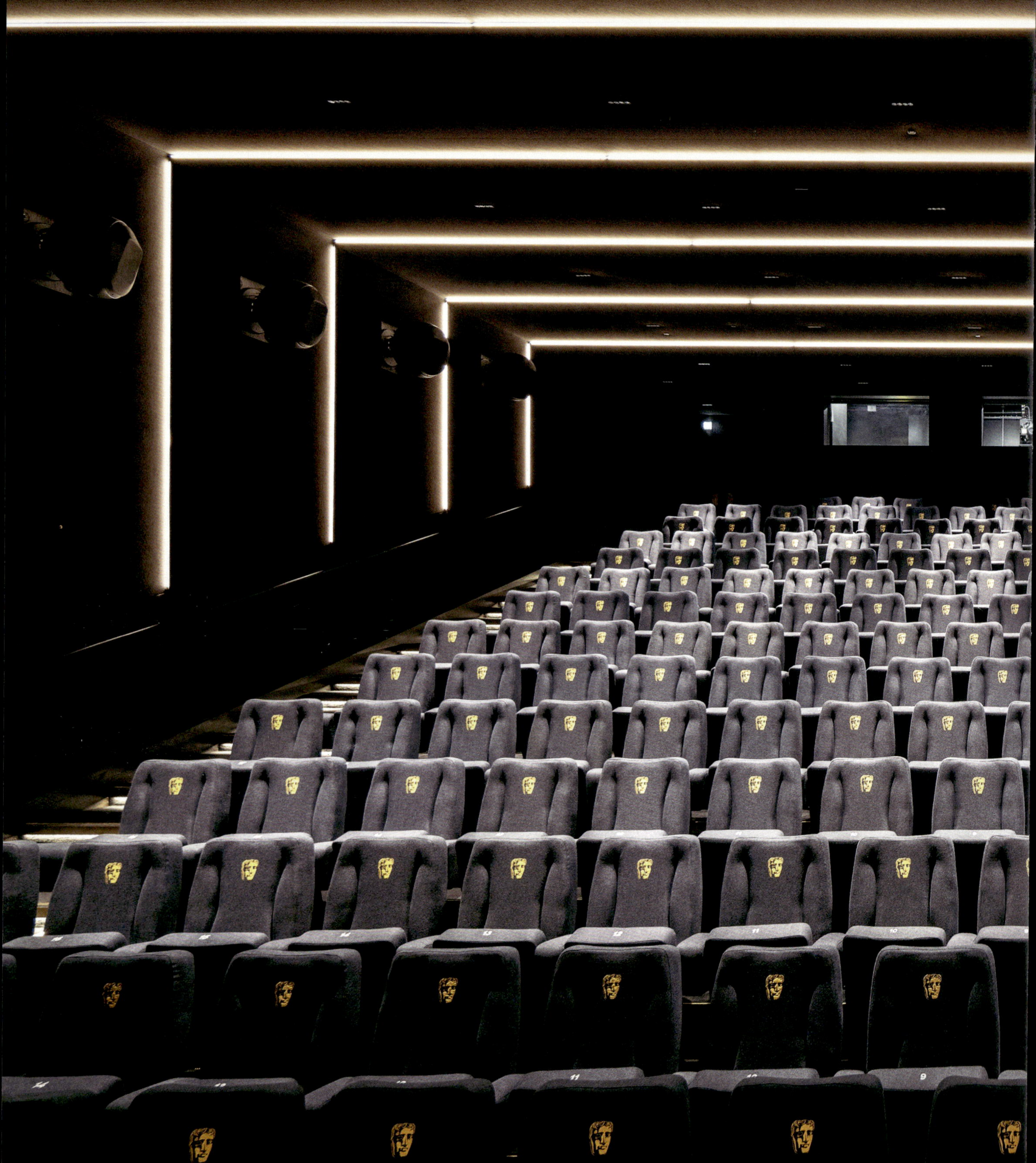

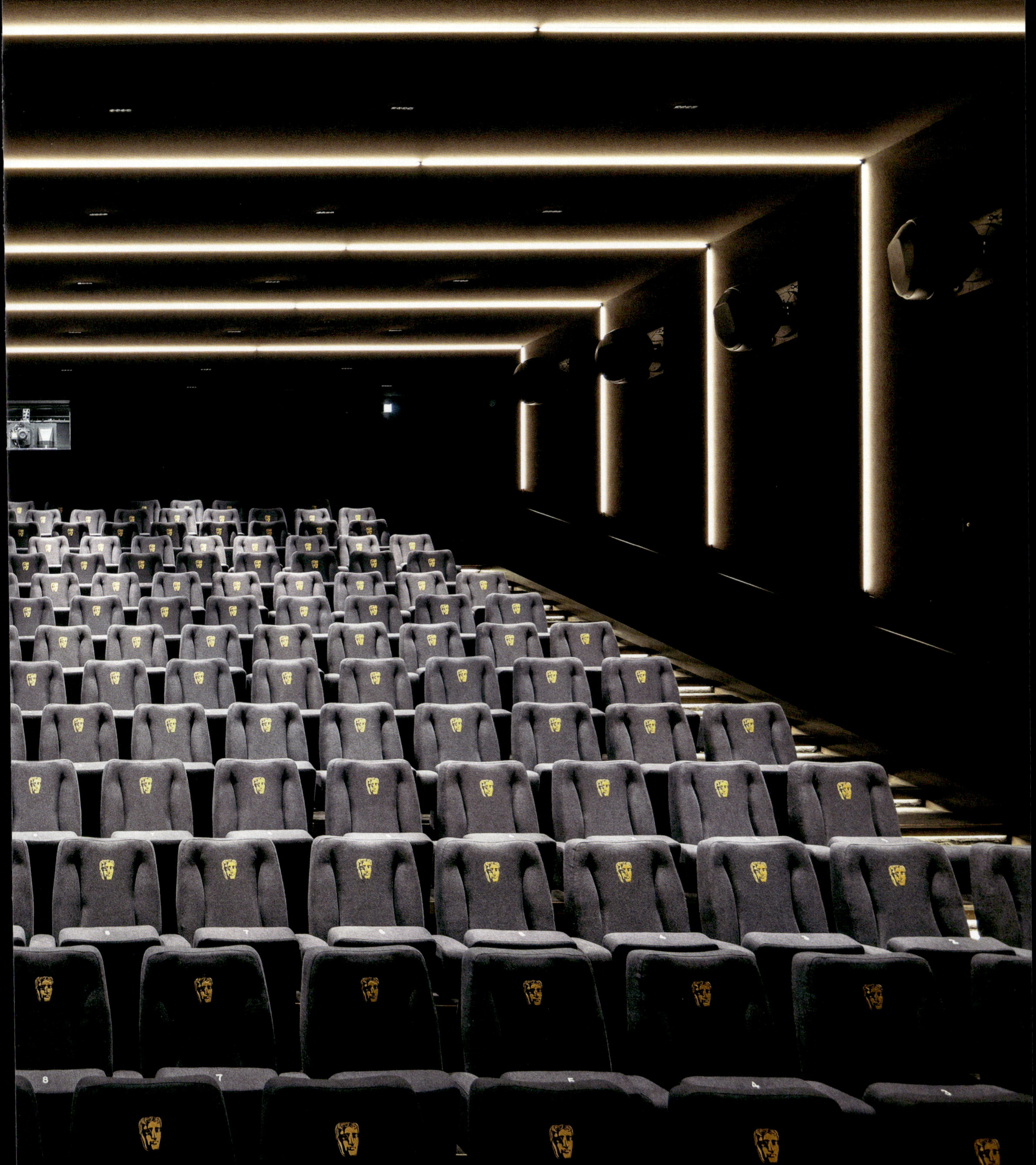

This approach moves freely across sectors. If a technology giant is one thing, an opera house – especially the Sydney Opera House – is another. The Charcoalblue involvement there was a concept for the upgrading of the venue's recording and broadcast spaces, streaming to people's homes.

'We make no distinction in the ways people tell their stories', Stickland concludes. 'It could be a theatre, a conference centre, a technology company HQ. It's a matter of finding out how people operate and would like to operate, and bringing the design and technology together to achieve that.'

LEFT Recording and broadcast control room at Sydney Opera House with Charcoalblue's Ian Stickland.
ABOVE Rack room at Sydney Opera House with Charcoalblue's Ian Stickland.

CBX: the parallel universe

Acknowledgements

Charcoalblue would like to acknowledge the traditional owners of the unceded lands we work on across the world. We pay our tributes to the traditional owners of these lands, and conduct our work with consideration and respect for indigenous peoples. We appreciate our position and opportunity to help continue irreplaceable traditions of art, storytelling and performance.

We would also like to honour the many partners, collaborators, risk-takers, creative minds, family members and team-players that we have been lucky enough to share our first 20 years of adventures with. Thank you to our very special clients, collaborating design team colleagues, lead architects, engineers, project directors and managers, and (even!) cost consultants.

You continue to inspire us.

Thanks most of all to the team of people that have built Charcoalblue. Do spend a moment to review their pictures in the appendix. Each one of them deserves their star in this hall of fame, for their creativity and contribution.

There are so many challenges in the world that we share together, not least ensuring its longevity, and we will try to share the next 20 years with these skilled and gifted people facing those challenges together.

About the author

Hugh Pearman was the architecture and design critic for *The Sunday Times* for 30 years and (overlapping with this) the editor of the *RIBA Journal*. His previous books include *About Architecture* (Yale University Press, 2023), *Cullinan Studio in the 21st Century* (Lund Humphries, 2020), *Equilibrium: the work of Nicholas Grimshaw and Partners* (Phaidon, 2000), and *Airports: a century of architecture* (Laurence King, 2004). He is an Honorary Fellow of the RIBA and in 2019 he was made an MBE for services to architecture. He is currently Chair of the 20th Century Society.

Picture Credits

Clemeth Abercrombie: 138t, 138b, 140; Martin Argyroglo: 159t, 160; Iwan Baan: 10–11, 50, 53; BAFTA/Scott Garfitt: 170–171, 177; John Bartelstone: 121b; Richard Battye for Feilden Clegg Bradley Studios: 4–5, 108, 110–111; Stephanie Berger: 77t; Brett Boardman: 84–85, 100, 102 bl, 103; Marco Cappelletti: 8, 9; Charcoalblue: 15r, 16t, 29, 34b, 45, 46, 60t, 66l, 67m, 67r, 71b, 73, 87t, 92b, 93, 99t, 105t, 133tl, 151b, 153, 154l, 155l, 158, 159b, 160, 163tl, 163tr, 163b, 164, 167b, 167tr, 173b, 176b, 180, 181; Peter Cook: 32, 34–35, 86; Dorothy Hong Photography: 131b, 133–134; Florian Eisele/AELTC: 174–175; John Gollings: 62, 64; Gavin Green: 19t, 25t, 28b, 31m, 33, 42t, 49, 58, 63t, 71t, 75, 81t, 91b, 96t, 96b, 99l, 111t, 128tl, 128b, 131tr, 136, 149, 172, 175t; Jag Gundu: 139; Ben Hanson: 37, 39, 42b, 43, 66r, 82t, 152r, 153r; Jenni Harris: 59t; Byron Harrison: 16b, 23bl, 23tr, 102tr, 102br, 166, 167tl; Haworth Tompkins & ARC: 142, 144; Andy Hayles: 15l, 54b; Stewart Hemley: 70, 72, 73, 74–75, 87b, 90, 91t, 92t; Hopkins Architects: 148; Hufton+Crow: 40, 41; Owen Hughes: 14, 20–21, 118–119, 120b, 130, 131tl; Jasmax: 104, 105b; Jesse Judd, ARM: 12–13, 65; John Bartelstone Photography: 120t; Hannah Kennedy: 28t; Eric Lawrence: 101t, 101b, 102t, 106b, 106t; Eric Magloire: 146; Greg Maka: 156–157, 162, 165; Paul Masck: 145t, 145b, 147; Julian Messer: 63b, 65b; Scott Norsworthy: 134–135, 141; Lucy Osborne: 67l; Tom Pearl: 23br; Elina Pieridou: 51t, 52t, 124l, 124r, 168; Luca Piffaretti: 176t, 178–179; Chris Plevin: 25b; Lindsay Ricketts: 121t; RSC/Gary Wright: 77b; Peter Ruthven Hall: 110, 126–127; Jon Sivell: 48, 51b, 52b, 54t, 55; Gary Sparkes: 59; James Steinkamp: 18, 22, 23tl, 26–27; Jim Stephenson: 78; Jon Stevens: 17, 30, 31t, 31b, 79, 82b, 122, 123; Ian Stickland: 154r, 173t; Bryan van der Beek, Courtesy of Esplanade – Theatres on the Bay, Singapore: 168–169; Philip Vile: 2–3, 7, 36, 38, 68–69, 80–81, 83, 95, 97, 115, 128tr, 129, 152l, 155r; Alex Wardle: 44, 47b, 98; Teddy Wolff: 19b.

Special thanks to Paul Tucker for all his support and patience across the years in taking many of our staff portraits and yearly team shots.

Index

@sohoplace, London 44–7
Acoustic Dimensions 90
AHMM 46
Alexandra Palace, London 4–5, 108–11
All England Club, Wimbledon 174–5
Allen, Greg 92, 93
American Repertory Theater (ART), Harvard University 142–5, 149
Andrews, Dave 113
Andrzej Blonski Architects 113
AOC Architecture 174
Architects 61 166
ARM Architects 62
ArtsEd, Chiswick 124
Arup 46
AS+GG 23, 24, 29
Assemble 78
ATG Entertainment (Ambassador Theatre Group) 113, 127, 129, 130
August Wilson Theatre, New York 129
Aviva Studios, Manchester *see* Factory International, Manchester
Aydon, Deborah 152, 154
Badgley, Sidney 139
Banakis, Brett 130
bb+c architects 124
BBC 6, 109, 110
Beestone, Gary 127, 129, 130
Benedetti Architects 176
Bennetts Associates 10, 32, 70, 76, 87, 90
Bentley, Andrew 32
Beyer Blinder Belle 119
BIG 171
Bodinetz, Gemma 154
Boepple, Maggie 48, 52, 54
Borger, Diane 143
Boyd, Michael 69, 74, 76, 86, 87
Bridge Theatre, London 143
Bristol Old Vic 113–14
British Academy of Film and Television Arts (BAFTA), London 176–9
Brook, Peter 119, 158
Bundy, James 147
Burns, Nica 46, 47
Cameron, Deane 138, 140
Carmody Groarke 127
Centre for Music, London 10–11
Chapman Architects 36

Château d'Hardelot, Normandy 157–9
Chicago Shakespeare Theater (CST) 22, 24–9, 143, 164
Chichester Festival Theatre 78
Church, Jonathan 78
Clifton, Alex 32
Cornell, Mark 127, 130
Courtyard Theatre, Stratford-upon-Avon 10, 14–15, 24, 29, 70–3, 74, 76, 80, 85–90
Daldry, Stephen 6, 69
David Brownlow Theatre, Horris Hill School, Berkshire 124–5
David Chipperfield Architects 154
David Geffen School of Drama, Yale 140, 146, 147
Davies, Siobhan 122
Derwent London 46
Diller Scofidio + Renfro 11
Dorfman Theatre (Cottesloe), National Theatre, London 66–7, 79–80, 94–9
Ebert Room, Glyndebourne 30–1
Edith Cowan University (ECU), Perth 150–1
Eric Harvie Theatre (Jenny Belzberg Theatre), Banff 147
Esplanade Co Ltd 166
Everyman Theatre, Liverpool 66, 152–5
Factory International, Manchester 8–9, 48, 56–9, 60–1, 143
Feilden Clegg Bradley Studios 109
Feldman, Susan 14, 15, 16, 17
Finch, Alan 78
Ford, Robert 162, 163, 164
Foster, Tim 36
Fretnall, Rebecca 127
Gaines, Barbara 24
Geelong Arts Centre Phase 3 62–5
Gill, Gordon 23, 24
Google 171–2, 172–3, 175
Gordon, Alex 85
Gropius, Walter 13
Gwyn, Eleanor (Nell) 135
Harper, Simon 90
Harris, Henry B. 112–13
Harris, Renee 113
Hassell 101, 103

Haworth Tompkins Architects 6, 14, 46, 66, 69, 78, 79, 94, 98, 99, 113, 114, 124, 135, 143, 150, 152
Heatherwick Studio 171
Henderson, Criss 24
Hepworth Gallery, Wakefield 154
Heritage Lottery Fund 109
Herzberg, Amy 163
Heywood, Vikki 69
Hopkins Architects 148, 149, 150
Howell, Bill 15
Hudson Theatre, Manhattan 109, 112–15
Hughes, Owen 15, 121, 164
Hytner, Nicholas 79, 94
Iwuji, Chuk 72
Jasmax 104, 105
John Morris Architects 24
Jonathan Tuckey Design 124
Jones, Christine 130
Kamara, Khady 49
Kenny, Sean 13
Kiln Theatre, London 32, 36–9, 101
Kirwin & Simpson 66, 66
Kit Kat Club, Playhouse Theatre, London 126, 127–9
Koolhaas, Rem 56
Kostow Greenwood Architects 129
KPMB Architects 138, 140, 147
La MaMa Experimental Theatre Club, New York 118, 119–21
Lan, David 6–7, 10, 48
Langford, David 53
Lasdun, Denys 79, 94, 98
Lavey, Martha 24
Lecat, Jean-Guy 119
Libeskind, Daniel 48
Library of Birmingham 154
Linbury Theatre, London 40–3
Liverpool and Merseyside Theatres Trust (LMTT) 152, 154, 155
Liz and Eric Lefkofsky Arts and Education Center, Chicago 23, 24
Lloyd Webber, Andrew 135, 137
London Astoria 45
London Palladium 135
Lyons Architects 150
Lyons Israel Ellis 98
Lyric Theatre, New York 130–3

Lyttelton Theatre, National Theatre, London 98
Mackintosh, Iain 36
Manchester International Festival 8, 56
Martinez + Johnson Architecture (OTJ) 113
Marvel Architects 17, 20–1, 130, 164
Marvel, Jonathan 130
Massey Hall, Toronto 138–41, 147
Massey, Hart 139
Matcham, Frank 135
Max Rayne Centre, National Theatre, London 94, 99
McAslan, John 74
McGrath, John 56
McIntyre, Michael 136
McIntyre, Patrick 103
Mecanoo 154
Metropolitan Opera, New York 171
Michael Van Valkenburgh Associates 20
Miller Bourne 30
Miller, Martin 163, 164
Museum of London 10
National Archives, London 174
National Theatre Studio, London 98
National Theatre, London 79, 80–1, 85, 94–9, 171
New London Theatre 13, 45
Nimax Theatres 46
Old Malthouse Theatre, Canterbury 124
Old Vic Theatre, London 98
Olivier Theatre, National Theatre, London 98
OMA 8, 48, 56
Parry, Eric 124
Paulus, Diane 143
Perelman Performing Arts Center (PAC), New York 7, 9, 10–11, 48–50, 48–55, 56
Perth Theatre, Scotland 114
Piper, Tom 74, 76, 86, 87
Quinn, Diane 143
Race Furniture 67
Rauch, Bill 49, 54
REX Architects 7, 9, 48, 49, 54
RIBA 6, 85, 152, 176
Richard Murphy Architects 114
Ritchie, Ian 10, 14, 15, 70
Roundhouse, London 6, 74–5, 74–5

Roundyard, London 74–5, 76
Royal Albert Hall, London 139
Royal College of Art, London 150
Royal Court Theatre, London 6, 10, 69, 152
Royal Opera House, London 40, 43
Royal Shakespeare Company (RSC), Stratford-upon-Avon 10, 14–15, 69–77, 85, 87, 90–1, 93, 152
Royal Shakespeare Theatre (RST) 32, 67, 70, 73, 76, 85, 86, 86, 90, 154
Rubasingham, Indhu 36, 101
Sarah Wigglesworth Architects 10, 122
Schwarzman Centre for the Humanities, Oxford 148–50
Schwarzman, Stephen A. 148
Scott, Elisabeth 70, 86
Scutt, Tom 127, 129
Shakespeare Memorial Theatre, Stratford-upon-Avon 70, 135
Shapiro, Anna 23, 24
Shed, National Theatre, London 2–3, 79–81, 98, 154
Sheridan, Richard Brinsley 136
Silver Thomas Hanley 150
Singtel Waterfront Theatre, Singapore 166, 166–9
Siobhan Davies Studios, London 6, 10, 122–3
So, Lissa 130
St Ann's Warehouse, Brooklyn 14–22, 86, 143, 157
Stanton Williams 40
Starr, Nick 79, 94
Steppenwolf Theatre, Chicago 22–4, 29
Stewart, Ellen 119
Stirling Prize 152, 154, 155
Storyhouse, Chester 32–5
Stubbins, Hugh 143
Summerton, Geoff 46
Sydney Opera House 180–81
Sydney Theatre Company (STC) 85, 101
Tate Modern, London 57
The Leys, Cambridge 124
The Other Place, Stratford-upon-Avon 15, 29, 70, 72
The Perse, Cambridge 124

The Scarlet and Gray Stage, Park Avenue Armory, New York 76, 77
The Yard, Chicago Shakespeare Theater 24–9, 146
Theatre on the Fly, Chichester 78
Theatre Projects 10, 69
Theatre Royal, Drury Lane, London 135–7
TheatreSquared (T2), Fayetteville 162–5
Tim Ronalds Architects 124
Todd, Andrew 157, 158
Tompkins, Steve 6, 47, 99, 145
Tricycle, London see Kiln Theatre
TTW Engineers 101
Tvrtković, Paul 13
Unusual Rigging 136
Waikato Regional Theatre, Hamilton 104–5
Wallin, Erik 15
Walton Family Foundation 162
Watts, Roger 6
Wells Cathedral School, Somerset 124
Western Australian Academy of Performing Arts (WAAPA) 150–1
Wexner, Leslie 76
Wharf Theatres, Sydney 85, 101–103
Williams, Kip 103
Wilson, Peter 90
Wilton's Music Hall, London 67
Woodman, Ellis 98
World Trade Center, Manhattan 6, 9, 48, 54
Wyatt, Benjamin Dean 135
Yale University Dramatic Arts Building 146–7
Young Vic Theatre, London 6, 7, 10, 14, 15, 22, 152, 154, 158

Charcoalblue

Who we are

We create amazing spaces where stories are told and experiences are shared. We are passionate about our work and our commitment to our clients' vision. We bring the best ideas from our global experience to every one of our projects.

Our work draws people together and celebrates creativity across the performing arts, music, media and technology, education, experiential, hospitality, workplaces, leisure, civic, public and cultural projects, sports and live entertainment.

We provide a full spectrum of consultancy services from strategic analysis and creative concepts through to detailed design and project leadership, integrating world-class acoustic, technical, digital and experience design.

Our hybrid working approach keeps our carbon footprint as low as possible and enables us to engage a diverse global team, anchored around studios in the UK, Americas and Australia. We are committed to inclusivity, recognising that bringing the right mix of perspectives to our projects makes them better.

We love what we do, and we couldn't have got where we are without the support of those closest to us. Special thanks to Anna, Chris, Clare and Pablo — we owe you everything.

Abigail Alltimes	 Abigail Harris	 Alex Dietz-Kest	 Alex Judd	 Alex Wardle	 Alistair Grant	 Allie Glonek
 Allora Livingston	 Amanda Brecknell	 Andrea Dohar-Corbett	 Andrew O'Rourke	 Andrew Woodhead	 Andy Hayles	 Angelica Lucero
 Angie Fullman	 Anna Cole	 Anne Marie Woodley	 Ayesha Ali	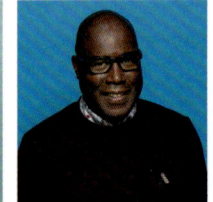 Ayo Daramola	 Becca Pearce	 Becky Daley

Becky McAuley	Beky Stoddart	Ben Hanson	Ben Truppin-Brown	Bernardo Gollo	Bradley Fritz	Breanna Ross
Brian Law	Brian Shaughnessy	Bruno Cardenas	Byron Harrison	C Wrenn	Carmen Almeida	Carol Feeley-Vario
Caroline Andrew	Caroline Rouse	Cassie Fraser	Catherine Jones	Charles Quayle	Charlotte Jakes	Charlotte Kenny
Chris Dales	Chris Daniel	Chris McDougall	Chris Plevin	Chris Spurgeon	Christian Wallace	Christina Keryczynskyj
Cindy Murray	Claire Hewitt	Clark Henry Brown	Clemeth Abercrombie	Cordy Chrisholm	Dan Dando	Dan Roncoroni
Dan Rousseau	Daniel Faro	Dara Tauss	Daric Warneke	David Beam	David Beidas	David Millman
Dicky Burgess	DJ Husted	Doug Storm	Eleanor Szarka	Elena Giakoumaki	Elina Pieridou	Elinor Wood

Elizabeth Stewart	Ellen Gruber	Ellie Kneissl	Elyse Desmond	Emilie Lemons Golding	Emily Rae	Emma Chapman
Emma Savage	Eric Furbish	Eric Lawrence	Eric Magloire	Erin Shepherd	Ethan Jackson	Euna Pae
Eva Von Dell	Evelyn Way	Flip Tanner	Fran Dewar	Fred Gollo	Freya Martin	Funmi Akinsanmi
Gabe Weisberg	Gabriel Bennett	Gabrielle Zachery	Gary Sparkes	Gary Wright	Gavin Green	Gavin Owen
Geoff Goddard	George Birch	Georgia Heath	Giles Favell	Gracie Becker	Graeme McGinty	Graham Keith
Gregory Allen	Harry Gill	Helena Jack	Hellena Schiavo	Holly Burnell	Ian Baldwin	Ian Hoffman
Ian Stickland	Indira Durakovic	Ines Cruz	Jack Tilbury	Jake Katz	Jake Loveday	James Mitchell

James Nowell	James Oakley	James Thomas	Jamie McIntyre	Jay Sterkel	Jean Gonzalez	Jenni Harris	
Jenny Radar	Jerad Schomer	Jessica Holgate	Jez Morris	Jo Manning	Joachim Fainberg	Joanna Kaszuba	
Joe Boxshall	Joe Mapson	Joe Schermoly	Joe Stansfield	Johan Slabbert	John Owens	Jon Morgan Heath	
Jon Sivell	Jon Stevens	Jon Woodley	Jonah Dutchman	Jonathan Zencheck	Josh Loar	Josh Scherr	
Joshua Ekekwe	Jaz Sandalli	Julian Messer	Julian Sleath	Kabir Naidoo	Kaitlyn Kistler	Kaliym Hill	
Karl Allen	Kascey Haslanger	Kate Groener	Kate Hardisty	Kathryn Nolan	Katy Winter	Kim Vermaak	
Kristen Tunney	KyLee Hennes	Kyrie McCormick	Laudan Nooshin	Lauren Shapiro	Leah Barish	Lee Youngson	

Linda Roger	Lindsay Ricketts	Liz Blessing	Louise Barclay	Louise Difford	Louise Dooris	Luca Dellatorre
Lucy Fineberg	Lucy Osbourne	Lucy Taylor	Lyndsay Burr	Mark Lovell	Mark Thomas	Martina Fatato
Mason Lev	Matt Berry	Matt Hall	Matt O'Leary	Matt Smee	Meg Willmott-Geary	Megan Watters
Meghan Milliken	Melissa Tripoli	Michelle Gunn	Mike Harvey	Milo Fox	Molly Faloon	Naia Martin
Nathalie Maury	Neena Thakkar	Neil Keane	Neil Kutner	Niall Black	Nicholas Correa	Nicholas Smith
Nick Royce	Niles Ray	Oliver Beetschen	Ollie Wade	Owen Hughes	Pablo Romero	Parminder Bamra
Paul Clay	Paul Crosbie	Paul Davies	Paul Franklin	Paul Halter	Paul Masck	Peter Longman

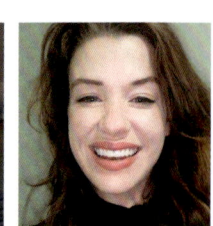

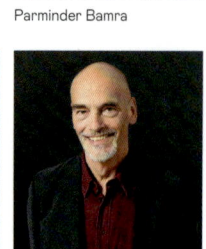

Peter Ruthven Hall	Phil Hampton	Phil Nicolaou	Pip Robinson	Rachel Morgan	Rhys Ansah	Rich Garfield
Richard Ingraham	Rob Halliday	Robin Townley	Rosina Kent	Russell Proud	Ryan Seelig	Sam Gosling
Sandy Beaunay	Sarah Hazelgrove	Sarah Nathan	Sarah Ramos	Sarah Ruston Reed	Sarah Turney	Scott Stewart
Sian Thompson	Simon Bond	Simon Brown	Simon Denman Ellis	Sonya Baker	Stan Pressnar	Steph Barrow
Stephanie Birdsell	Stephen Murphy	Steve Green	Steve Roberts	Stojan Djordjevic	Tanya Burns	Tessa Bagshaw
Tina Torbey	Tom McEwen	Tom Snell	Troy Colson	Tyler Glass	Umairah Farooqi	Vangelis Koufoudakis
Will Bowen	Yaya Zhou	Zane Beatty	Zoe Freezor	Libby Penn		

First published in 2024 by Lund Humphries

Lund Humphries
Huckletree Shoreditch
Alphabeta Building
18 Finsbury Square
London EC2A 1AH
UK
www.lundhumphries.com

Charcoalblue: Designing for Performance
© Charcoalblue, 2024
Text © Hugh Pearman, 2024
All rights reserved

ISBN: 978-1-84822-661-6

A Cataloguing-in-Publication record for this book is available from the British Library

All rights reserved. No part of this publication may be reproduced, stored in a retrieval system or transmitted in any form or by any means, electrical, mechanical or otherwise, without first seeking the permission of the copyright owners and publishers. Every effort has been made to seek permission to reproduce the images in this book. Any omissions are entirely unintentional, and details should be addressed to the publishers.

Hugh Pearman has asserted his right under the Copyright, Designs and Patents Act, 1988, to be identified as the Author of this Work.

Copy edited by Julie Gunz
Designed by Myfanwy Vernon-Hunt, this-side.co.uk
Set in Mabry and Mabry Mono
Printed in Belgium

Cover image: Free Your Mind, 2023, opening production, directed by Danny Boyle, Aviva Studios, home of Factory International, Manchester

Pages 2-3: The Shed, National Theatre, London

Pages 4-5: Alexandra Palace Theatre, London